CHANGING PLACES

Changing Places

THE SCIENCE AND ART OF
NEW URBAN PLANNING

JOHN MACDONALD

CHARLES BRANAS

ROBERT STOKES

PRINCETON UNIVERSITY PRESS

PRINCETON & OXFORD

Published by Princeton University Press
41 William Street, Princeton, New Jersey 08540
6 Oxford Street, Woodstock, Oxfordshire OX20 1TR

press.princeton.edu

ISBN 978-0-691-19521-6
ISBN (e-book) 978-0-691-19779-1

British Library Cataloging-in-Publication Data is available

Editorial: Meagan Levinson and Jacqueline Delaney
Production Editorial: Kathleen Cioffi
Jacket Design: Layla Mac Rory
Production: Erin Suydam
Publicity: Tayler Lord and Kathryn Stevens

Jacket image (background): Empty lot and homes in the Fishtown
neighborhood of Philadelphia, PA. © Frances Roberts / Alamy Stock Photo

This book has been composed in Arno

Printed on acid-free paper. ∞

Printed in the United States of America

10 9 8 7 6 5 4 3 2 1

CONTENTS

PREFACE

THIS BOOK is designed to get us thinking about the fundamental importance of "place" in designing healthier and safer cities. A seemingly obvious concept, place is of course all around us, all the time. Place is not an abstract theory or an academic daydream. Place is our homes, our workspaces, our backyards, and our streets. Place reflects the ambience, conditions, and situations we encounter every day that profoundly shape our daily routines. The context of place may be more important to our health and safety than policy makers and the public realize. The design of streets and sidewalks, the amount of trees, grass, and other green space, the physical environment of our housing and schools, and the businesses and parks we go to shop, work, and play—these all profoundly affect how we navigate our lives, how safe we are in a world of traffic and crime, and ultimately our most basic health outcomes.

Despite its importance, too often policy makers forget that the design of places is a viable, leading opportunity for positively shaping people's lives. Some of the greatest influences on the human condition emerged a century ago, in an era when city planners and policy makers used placemaking as bold first-line options to improve health and safety. The creation of public water and sanitation systems, zoning of municipal land, building codes, and roadway redesign did more to enhance the health of the public than many other programs, including medical care. But, at some point, focus shifted primarily away from places to lifestyles and personal responsibility, placing the onus on individuals to improve their own situations, despite being deeply entrenched in environments that continually thwart such improvements. Expecting people to access far-off hospitals or call police *after* they experience an illness or crime ignores the importance that place environments has in shaping their lives and choices, not to mention the great benefits to health and safety that occurred a century ago, when city planners, physicians, sanitarians, and civil engineers collaborated to design cities.

In recent years, the idea that place matters for health and safety has received renewed attention in academic and policy circles. Urban research from multiple disciplines shows that obesity, chronic disease, stress, and insecurity all thrive when places are poorly designed. Placemaking is now a term used to advocate for the planning, design, and management of public spaces in ways that maximize community benefits.[1] In this way, placemaking is a form of city planning that directly engages the community in the design of places and fits with calls for city planning approaches that focus on reducing inequalities across neighborhoods.

While community input is key, figuring out whether the redesign of a place will lead to healthier activity, increased social connection, and reduced street crime requires scientific testing. With the advent of experimental and quasi-experimental approaches we can actually test how different designs of places improve the health and safety of populations. The opportunities for place-based remedies that can be shown to improve our health and safety problems are growing. This book is dedicated to helping think through some of the mechanisms that explain why place-based remedies to health and safety in urban communities work and which ones have the best scientific evidence.

Consider the effort and scientific resources that are devoted to finding out if pills, personal therapies, and surgeries are effective. Why not do the same to determine the effectiveness of different designs of parks, transit systems, and sidewalks, as potential therapies? Despite the potentially awesome power of place, science has played a comparatively small role in how we design places for our health and safety. Questionable science has led to mass relocation, neighborhood exclusion policies, disruption of entire communities, and, over time, an increasing segregation of our most resource-deprived citizens, cut off from the benefits of economically diverse neighborhoods.[2] It should come as no surprise that citizen-advocacy groups and urban-planning theorists have questioned the use of science to solve the health and safety problems of economically disadvantaged communities.[3]

Indeed, many have asked whether science itself is just another language of exclusion, a process for reaffirming the beliefs of experts and elites in the planning process. Culturally sensitive, thoughtful use of science to answer policy questions is a critical concern, but it is equally critical not to simply jettison the scientific method altogether, as it offers one of the most powerful tools for understanding how the human-built environment can best impact the health and safety of communities. A model of science where scientists, planning practitioners, and citizens work together can be applied to the larger interests of the population and can benefit the most economically disadvantaged. This coproduction of science should involve consistent community input across the life course of place-based policy and design interventions, from idea generation to rigorous scientific testing to implementation, all with the vision of redesigning neighborhoods and cities for optimum health and safety.[4]

Urban planners should work directly with community end-users in the planning phases so that the design of places promotes effective changes that are more democratic and give would-be beneficiaries of these changes a greater sense of place. Well-chosen changes to places, from small neighborhood gardens to major public building projects, can be powerful influences on our lived experiences and our sense of place. Focusing on increasing that sense of place for the people who most use newly created spaces is a key design component that can itself be successfully tested. Nevertheless, a disconnect still exists between those who implement place-based changes and the community of scientists who are now starting to rigorously evaluate them. Architects, planners, and real-estate developers need to recognize the value of thorough and drawn-out scientific testing; scientists need to embrace the action-oriented work of practitioners who are routinely changing places in cities on a daily basis. After all, both groups are part of a professional class that ultimately wants the best results for people and places. Lasting partnerships between urban-design professionals and today's scientists could ultimately surpass the place-based successes of a century ago, leapfrogging our cities into the healthy and safe places that are worthy of the new millennium.

As both scientists and planners, we've written this book to be of interest to those with little to no technical background in research. Our goal is to promote a new middle ground between researchers and practitioners around truly transformative place-based changes. While the level of engagement between those making the places and those studying placemaking has already grown more robust and fruitful, our hope is that the cases presented here provide a framework for further expansion of these partnerships.

Chapter 1 ("Our Surroundings, Ourselves") examines how the features of our built environment affect our health and safety. In this chapter we focus on why and how the design of places shapes our lived experience. We also introduce an emerging scientific movement concerned with the way changes to our built environment, from buildings and parks to streets, impact health and safety.[5] We argue that changing places is one of the best ways to produce sustained improvements in well-being for large groups of people over long periods of time. Certain characteristics of place-based designs can be chosen to maximize success. Altering the structures of the built environment to basic principles of simplicity, scalability, and ease of use can be employed as a model for producing place-based changes that have the most significant and lasting impact. This chapter illustrates why place-based strategies should be among the first set of policy choices for enhancing the health and safety of urban residents.

Chapter 2 ("A New Movement") summarizes the history of select endeavors that focused on place-based changes as a mechanism to improve the health, safety, and well-being of urban residents. Unfortunately, these endeavors evolved in silos, with urban planners and public-health and criminal-justice practitioners working largely in isolation from one another. The successes and limited uptake of these isolated endeavors are brought to light as we look at how they were overshadowed by individually focused therapies and interventions. Many people probably think that good science is already inherently involved when a place gets altered or a development gets built; this is perhaps the case with respect to the physical science of certain placemaking endeavors. For instance, a suspension bridge can't be built without the right load and compression calculations. But the health and biological impacts of buildings and larger developments are very often left out, or only modestly considered as part of environmental or health-impact assessments. There is a need to invigorate a new movement that connects social scientists, planners, and policy makers as we build the world around us. The best science is produced in the real world and thrives when it is combined with individuals who have practical knowledge. The best placemaking occurs when it is supported by empirical evaluation of its impacts on humans with the active involvement of scientists.

Chapter 3 ("Got Evidence?") provides a guide to scientific evidence and explores how field experiments can be used as a scientific standard for determining what place-based policies to adopt, refine, or abandon. This chapter also discusses what sorts of evidence to rely on when experiments are not possible for various ethical or pragmatic reasons. Experimentation is at the very heart of science, and relying on a scientific model for deciding how, and in what forms, the built environment should be modified is a dynamic process that can ultimately inform the efficient and effective expenditures of limited resources by policy makers. Rather than provide a treatise on the scientific method and the value of experiments, we provide a short discussion of the benefits of different methods of evaluation and focus more attention on the utility of a science-based policy agenda for changing places. The scientific model allows us to evaluate the influence that environments may have on our health and safety while also encouraging us to pursue discoveries of innovative new place-based strategies that can achieve the greatest health and safety benefits at relatively low costs.

Chapter 4 ("Cities as Ruins") is the first of a series of chapters that discuss specific ways to alter the built environment to improve our health and safety. This chapter focuses on urban building and housing interventions that have been evaluated at some of the highest levels of scientific evidence. Building and housing interventions strongly appeal to policy makers and the public who intrinsically recognize the basic human need for shelter. The most blighted and neglected human dwellings in cities provide a strong basis for motivating action. After all, one can clearly see a significant change in an area when old buildings and physical structures are razed and new ones constructed. Questions arise, though, in terms of the actual need for complete replacement with new structures, as opposed to more widespread renovations and preservation of old buildings. It is equally important to consider the effect that urban-revitalization activities, especially in residential districts, has on gentrification and the possible reduction of a city's affordable housing stock, which itself influences health and safety. We discuss examples of building interventions that have failed to produce positive evidence and ones that have shown success without causing significant dislocation or displacement.

Chapter 5 ("The Nature Cure") turns to interventions for land and open spaces and their impact on public health and safety. Abandoned, vacant, and neglected land is of great and growing concern in many cities. We discuss recent efforts to address this sort of land-based blight and how planners can partner with scientists to implement and evaluate land-remediation and zoning strategies to best improve public health and safety. In many ways, these changes represent our innate human desire for nature and green spaces. Without action from planners and landscape architects, such natural spaces wouldn't exist in many of our cities. We also showcase several studies that provide evidence that the mere presence of green spaces have healing and calming effects, an effect that occurs even if residents do not actively use these spaces. Indeed, there have been myriad efforts over the past decade or so by cities to revisit and reinvigorate their green and open-space planning efforts. Much of this effort has been to insert managed green spaces into smaller parcels and equitably distribute them across neighborhoods that lack access to larger green spaces. This pocket-park movement has economic drivers but, in some cities, also seeks to leverage the likely health benefits to local residents.

We discuss the body of scientific evidence that has been developing to investigate how the design of land, grass, and tree planting in cities can reduce crime and improve health in communities.

Chapter 6 ("Driving Ambivalence") discusses the role of transportation and street environments in our lives and how reliance on the automobile has shaped the United States and other parts of the world. Our century-long evolution into a car-dependent culture has had its benefits in terms of commerce and regional mobility, but has also had devastating effects on our health and safety. Rather than discuss the negative impacts of cars on air pollution, we focus on the place-based health impacts of reducing our reliance on the automobile by increasing the walkability of areas and expanding access to public transit. Younger adults are increasingly ambivalent about whether they should even own a car and are moving to cities in search of more efficient and human-scale mobility options. These options include having access to a street network with safe and efficient pedestrian and bike infrastructures as well as public-transit options. Public officials in numerous cities are talking about the benefits of expanded transit systems and walkable street grids to encourage more active lifestyles and attract tourists, families, and entrepreneurs who are tired of traffic congestion and car commuting and interested in a lively street experience that is not simply seen from behind a windshield. We discuss why these new transportation and streetscape changes have grown and highlight case studies showing how new place-based transportation and streetscape changes can be a tool for improving health and safety.

Chapter 7 ("Good Clean Fun") is an in-depth examination of how the design of entertainment districts and public parks impacts the health and safety of neighborhoods. Many place-based changes are initially spurred on by commercial interests in and around business districts. However, little attention has been placed on the role that commercial and business design can have on our health and safety outcomes. Commercial corridors and business districts that actively choose to enhance the place-based experience for their customers generate bustling streets that improve commerce and reduce crime. Parks were originally designed for leisure, and large infrastructure changes to parks are expensive and generate little change in overall use and exercise. However, small strategic changes can be made to parks to provide subtle motivational signs that stimulate greater physical activity among park users. We provide several studies based on rigorous scientific evidence that highlight how such strategic designs and governance arrangements of business districts and parks can improve the experience of people in search of places for shopping and recreation.

Chapter 8 ("Embracing Unintended Consequences") takes the evidence from our prior discussions of building, land-use, transit, and recreational interventions and discusses how these place-based changes can bring about unintended consequences. We argue that unintended consequences are a key element in any scientific endeavor, including the study of place-based changes, and that unplanned consequences should be thought through and embraced by implementers of place-based changes. Successful changes to places will inevitably lead to increasing desirability for their use. Any sustained change to the built environment of a place creates the potential for multiple outcomes. There will always be potential negative tradeoffs to changing places. Unintended negative consequences should be planned for and discussed ahead of time, so that efforts can be made to mitigate against their occurrence. Fear of change or negative impacts can create an inescapable status quo for many poor and neglected communities who could benefit from place-based change. This status quo can lead to dangerous and unhealthy conditions persisting for too long, producing negative legacy effects for these communities. As a solution, negative externalities of placemaking interventions are more readily anticipated through research. In this way, early scientific involvement can greatly inform proactive planning and thoughtful place making, easing any apprehension among local policy makers and residents.

The book's epilogue ("Where Next?") ties together the chapters and summarizes the agenda for a placemaking initiative guided by scientific inquiry. This chapter reviews a number of the theoretical perspectives, suggests areas that are rich for future investigation, and calls for planners and scientists to work together to make places a central part of the agenda for positively shaping the future health of communities. We discuss avenues by which scientists at local universities and think tanks can partner with planners when it is time to redesign places and set up a framework for figuring out what works, what doesn't, and what shows promise. Researchers working in the field with community groups and practicing planners can generate ideas about the design of communities, scientifically evaluate those ideas, and then see which ideas can be expanded to benefit entire communities. The public is thirsting for knowledge of ways to redesign places with the broadest benefits for their own communities, as well as serving as models for communities outside their own.

ACKNOWLEDGMENTS

MANY PEOPLE AND PLACES made this book possible. We begin with a special thanks to the University of Pennsylvania for the sabbatical faculty research leave provided to John MacDonald and Charles Branas that started this book. We are greatly indebted to multiple colleagues at Penn and the RAND Corporation who contributed to many of the projects we discuss here. In particular, we would like to thank Rose Cheney, Vicky Tam, Michelle Kondo, Phillipe Bourgois, Keith Green, Bob Grossman, Deborah McColloch, Jamillah Millner, Gina South, Bernadette Hohl, and the late Tom Ten Have for their collaborations on our vacant-land and housing studies. We would also like to thank Ricky Blunthenthal, Aaron Kofner, and Greg Ridgeway for their collaborations on the business-improvement-district and light-rail studies. Phil Cook deserves special mention for his collaborations and insights into thinking more about business improvement districts as an economic model of crime prevention. Our respective spouses and children of course deserve the lion's share of thanks for their patient support over the past decade of research and writing. Multiple research projects discussed in this book were also conducted with the support of grants from the Centers for Disease Control and Prevention, the National Institutes of Health, the US Department of Agriculture, and the Robert Wood Johnson Foundation. This body of work, and the many other projects we cite, gave us confidence in the idea that the design of places is fundamental to our well-being, and that good science can help us create safer and healthier cities.

CHANGING PLACES

1

Our Surroundings, Ourselves

CONSIDER THESE TRUE and all-too-common stories. A woman walking on the South Side of Chicago is accosted by a man who puts a gun to her neck and takes her to a nearby abandoned building. When he is unable to get into the boarded-up building, he forces her into an empty lot and sexually assaults her.[1] A boy in East Saint Louis is laughing one minute and breathless from an asthma attack the next. An ambulance rushes him to the hospital, but, in a city where garbage collection can be sporadic and raw sewage backs up into people's homes, his asthma will only return.[2] A young man in suburban New Jersey is killed when the car in which he is riding crosses a roadway divider and hits oncoming traffic. The car, which was driven by another young man, is so badly damaged that firefighters need to forcibly extricate both driver and passenger.[3]

These are all tragedies that could have been avoided. Now consider the following true stories. A woman in Southwest Philadelphia decides to do something about the vacant lots in her neighborhood: eyesores created when abandoned homes were torn down and nothing replaced them. She transforms these spaces by picking up the trash and debris and planting grass. The abandoned space becomes a pocket park that is used for picnics, community meetings, and arts and crafts for local kids. With the transformation of these formerly vacant lots, crime drops in her neighborhood and her neighbors feel less stressed.[4] A boy in the High Point neighborhood of Seattle moves into a home that has been specially designed to prevent asthma and other breathing problems. He is happier, healthier, and can breathe much better here, while his parents can finally get a restful night's sleep.[5] A young man in Charlotte's Uptown neighborhood no longer needs to drive his car to work because he lives near a new light-rail line and a no-traffic bikeway. He is part of a new generation, less exposed to the dangers of the road because new transit options have made personal cars less attractive.[6] An immigrant family in Los Angeles that lives near and works in a newly revitalized, well-managed, and now thriving commercial district finds that they suddenly have a greater choice of goods and services, many of which are locally sourced, and their home neighborhood has become safer and more vibrant due to deeply invested community stakeholders and place managers.[7]

Real lives are changed in positive ways with thoughtful rehabilitations of places. Real lives are marred when we let places deteriorate and urban blight worsen. While it is easy to point to ways that urban environments are harmful, cities are already some of our safest places and ripe for further improvement. Accidents, poor health, and victimization are not always unavoidable mishaps that occur as a matter of poor luck or lack of individual determination.[8] When someone in a disadvantaged neighborhood manages to live a safe and healthy life, it is easy to credit their personal drive in making the best out of their hard-scrabble surroundings. But that's only part of the equation, maybe even just a small part. Good health and personal safety result from more than just good individual choices and what we teach our children, especially for those living in dangerous and unhealthy surroundings.[9] Paying close attention to those surroundings, as a first order of business, could be the path to lasting community benefits that even the best teachers and a load of gumption can't provide.

Why Places Profoundly Matter

Interest in reshaping places to improve the health and safety of the people who inevitably live, work, and play in them has grown over the past two decades.[10] In many ways, these place-based programs are a departure from business-as-usual approaches in many fields (e.g., medicine, law enforcement, psychology) that have focused primarily on the characteristics of individuals and the myriad ways to get these individuals to modify their lifestyles in positive and sustained ways. Despite massive resource investments, individually focused intervention programs that seek to encourage better eating, more daily exercise, and safety precautions have fallen far short of expectations. While there are certainly examples of success, more can be done to supplement, or even supplant, individual-based programs with place-based programs that hold significant promise and, in some cases, have already been proven successful under rigorous scientific testing.

Even when they work, individually based programs can lose sight of the bigger picture. Medicine produced by pharmaceutical companies only works if people take it according to the correct timing and dosage. Twelve-step programs only work if individuals consistently show up for their group sessions and stay committed to the behavior-change regimens they pledged. These programs are often so focused on the particular circumstances of each individual that they are difficult to deliver to large populations, thus often touching relatively few lives and ignoring how broader environmental influences can so strongly dictate individual decisions. Episodically treating small numbers of people for chronic stress, obesity, or lack of daily physical activity, while ignoring the unhealthy social and physical environments where they work, live, and play, has led society on a fifty-year wild-goose chase for individual "cures" and delayed efforts to create policies that address the causes of poor health and safety that are often rooted in the very places and mundane surroundings where we dwell.

Changes to the built environment of places can impact the health and safety of everyone living or working in an area, influencing individual choices often by default and leading to positive and sustainable changes. Take the example of daily exercise. It is far easier to sustain an active lifestyle by walking to work as part of one's daily commute than it is to get up early each day before work and drive to a gym. Driving itself offers no exercise benefit, and education campaigns and reminders from your doctor to get to the gym and exercise have been shown to be unsuccessful for the vast majority of us. By contrast, for people who live in an area where walking to work is feasible, or maybe even preferable because the physical environment around them promotes it, the choice to be active becomes much easier, more maintainable, and more successful as a personal health strategy.

A simple strategy in choosing place-based programs is to consider whether a program is making basic structural changes to places, whether the changes are scalable to multiple places and large groups of people, and whether it can be sustained over long periods of time. Successful programs that redesign places should be disseminated and replicated across cities. Unsuccessful place-based programs should be abandoned or retooled as part of a larger learning cycle to design cities in ways that best improve the health and safety of large populations.

Programs that focus on making changes to the structural features of the built environment where human activity occurs, such as creating new buildings or street infrastructure, can influence more people for longer periods of time than those that focus on individually based interventions. Leading researchers at the National Academy of Sciences have pointed out that it is unreasonable to expect peoples' health to improve when the basic environment around them is, by design, working against such improvements.[11] If the basic structures producing negative health in peoples' surroundings cannot be changed, the likelihood of truly transformational improvements is stunted right from the start.

Structural changes to places impact everyone using a space, not just those most affected or those most in need. Street grid adaptations, such as those pursued by the Smart Growth Coalition with their Complete Streets concept, seek to build healthier places through a broader public program to fix our unhealthy, car-centric transportation and mobility systems.[12] Complete Streets seeks to integrate pedestrian, bicycle, and mass transit in encouraging active living, an issue that is particularly important as aging populations become more and more sedentary.[13] In making changes to the physical environment of cities, Complete Streets redesigns can be structured for widespread impact and greater access for all.

Other place-based programs, such as the US Department of Transportation's Safe Travel to School programs, have created safe corridors for pedestrians and bicycle travel to and from schools. In cities, the Safe Travel to School program tends to focus on crime and other safety issues for students, while its suburban and exurban versions are focused on safety issues related to poor road designs and dangerous crossings, lack of sidewalks or paths, inadequate lighting, and unsafe vehicle speeds.[14] Regardless of where they get implemented, place-based designs that reduce the need to use a car and encourage more walking and bicycling positively impact everyone, young and old, students and workers, long-time residents and visitors alike.

The "popsicle test" is a great example of a health-and-place-focused metric. The basic metric measures the ability of an eight-year old child to walk safely to buy a Popsicle in their neighborhood and return before it melts. This concept captures many of the elements of a healthy place, including walkability, pedestrian safety, a connected community that looks out for their children, and mixed-use planning where people can walk to stores from their homes for simple items. Designing places with the health and safety of children in mind has become one of the more compelling themes in modern planning discussions. A recent movement toward "free-play" spaces for children rather than overly structured parks and organized athletics has also entered the planning realm. A recent book advocates for "playborhoods" where children's play is unstructured and aims to reduce fear and apprehension among parents about allowing children to use their neighborhoods as play spaces.[15]

In addition to changing basic structures, place-based programs also need to be focused on widespread impact if they are to be most effective and transformational. To have widespread impact, place-based programs need to be scalable to entire populations, offering health benefits to people with a political voice as well as to those without. Think chlorination of public water. The painstaking scientific and political processes that led to widespread chlorination of drinking water is a prime example of structural, place-based change that was scaled to entire cities, with profound impact.[16] Chlorination of public drinking water has saved millions of lives. Although such programs are undoubtedly ambitious, they need not to be overly complex or expensive if they are to be scaled up from one place and tailored to the needs of other places in producing widespread returns on health and safety. For instance, simple changes to sidewalks or streets to encourage walking are readily reproducible and scalable fixes that can have profound impact primarily because of the ease with which they can be transplanted from one place to the next. Scalability is thus defined by the likelihood of reproducing a program in additional places, a cardinal feature of truly transformational place-based programs.[17]

As a third cardinal feature, place-based changes must be sustainable, without the need for constant and conscious maintenance of positive behavior or the perpetual persuasion of individuals to be safe and healthy. Employee exercise programs, for example, require employees that are committed to volunteering and maintaining their involvement in the program.[18] But what happens when people switch jobs? When people lose interest? When people forget or vary to adhere to exercise regimens? Maybe an employer is willing to pay their employees to be in the exercise program, but what if the payments aren't enough to motivate the employees? What if the economic situation of the company changes and they cannot continue the payments? Maintaining programs that target individuals and then sustaining the healthy and safe behaviors of these individuals is a big challenge. In many ways, place-based programs get past this sustainability problem because they often cost less, require little if anything of would-be beneficiaries, and are immersive, offering their benefits by default to those entering a newly improved space. But simplicity and cost are only part of the sustainability equation. Studies show that the more effort someone is required to make the less likely they are to make a healthy choice.[19] People have an easier time making marginal changes in their lives than making major lifestyle changes. When a change is made to a place that makes it easier to walk rather than drive, to socialize with their neighbors, to access healthy food, or to experience green space, it is more likely to be successful than public education campaigns that repeatedly alert people to make the right decisions, ultimately fatiguing them into disregard.

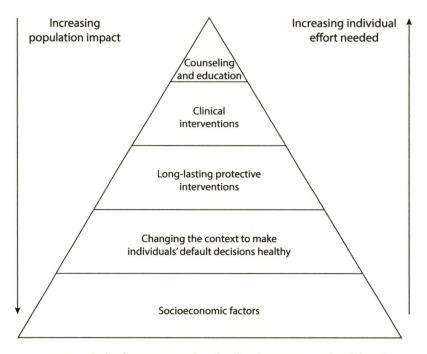

FIGURE 1.1. Scale of interventions directly affects how many people will benefit. *Source*: Frieden, Thomas R., "A framework for public health action: the health impact pyramid," *American Journal of Public Health* 100, no. 4 (2010): 590–95. © The American Public Health Association.

Public-health professionals have long recognized that filling in a brackish tidal pool is far more likely to reduce malaria years after funding has ended than the expectation that local community members will continue regular applications of larvicide.[20] Stemming from this sort of thinking, the Centers for Disease Control and Prevention (CDC) are now promoting the motto "making the healthy choice the easy choice" as a way of touting the importance of changing people's contextual surroundings and promoting high-impact pathways to health. The CDC's "health impact pyramid" (shown in figure 1.1) lists changes to contexts and places as among the highest impact interventions available—higher than counseling, education, health care, vaccinations, and other more traditional, individual-based approaches to improving people's health and safety.[21]

The idea of "making the healthy choice the easy choice" is analogous to work that cognitive psychologists and behavioral economists have argued for "default"

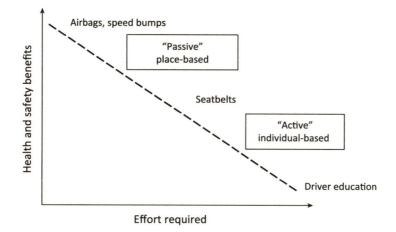

FIGURE 1.2. Interventions more likely to be successful require less effort. *Note*: Adapted from Baker, S. P., "Childhood injuries: the community approach to prevention," *Journal of Public Health Policy* 2, no. 3 (1981): 235–46.

interventions, sometimes referred to as "nudges."[22] These concepts are basically the same. The less you ask of would-be beneficiaries in terms of personally being responsible for their own health and safety, the more likely the program is to be successful in terms of actually improving health and safety. It's an inversely proportional relationship between effort and success that can be illustrated via a number of salient examples.

We use a motor vehicle safety example here and in figure 1.2 because it provides a clear example, but there are a host of others in which places can be redesigned to passively protect people's health and safety without asking them to make conscious changes to their habits or choices. Consider airbags. Airbags have been highly successful in many ways because they ask nothing of the people whom they benefit during a car crash. When someone crashes a car, an airbag deploys and can save a trip to the hospital while requiring no active knowledge or maintenance or actions on behalf of that car's occupant. The same cannot be said, however, of driver-education programs that multiple scientific studies show have minimal impact.[23] Our physical environments can be similarly changed to require less of us, but still provide intense benefits. If done right, well-designed places can protect people as part of their daily lives. However, these changes require forward-thinking societal investments in the science of optimal design and the restructuring of our greatest opportunities for place-based change: the built environments of our cities.

Places Change Us in Fundamental Ways

"Making the healthy choice the easy choice" is an important way forward in creating high-impact, sustainable changes to people's health and safety.[24] This follows a long history of so-called "passive" interventions that public health and engineering professionals have been promoting for decades, albeit without sufficiently widespread uptake.[25]

Perhaps the concept of "making the healthy choice the easy choice" via place-based interventions is anathema to those who favor focusing on personal responsibility over what might seem to be a paternalistic approach to health and safety. However, place-based interventions need not threaten personal liberties. If done right, place-based changes have the potential to enhance personal freedoms and open up new opportunities and locations that might once have been uninhabitable or inaccessible. Place-based interventions also need not be seen as sterile engineering solutions in situations one might argue need more connections between people. Place-based changes are fundamentally about people and augment how they interact with their surroundings. An appropriately engineered place is, by its very nature, designed to bring people together for as much interaction as possible. To be successful, however, place-based designs need to engage the public and know what will draw people to use newly created spaces.

With varying degrees of success, planners have long sought to engage the public in the placemaking and redesigning process. Emerging from the politically turbulent 1960s and concerns with the "top-down" planning models encouraged by federal urban renewal programs of that period, planners sought to build on the idea of a democratic planning process.[26] Planning educators began to suggest engagement models based on the principle that more citizen voices make for better places.[27] Public participation in the planning process has been used successfully in the past to block the construction of freeways that would have dissected and disenfranchised entire city neighborhoods.[28] Jane Jacobs's famous battle to prevent New York City Planning Commissioner Robert Moses from building a highway through lower Manhattan is a prime example of successful community opposition to what is now seen as reckless top-down planning. One should consider this a success, as many cities today are tearing down expensive and divisive highway systems and replacing them with promenades, biking trails, parks, and housing.[29] Sustained citizen engagement, however, has been difficult to achieve in practice, as citizens are busy and often lack information and the political power to influence larger planning processes that seek to change the built environment around them. Still, involving citizens in the planning process can provide the benefit of generating a marketplace of ideas and testing the best plans to ensure that they are maximally beneficial to the public.

With effective public engagement, well-designed built environments allow individual and lifestyle programs to work as intended, making place-based changes a linchpin that must be addressed *first* in order to make truly consequential advances for the health and safety of cities. Despite efforts to educate, medicate, vaccinate, or police our way out of the negative consequences of the physical environment on people, we continue to be faced with a striking and unavoidable reality. If the environment that surrounds much of the population is decrepit, dangerous, and unhealthy, then it is self-evident that our best efforts to lift up these same people will be stymied and undone by toxic places that reduce their chances for success.

Unfortunately, place-based programs have been primarily viewed as mere adjuncts to programs that focus on individuals. For instance, policy makers have incorrectly thought of small changes to places as an accessory to individually based efforts such as erecting neighborhood-watch signs to warn potential burglars that a neighborhood is not fair game, exercise signs in parks to remind people that the space can be used for physical activity, and municipal signs to inform people that their dogs need to be leashed and they have to clean up their waste. Public education campaigns can certainly be beneficial, but they should be complements to place-based changes to the basic structures that necessitate educational signage in the first place. New streets and parks structured specifically for better health and safety are not simply adjuncts to educational campaigns. Quite the opposite: they represent major opportunities for positive change that can stand on their own and, in some cases, may not need follow-up education and training.

The federal government during the Clinton and Obama administrations did recognize the importance of place.[30] They promoted several high-profile community development initiatives through the Department of Housing and Urban Development that targeted federal money to highly distressed neighborhoods in the form of direct grants to cities or nonprofits for extra services (e.g., police, social workers), tax benefits to businesses for hiring local community members, and tax credits to real-estate developers for building mixed-income developments.[31] These federal programs were general mechanisms for funding place-based economic development, although the design of the places was not always a central element in what ultimately emerged. While there is evidence that the Empowerment Zone initiative helped create jobs in targeted areas, they came at a high cost of more than $100,000 for each job created.[32] And housing prices rose in Empowerment Zones, suggesting that the benefits of job creation came at the cost of higher rents, which arguably hurt longer-term residents who were renters.

There is little evidence of lasting benefits of federally initiated place-based economic development initiatives. This is not surprising, as many place-based economic-development initiatives primarily focus on directing money to promote job growth in places that are no longer growth centers.[33] When place-based economic development is successful, it may spur migration from outsiders seeking jobs. This in-migration of outsiders tends to increase property values, as there is more competition for housing. While increasing property values has largely been seen by planners and city budget managers as a positive outcome related to place-based revitalization strategies, it is important to recognize the dangers of displacement faced by long-term renters and fixed-income residents when housing values increase.

Federally supported place-based economic development initiatives are rarely guided by scientific evidence on what will likely work to improve the well-being of residents in a given neighborhood. When urban renewal policies have been funded to address blighted land and rehabilitate neighborhoods, they have most often taken the form of slum clearance, the development and demolition of high-rise public housing, and the development of scattered-site developments.[34]

The Choice Neighborhoods initiative launched under the Obama administration is a recent exception to traditional federally supported place-based economic development in that it specifically advocates for neighborhood designs.[35] Choice Neighborhoods most closely resembles the place-based approaches discussed here, as improving the physical design of places can be an indispensable precursor to enhancing people's wellbeing. The goal of this initiative was to leverage public and private dollars to implement a comprehensive design plan for select neighborhoods. The design plan was supposed to come from a collaboration of local leaders, residents, nonprofits, the public housing authority, and other stakeholders seeking to revitalize blighted neighborhoods into mixed-use, mixed-income areas. Cities like Atlanta, Boston, Denver, and St. Louis were beneficiaries of these plans, and the areas they created were intended to draw new residents and allow longer-term residents to benefit from the neighborhood improvements.[36]

Choice Neighborhoods recognizes that many communities contain contributors to health and safety: for example, housing, roads, schools, medical clinics, parks, and shops. They also contain the embedded social and cultural understandings related to building a healthy, safe, and connected society. At some level, most people inherently understand that places matter and that our surroundings impact us. Structuring places to facilitate the healthiest and safest living situations should be a major focus of urban planning policy.

But how do we know if a place-based program is successful? That a community development model like Choice Neighborhoods works? How do we know if a place-based intervention will become an urban planning success, or, in the words of American urban planner Alexander Garvin, "a public action that will produce a sustained and widespread private market reaction"?[37] Relevant scientific evidence should be used for guidance on which place-based changes to cities will have the greatest health and safety benefits. Interest groups will of course advocate for designs that meet their own agendas. For example, land developers will push for mixed-use zoning when commercial construction projects are more lucrative or financeable than residential ones. Yet choices should be guided by evidence from scientific studies testing how changes to the design of places impacts health and safety.

Despite this, evidence from scientific testing alone may be insufficient to justify a change to the design of neighborhoods, streets, and transit options. Cost is likely to be become an obstacle to making design changes. Evidence of the cost-effectiveness of a place-based initiative can be used as a justification for upfront and scalable investments to entire neighborhoods or even entire cities. For example, work showing that the investment of one dollar in the remediation of abandoned housing results in a first-year return of five dollars to taxpayers and seventy-nine dollars to society has caught the eyes of policy makers, perhaps more so than the reduction in gun violence that fixing abandoned housing may generate.[38] Cost-benefit evidence, however, doesn't actually address how to finance place-based initiatives. Smaller-scale pilot studies could demonstrate effectiveness and be used to mobilize political support to overcome the resistance to financing and eventually implementing place-based interventions.

In this book we highlight examples of changes made in the places people live, work, and play that have been shown to be effective through scientific testing in the real world. Examples include a newly built light-rail system in Charlotte that lowered obesity and body mass index for users compared with car drivers, newly designed "breathe-easy" homes in Seattle that lowered asthma symptoms among children, business improvement districts that revitalized neighborhoods and reduced crime in Los Angeles, and thousands of newly greened vacant lots in Philadelphia that reduced violent crime, stress, and inactivity for nearby residents. These are just a few key examples of the kinds of changes that can be made to places and scientifically evaluated to show that they work before recommending they be implemented in other places and in other cities. At the same time, these are isolated examples, and more are needed in every city to figure out what place-based interventions work, are locally feasible, and can be taken to scale.

Place-based programs that sustainably change basic structures for large populations have long been in existence, but scientific evidence remains in short supply in determining what works and is most effective for improving health and safety. While it is impossible for all place-based changes to achieve their intended benefits, place-based policies for redesigning cities and neighborhoods should focus on those that achieve the greatest benefit for greatest number of people. Changing places can be used to protect the boy in East Saint Louis, the young man in New Jersey, and countless others that never make the news. If scientific evidence helps guide the choice of the best place-based programs, it is possible to improve the health and safety of the community at large in the coming decades.

Some place-based ideas have long been in existence and are in need of scientific testing, while others have yet to emerge. Discovery and testing of these ideas with rigorous scientific models is certainly in order to figure out what will work in different contexts and to mobilize community groups, practitioners, and policy makers to redesign basic urban structures and places with health and safety as a first consideration.

2

A New Movement
Based on Old Ideas

INDIVIDUAL DECISIONS are deeply rooted in the context within which we live, work, and play. There are meaningful opportunities to change that context in the form of the physical environments of even the most dangerous and blighted areas to produce healthier and safer living. Individual choices make a difference, but many life choices are heavily shaped by options one confronts in one's local environment.

In some ways, this is really nothing more than a reconstitution of thinking that has been with us for more than a century, but that became less relevant in the middle of the twentieth century as "better living through chemistry" and various programs focusing on lifestyle changes and individuals became prevalent, although with limited successes, as they ignored the difficult contexts surrounding individuals on a daily basis.[1] By comparison, the early twentieth century saw vast improvements in health and safety that occurred as a result of a direct recognition of place as important to human well-being and the cultivation of collaborations that today would be viewed as unusual—physicians and municipal managers, police and planners, sanitarians and civil engineers.[2] This teamwork resulted in the formation of public sanitation systems, electric power grids, municipal zoning and building codes, safety inspections of buildings, and health inspections of plants and restaurants.

Early zoning laws are great examples of place-based programs. The 1285 Statute of Winchester, for example, mandated that highways in Britain leading from "one market of town to another" be widened, that woods and brush be cleared within two hundred feet, and that parks have walls constructed so robbers wouldn't have access.[3] Municipal zoning codes were originally developed in Germany in the early 1800s but took a different form when they were applied in the United States.[4] The country's first comprehensive citywide zoning law—which has been hailed as one of the greatest single achievements in the history of city planning—was passed in New York City in 1914.[5] While many political interests sought zoning to protect the health and welfare of the working poor who were forced to live close to pollution-spewing factory districts, New York City's law had its genesis in a conflict over competing commercial retailers who wanted their stores physically separated from manufacturers. They wanted to spruce up the look of their stores, and they saw the manufacturers they relied on as a visual eyesore. Zoning was also focused on regulating the height of buildings, as the development of the elevator and the steel-framed building was crowding out the view of many NYC residents. There was broad support for the country's first comprehensive zoning law, from the city's average citizen to its banking and finance barons. While citizens were concerned over public health and overcrowding issues, the city's power brokers were trying to find a way to limit construction activities that were harming the general real-estate market in the city. Each individual's interest in maximizing the value of their own land by building a taller building had the potential to generate a collective disaster: an oversupply of office space and a drop in rental prices.[6] Zoning laws proved to be a highly effective tool to limit supply. Zoning laws expanded, and they were widely successful because they focused on places or structural changes while being cost-effective and readily scalable to cover entire communities, thus impacting large numbers of people over multiple generations.[7] Zoning was an absolute necessity in primarily industrial economies, with factory operations causing widespread air, water, and soil pollution that endangered the health of many urban dwellers. Zoning ordinances have since been based on ideas about how land use can impact health and safety, including separating different forms of residential and commercial land and regulating where potentially hazardous facilities can be located.[8] We still need to know more about how zoning can affect the health and safety of the population in a modern context, where cities are no longer manufacturing centers. Zoning has at times been a matter of contention, with some viewing zoning as an overreach of the government on individual property rights.

But the ability of municipalities to establish rules on land use through zoning is now a settled legal matter. In 1926 the US Supreme Court case of *Village of Euclid, OH v. Ambler Realty Company* settled the legal power of municipal governments to regulate the use of land. This case unfortunately also set the stage for the development of single-use zoning (also known as Euclidean zoning) in suburban communities, typically in form of single-family homes on large plots of land. Single-lot construction with large minimum lot sizes priced out the poor and urban minorities and limited the diversity of land use. The result was the growth of homogenous land use and populations that increasingly became dependent on car travel for daily routines. This suburban zoning practice is now one of the reasons that we have so many unhealthy places. Rather than consider the general social fabric of a community, single-use zoning treats each home like its own castle, complete with minimum lot sizes and setbacks. Thus, private architects and real-estate developers built places for individual families that came at the expense of designing neighborhoods with social and physical connectivity, providing fewer sidewalks, walking destinations, and playgrounds.

Riverside, Illinois, provides an exemplar of the power of zoning to shape the use of land in ways that promote car use over walking and public transit. Riverside, designed in 1869 by the famous landscape architect Frederick Law Olmstead had a curvilinear street pattern that utilized the natural shape of the Des Plaines River that meandered through the village for its design inspiration. Each house built in this master-planned community had a minimum price point and minimum lot size. The Riverside plan became the model for many suburbs built after World War II. Layered on top of this has been the tendency of suburbs to set restrictions on floor to area ratios, the setback distance of a house from the street, and forbidding multifamily or multipurpose buildings. Over time, the result of these planned unit-development suburbs has been larger homes, bigger lots, and a suburban sprawl design. In a sprawl, houses are further apart, sidewalks are few or nonexistent, and people drive to their destinations. This form of single-use zoning resulted in cutting people off from the natural interactions with their neighbors that occur when walking to a playground, restaurant, or shopping district.

Zoning—initially designed to protect society from what was once coming out of the industrial smokestack—was turned into a method of building single-family homes in isolation from apartment complexes and commercial uses. The legacy of single-use zoning in the suburbs has been to increase economic segregation, as the poor cannot easily enter these single-family housing markets.[9] There is also now mounting evidence that single-use zoning can undermine productivity, by limiting the available supply of housing or commercial businesses that can be built and preventing people from moving to more productive areas.[10] If you can afford to drive to work and accomplish daily tasks, the suburbs become the place to be. If you cannot, you remain dependent on public transit and cut off from more economically vibrant communities. On the other hand, those dependent on cars live a more sedentary life, which is a major contributor to obesity and related diseases.

Over the past twenty years, there has been a push for zoning reforms in urban and suburban areas. Inner-city economies have shifted from a basis on manufacturing to service and consumption. Downtowns are now hubs for entertainment and commerce and are increasingly also being seen as destinations for living. A new generation of people—empty nesters and young working professionals—want to live in vibrant, walkable downtown areas. This has created implications for removing single-use zoning and revitalizing former manufacturing sites into mixed-use zoning that permits residential and commercial buildings to be located near each other. Mixed-use zoning accommodates the desire of people to be within walking distance of shops, restaurants, or workplaces.

The move to mixed-use zoning has made its way to suburbs that were historically zoned for single uses. This is especially apparent in new suburban developments that have higher residential density and mixed uses, especially around retail agglomerations and rail transit stations. People want to live in suburbs that share some urban amenities and make travel to work and play easier.[11] While single-use Euclidian zoning has lost favor in many communities, its legacy remains embedded in our built environments, as most Americans still live in low-density, single-family neighborhoods. These historical land-use patterns have motivated planners to think creatively about how to redesign suburban communities that maximize human activity and promote public safety. There is now a larger movement in planning that supports "retrofitting" new suburban development to promote greater population density through zoning laws that require multifamily dwellings, commercial retail, and service uses and aim to cut down on automobile use by supporting expanded fixed rail mass transit and buses.[12]

While there is a negative legacy effect of single-use zoning, the benefits of many forms of zoning and other land-use changes that were regulated by government intervention are clear. Electric power grids, water treatment plants, building codes, and roadway redesign perhaps did more to enhance the health and safety of the public than many other efforts, including medical care and policing.[13] To be clear, we are not arguing for the cessation of key public services like medical care and policing. We need effective medical care and police. But these services occur largely *after* a health or safety problem has occurred. More consideration needs to be given to implementing place-based programs that can *prevent* health and safety problems from arising in the first place.

Programs that may prevent problems *before* they occur offer substantially greater return on our investment of scarce public resources. It's no secret that a big share of any municipal budget is the local police department and that, nationally, in the US and other countries, physician and hospital services also make up a big percentage of federal budgets. In times of financial crisis, though, investments in seemingly low-contribution programs—such as housing, parks, and playgrounds—are cut first, these programs may have more to contribute to tempering the negative effects that will eventually get addressed at either expensive hospitals or prisons.

A number of movements have sprung up in support of thinking more systematically about how changes to zoning can promote a healthier population. These have included New Urbanism, Green Living, Active Design, Crime Prevention through Environmental Design, and the Healthy Places movement. These movements provide a roadmap of sorts for why changing places is important for producing public health and safety solutions and address the need to inject more science into the actions coming out of these movements. Research into best practices in these areas will permit us to design and implement place-based solutions to health and safety concerns.

New Urbanism and Green Living

In 1961 Jane Jacobs published *The Death and Life of Great American Cities*, which details the superiority of traditional urban development patterns, such as those seen in her densely populated, mixed-land-use, and walkable neighborhood of Greenwich Village in New York City. Jacobs fought to resist planning efforts emphasizing suburbanization in the US, and the planning and design philosophies of federally funded urban redevelopment programs that started in the 1950s. These federal programs birthed the expansion of the concept of a "superblock," or a block with high-rise residential development surrounded by concrete and carpark access. These superblocks resulted in the development of sterile sites carefully planned for high-rise residential towers. Superblocks did not allow for any of the innovative uses of land that organically developed in places like Greenwich Village, where land uses were not carefully planned and governed.[14] Despite Jane Jacobs's powerful objections, high-rise development and the superblock became the dominant urban renewal form in the 1950s through the 1970s.

In the early 1990s, a long-simmering urban planning movement finally found its legs. For thirty years, a small group of urban advocates had grown weary of merely expounding the virtues contained in Jacobs's book and decided to get organized. In 1993, the Congress for New Urbanism (CNU) had their first meeting. Its founders included the influential architect Peter Calthorpe, the author of *The Next American Metropolis: Ecology, Community, and the American Dream*.[15] This book sought to reintroduce some of the planning concepts espoused by Ebeneezer Howard and his Garden Cities movement at the turn of the twentieth century, with regard to green, sustainable human habitats. The book also presented ideas from Andrés Duany, who had advocated against mass suburbanization and urban sprawl as unsustainable, unhealthy, and the "end of the American Dream." CNU created a mission statement that drew on Jacobs's: their goal was to "change the practices and standards of urban design and development to support healthy regions and diverse complete neighborhoods."

CNU's charter had organizing principles and a preamble that laid out their utopian vision of the future of the planning and design professions: "We stand for the restoration of existing urban centers and towns within coherent metropolitan regions, the reconfiguration of sprawling suburbs into communities of real neighborhoods and diverse districts, the conservation of natural environments, and the preservation of our built legacy."[16] The use of the term "healthy" in CNU's mission statement, rather than "wealthy," was no accident. The links between urban planning and public health goes back as far as human civilization itself. Urban planning and design as a social enterprise has always held public health as a key professional ethic and political outcome, as promoting healthy places through urban design also keeps capitalist societies working productively.[17]

Looking back at some colonial cities in the United States, like Philadelphia, Pennsylvania, and Savannah, Georgia, reveals some very fundamental efforts to create a healthy spatial order and avoid the dangers of ad-hoc development patterns that had occurred in earlier European cities. The inclusion of green space throughout their grid designs is a clear example of these early planned cities' efforts to promote healthy urban living. Philadelphia had five green squares; the center square would later become the site of City Hall. Savannah was planned with twenty-four squares organized around six administrative wards.

The superiority of the simple grid pattern as an urban design principle has found its way both into the popular lexicon of modern-day advocates for urban spaces and experts on urban planning. The choice of the name of a recent publication dedicated to urban environmental sustainability in Philadelphia points to this: *Grid*. Urban planners now measure sprawl by the number of street

FIGURE 2.1. Original plan for Savannah, Georgia, drawn in 1818 by Moss Eng. Co., New York. *Source*: From *Report on the social statistics of cities, Part II*, Compiled by George E. Waring Jr., U.S. Census Office, 1886.

crossings in an area. A city where the average intersection has at least three street segments crossing is now considered less sprawling and more of a grid design. Cities or town planning authorities who want to limit urban sprawl may now merely limit the number of nonintersecting street segments in any approvals for a major redevelopment. An early map of Savannah shown in figure 2.1 displays the power of the grid design to control land use. Savannah was a product of an early 1700s design by Oglethorpe.

At the turn of the nineteenth century another planning and design movement sought to impose spatial, social, and economic order on an industrial urban landscape that had become a public health menace. The Garden City movement arose as a response to the dangerous urban designs that mixed housing with industrial space in cities. Ebenezer Howard, the father of the Garden City design, writing in 1898, prescribed their size: 32,000 inhabitants

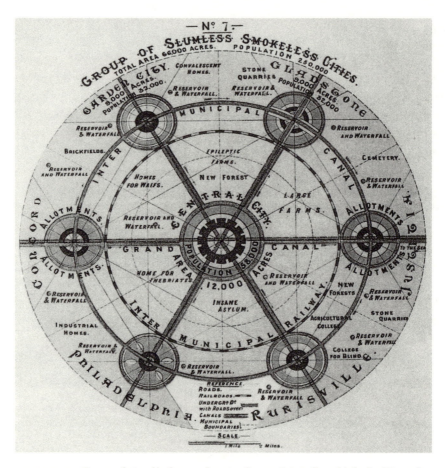

FIGURE 2.2. Proposed site plan for a garden city. *Source:* Originally published in Howard, Ebenezer, *Garden cities of tomorrow* (London: Swan Sonnenschein and Company, 1902).

with a radiating concentric use zoned around a town center with clear land-use separations and a surrounding greenbelt. The Garden City design was promoted to create healthier city environments; figure 2.2 shows a proposed site plan.

The Garden City idea found little traction as a large-scale development model, and only a few of these developments were built in the US and Europe.[18] The US government attempted to try this model in a new town-development scheme during the Great Depression. Seeking to build thousands of new "Green Belt" towns that incorporated many of the design and planning ideals of the

Garden City, they ultimately built only three: Greenbelt, Maryland; Greendale, Wisconsin; and Greenhills, Ohio.

Jane Jacobs would offer a critique of Howard's Garden City as being fundamentally antiurban for focusing too much on land-use separation, and as a heavy-handed expression of the planner's ideology over the people they sought to serve.[19] Like most utopian visions for human settlements through time, the Garden City movement failed. Indeed, the political and market difficulties in constructing total communities are legion. That said, the central idea of the Garden City was to design a largely self-sustaining economic, social, and environmental ecosystem in each city. Its design was a reflection of a desire to rid society of easily corruptible urban governments, which could be paid off to ignore environmental degradation caused by unfettered industrial use and the social ills brought on by crowding, poverty, and unhealthy living conditions. The title of the Garden City site plan graphic in figure 2.2 sums up the designers' larger goals: "A Group of Slumless, Smokeless Cities."

While New Urbanism takes ideas from Jane Jacobs, it also borrows ideas from the older Garden City designers. Urban planning historically has been tied to public health concerns, as threats such as widespread disease epidemics and fires have threatened cities. As we have previously discussed, overcrowded and unsanitary housing conditions, often commingled with urban factories, led to land-use zoning regulations in the United States during the twentieth century. The justification for the regulation of land use began with a desire to promote greater public health and safety.[20] This justification continues today in how we think about designing safer and healthier cities.

New Urbanism borrows many ideas from the efforts of the Garden City and other urban village designs of the nineteenth-century planners that were common before the advent of cars and the suburbanization of US cities.[21] New Urbanism at its core promotes higher residential densities, a mix of residential and commercial land uses in close walking proximity, and a grid street pattern that promotes closer distances between residential and commercial destinations.[22] Grid street patterns that have more intersections and smaller blocks also provide for multipurpose uses, like the creation of small neighborhood parks or green space adjacent to residential and commercial uses. The link between grid designs and health outcomes goes beyond simple land-use planning goals related to visual "coherence" or mixed-use enablement. Grids also provide prioritize pedestrian mobility, as they tend to generate more traffic stops that slow down car travel. Street grids, mixed-use zoning, modest street-segment length, and paved paths and sidewalks all make up part of the larger design that promotes multiple forms of travel in cities beyond cars. The grid system promotes walking, more sustainable forms of mass transit, and eclectic uses of spaces that encourage human activity.

At the turn of the twentieth century, civic groups around the US sought to do away with the grid systems that colonial planners installed as an American urban footprint. Suburban developments like Riverside noted above, as well as the City Beautiful movement that began with the Chicago's World's Fair and Exposition of 1896, and the subsequent plan for the federal district of Washington, DC, that was inspired by Haussmann's redevelopment plan for Paris, argued that the grid system invited crowding, visual monotony, and inefficient uses of land. Urban planning started to promote widespread redevelopment programs to beautify cores of cities. These projects sought to link newly developed civic buildings and public spaces to expanded landscaped park systems connected by parkways and grand boulevards.[23]

While there have been some social science endeavors to gauge the relative superiority of the grid street and mixed land-use designs, these designs were largely informed by a few key thinkers in urban planning. Science did not guide these ideas. The field of architecture that guides many urban planning decisions has long been informed by what might be called good design principles, which have emerged through an ideology of human habits along with trial and error. Seldom have good design principles been rooted in any empirical testing. The most important empirical test in the history of US development is the one supplied by the market and the question of whether the design will sell. This is a mistake that must be corrected. Basic science can help us figure out what works, what doesn't, and what is promising for designing safer and healthier cities.

Active Design and Healthy Places

A new mentality of active design and healthy places has arisen in modern urban planning: design focused on promoting physical activity. Initiatives like "Active Living by Design"[24] and the American Planning Association's "Planning and Designing the Physically Active Community" recognize the idea that urban planning should focus on designs that promote physical activity as a part of everyday life.[25] Gone is the sole focus on urban design informed by values related to comfort, relaxation, and construction efficiency (e.g., concrete is stronger and cheaper than brick). Cars, home appliances, home television, and city parks were originally promoted as a break from a life of hard manual labor. Now there is a growing awareness in urban planning that the physical design of places should promote physical activity.

The change in the nature of work for the vast majority of Americans over the past forty years has resulted in a more sedentary life. It's now common to see people running for their own fitness or going to the gym. But the jogging and fitness craze didn't take hold in the US and elsewhere until the 1970s, a decade when modern capitalist economies went through a period of massive restructuring away from manufacturing jobs to employment opportunities in the service sectors. As our economy became more automated, our chances of physical exertion during working hours became far less likely. In contrast, during the industrial age, housing for workers was often designed close to factory or port facilities. This was done out of pure necessity, as workers were too poor to afford private transportation and public transit was underdeveloped. People walked to work, performed several hours of physical labor, returned home, ate a home-cooked meal, slept, and did it all over again. Compare that to today's typical worker, who drives alone thirty minutes to work, sits for eight to nine hours, drives home another thirty minutes, eats processed food, watches television for three hours, sleeps, and does it all over again. And, instead of going to a park on the weekend to relax, the average worker watches six more hours of television and tries to get to the gym on Saturday afternoon. There is a clear connection between our sedentary modern lifestyles and the obesity epidemic.

Active living seeks to combat the negative health impact of sedentary living by designing and promoting healthier lifestyles. The active-living agenda promotes the idea of attaining some minimum level of physical activity through routine daily activity. Minimum standards have been devised and promoted by the Center for Disease Control and Prevention in the United States, which get promoted in schools and public service announcements, as well as by healthcare insurers and by doctors. Cities and towns have also built physical-activity promotional campaigns around athletic and social events, such as foot or bike races. Companies now have a "take the stairs" week as a way to entice workers to be more cognizant that exercise opportunities exist in even the most sedentary environments.

The active-living agenda also acknowledges that individual behavioral modification programs and messaging are hard to maintain in the face of the structural organization of our society around driving an automobile and taking an elevator to work. Active-living design programs seek to restructure the sedentary aspects of modern life by redesigning the built environment away from suburban sprawl and a dependence on car travel to denser development patterns organized around mass transit nodes. The basic idea is to promote walking to transit or to nearby entertainment districts as a way to obtain a minimum amount of needed physical activity. Active living also seeks to promote physical activity by designing local trails, walking paths, sidewalks, improved lighting, and landscaping spaces to make walking more attractive to pedestrians. While New Urbanism also promotes design principles that result in more walkable neighborhoods, active living seeks even a more explicit focus on designing the built environment of cities in ways that promote physical activity. New Urbanism and active living are not the only ideas motivating planners to change the design of cities. Public safety is also an important component of urban design.

Crime Prevention through Environmental Design

While the planning models of New Urbanism and Active Living by Design have gained greater traction in urban planning circles, within the field of criminology, Crime Prevention Through Environmental Design (CPTED) has been the primary model for explaining how the built environment of places influences crime. Coined in 1972 by C. Ray Jeffrey, CPTED refers to the idea that crime can be prevented by adapting elements of the built environment.[26] The basic model builds off the ideas of Jane Jacobs, and her observations that the physical designs of streets and housing are central to encouraging active guardianship by residents and business proprietors in their neighborhood. Simple examples include designing houses with porches or windows close enough to the street for residents to keep a watch on sidewalks. Designing residential apartments with commercial property on the street level of buildings was thought by Jacobs to reduce crime because merchants during the day would guard entrances to buildings and maintain order. The crime prevention benefits of the types of changes to the built environment of places may be subtle in nature. Less subtle changes to an area using a CPTED approach could include adding lighting to a parking lot or closed-circuit cameras to prevent motivated criminals from thinking they can break into cars without being seen.

Some key ideas from CPTED include modeling the design of the built environment to maximize surveillance, limit access, and enhance signs of territoriality (i.e., communicate ownership of the area). Surveillance can be maximized in countless ways. Streets can be designed to increase pedestrian and bicycle use. This will mean there are more "eyes upon the street," reducing the chance that an offender is alone on the street with an isolated victim. Setback distances for buildings should also be minimized so that it is easier for individuals in a building to see the street.[27] Some have also argued that reducing brush and overgrown trees on streets is important. [28] In commercial areas with high-value targets, like ATM machines, convenience-store cash registers, or jewelry stores, it is important that potential targets are located in plain view of the public.[29] This means using two-way glass and putting high-value targets in an open area that passing traffic can see. Changes to the built environment that reduce access include guarded entranceways to buildings, limiting the number of doorways at street level, and installing fences around properties. Some designs can also facilitate both surveillance and access control, such as cul-de-sacs, because they provide only one way in and out of a neighborhood but opportunities for residents to view passersby.[30] Territoriality can be promoted by signs that indicate a security system is installed in a home, or that trespassing is not allowed on a property. Short picket fences along property lines may also limit access while also providing neighbors with a sense for who is and is not permitted in a property. If there are clear signs that a space is maintained and controlled by the owners, criminals are less likely to enter it. Note that this model does not address the fundamental motivations behind crime; rather, it tries to make crimes inconvenient. The idea is that there are easier targets elsewhere. Some have criticized CPTED because it does not address underlying root causes that make someone likely to commit a crime in the first place. This misses the point.

CPTED is not an explanation for why crimes occur. Rather, CPTED is a prescription for designing the environment in ways that minimize crime among those most predisposed to committing it. CPTED suggests that certain design characteristics of the built environment, such as poor visibility, unguarded entry points, and a permeable street network that make entry and escape easier, can predict what kind of place will be attractive to criminal victimization. CPTED offers a recipe for reducing crime by shifting the availability of easy targets. This does not mean that an offender's motivations to commit crime have been erased; it simply means that some offenses won't occur in given areas because offenders either choose to go elsewhere or to not commit the crime. If one assumes that not all crimes are easily replaceable (e.g., many crimes occur close to where people live) then the crime rate can go down by shifting the built environment without addressing the underlying causes of criminal motivations.[31] The goal of CPTED is simply to reduce the demand for crime by making an area less appealing to the offender because the chances of getting caught have increased while the chances of successfully pulling off the crime have decreased.[32]

But how well does CPTED work in practice? There are many case studies that highlight apparent examples of where CPTED appeared to work in reducing crime. For example, a North Miami neighborhood installed street barricades to reroute traffic and found that burglaries, car thefts, and robberies decreased.[33] There is also a cottage industry of vendors selling CPTED products with promises of crime reduction.[34] But most of these successes provide either no statistical test of whether the differences merely occurred by chance or a comparison group of places that were similar but did not receive a CPTED design change.[35] Despite the lack of high-quality evidence of the effectiveness of CPTED, it remains a popular crime prevention model because it is easy to conceptualize, and the case studies discussed have an instinctive appeal to the public.

Like New Urbanism and Active Living by Design, CPTED is appealing because the model is clear. Make sensible changes to places and people will change to adapt positively to their new environment. Criminals will be deterred, just as people will walk instead of drive in an Active Living by Design area, and stress and poverty will decline in a New Urbanism design, where mixes of land uses and residential incomes lead to better connected and economically integrated neighbors.[36] While such models are attractive, they have been espoused in isolation of rigorous evidence. Linking these models to evidence is important if they are to be useful policy prescriptions for changing places.

It's unfortunate that these previous movements have evolved in mutually exclusive silos—city planners doing their own thing in isolation from public health and public safety practitioners. These uncoordinated endeavors have had limited success and impact, though there is a growing emphasis on all three models in the American Planning Association's policy guidance on "Smart Growth," "Healthy Communities," and "Security."[37] While it is reasonable to think that good science is already involved when a place gets altered or a venue gets built, this is rarely the case. With the exception of the physical-engineering science of constructing buildings, bridges, and roadways, the human health and safety impacts of urban design are seldom informed by scientific testing.

There is a need to invigorate a new movement that connects scientists, urban planners, and policy makers to design safer and healthier cities around the world. The best science is produced in the real world and thrives when informed by individuals who have practical knowledge. The importance of innovation and creativity in implementing meaningful place-based interventions cannot be understated. Community-embedded practitioners who possess the real-world experiences necessary to make smart design choices need to engage with scientists to produce the greatest health and safety benefits to society.

The best placemaking can occur through scientific evaluation of human settlements. Just like those who conceive innovative new place-based programs, the importance of involving scientists "early and often" in these programs is a key ingredient to building safer and healthier cities. Policy makers need to embrace science in determining what works and what doesn't. This means sometimes overriding your prior understanding, when evidence suggests another course of action or goes against the profit needs of a powerful interest group. A new "changing places movement" that overtly connects planners, policy makers, and scientists can provide the foundation for this kind of conviction. So how do we know that the evidence before us is bona fide?

3

Establishing Evidence

IN THE SUMMER OF 1854 the Soho neighborhood of West London was in the middle of an unrelenting outbreak of cholera. In about a week, some five hundred people died. At the time, popular wisdom contended that the disease was being transmitted via miasma, or "bad air." Even among physicians, it was largely inconceivable at the time that infections could be transmitted through contaminated water, which, as we know today, was the source of this outbreak.[1]

John Snow, a highly regarded physician, decided to investigate Soho water sources as a potential cause of cholera. Snow compiled data about neighborhood residents who had died from cholera and other members of their households. After mapping these data, it looked to Snow like most of the deceased lived nearby the Broad Street water pump; given this evidence, Snow petitioned the local authorities to shut it off. In his own words, "I had an interview with the Board of Guardians of St. James's parish, on the evening of Thursday, 7th September, and represented the above circumstances to them. In consequence of what I said, the handle of the pump was removed on the following day."[2] After people living on Broad Street could no longer drink water from the pump, cholera deaths waned. From this intervention, Snow's theory developed: that cholera was a waterborne disease. It would take decades for the idea of water-based oral-fecal transmission of disease to be accepted as reality by local officials and the public.

Snow's actions to remove the Broad Street pump handle and to challenge miasma theory of "bad air" have become the stuff of legend in modern public health. Snow is widely regarded as the father of epidemiology and was voted the "greatest doctor of all time" in a March 2003 survey by *Hospital Doctor* magazine.[3] Removing the handle of the Broad Street pump is a prototypical example of a place-based intervention to improve health. Snow relied on a method of scientific evaluation to reach his conclusions, showing that deaths from cholera were higher among people living near the Broad Street water pump than those living nearby who drew their water from other wells. The story of John Snow is an important demonstration of the kind of action that, if undertaken, can change places and impact the lives of real people in a positive way.

Today's epidemiologists largely agree with Snow's actions. In many ways, what Snow accomplished was remarkable, given the absence of a known biological basis for cholera and the relative infancy of the use of statistics to describe disease risks.[4] By today's standards of scientific evidence, though, certain inconsistencies in Snow's investigation are instructive. For instance, geographers have reconstructed maps based on Snow's original data and show that the cholera outbreak could have been much more effectively displayed and acted upon with modern geographic information systems.[5] Compare Snow's original map of the cholera outbreak and the pumps with this new map made with the latest technology and one can see that the more modern map makes the source of the outbreak even more apparent.

Snow was likely correct in concluding that the pump was the source of the cholera, but it could have also been some other factor. We only conclude that he was correct because the outbreak dissipated after the removal of the pump. But did removing the pump handle really produce the subsequent reduction in cholera cases, or was the epidemic already in decline, perhaps because of the natural course of the disease or because the number of individuals who were still susceptible had substantially dropped, having either fled the neighborhood or been infected? As Snow himself later noted, these alternative explanations were possible.[6] Modern chemistry tells us that cholera is caused by water contaminated with bacteria Vibrio cholera.[7]

The power of a place-based intervention is evident in the story of the Broad Street pump. Even Snow's detractors at the time acknowledged as much: "I must not omit to mention that if the removal of the pump-handle had nothing to do with checking the outbreak which had already run its course, it had probably everything to do with preventing a *new* outbreak."[8] Through stories like the Broad Street pump and many others, the idea that our surroundings are important to human health and safety has long been recognized. It's less clear, however, which specific place-based interventions should be undertaken to most acutely change the health and safety of large groups of people. One could argue that our lack of funding for scientific studies to convincingly identify how to change key aspects of places and improve health and safety has thwarted societal efforts to make even more transformative place-based interventions. By contrast, the pharmaceutical industry starting in the 1950s, invested in scientific

FIGURE 3.1. Snow's 1854 map of cholera around the Broad Street Pump compared to computer software. *Source*: (Top) Snow, John, *On the mode of communication of cholera*, 2nd ed. (London: John Churchill, 1855).

studies and the "Better Living Through Chemistry" movement to fundamentally alter public views and policies to rely primarily on drugs in responding to many of society's biggest health problems. Whether this movement has actually delivered better living is debatable, but it is illustrative of the way we as a society can make a significant scientific investment in a field and develop programs to intervene and improve population health and safety.

Today, decisions about changing places are often made within fleeting political contexts informed by public opinion focused on what is desirable at the moment, as opposed to what could be shown to offer the greatest long-term results. Rarely are zoning or land-use laws changed or amended in a given municipality because of scientific studies that show they will improve health and safety outcomes.[9] When cities change their built environments and add new buildings, parks, streets, and sidewalks, these changes may reference public health impacts but are only loosely connected. Rarely does a city change the built environment with a specific emphasis on safety and health generated from evidence derived from scientific studies. Yet the impression persists that such land-use and zoning changes are tied to scientific evidence and not just to stylistic preferences.

Why is scientific evidence important for understanding how to change the design of places to improve safety and health in cities? Don't we know already what needs to be done from successful case studies of places that have been changed? Unfortunately, decisions around changing places are often driven by isolated, unsystematic examples of apparent successes, many of which may actually have little bearing on what works. These case studies, while often offering valuable preliminary guidance and proofs of concept, are conducted in small areas and affect too few people to justify wider action and satisfy two key aspects of scientific validity: causality and generalizability. In table 3.1 we outline key terms that will guide our discussion of establishing levels of scientific evidence, or evidence used to support a theory based on the scientific method.

Causality and Place

Terms like scientific evidence and evidence-based policy are often discussed with little explanation, as if the existence of evidence is self-evident. Although it is easy to find a published study showing that people living in different environments have different health and safety outcomes, this is not sufficient evidence to take action or make policy. How well a study informs action rests

TABLE 3.1. Key Terms

Causality =	Input produced the effect (63) according to probability that an effect will occur (65) and theory of action that explains the sequence (80).
Reason for establishing causality =	Make predictions about the future and take corrective action (64).
Causal relationship requires =	The treatment *preceded* the observed effect; the treatment is *related* to the effect observed; and there are *no other likely explanations* for the change one observes other than the treatment (73).
Experiment =	"A test under a controlled conditions that is made to" "demonstrate the efficacy of something."
Randomized controlled trials =	Experiments where subjects are randomly assigned to treatment or control groups (70). Random assignment assures all groups have equal chance of receiving treatment and removes bias.
Counterfactual comparison =	Condition people or places if they had not received the treatment (67).
Balance =	Treatment and comparison groups are comparable on average to factors that are measured (73).
Natural experiments =	Random assignment happens outside of the control of the scientists, through nature or by a policy intervention that resembles an experiment (78).
Quasi-experiment =	A controlled trial without random assignment (79).
Generalizability =	The ability of the results from the experiment to apply in another context (81).
Random sampling =	A scientific process of randomly selecting subjects so that they represent every person or place in the population (5).
Systematic review =	A synthesis of studies based on clearly detailed criteria (89).
Meta-analysis =	A method of combining estimates from multiple studies into a single estimate (90).

Source: Shadish, William R., Thomas D. Cook, and Donald Thomas Campbell, *Experimental and quasi-experimental designs for generalized causal inference* (Boston: Houghton Mifflin, 2002).

both on the quality of the evidence it contains and how translatable it is to actual policy.

Readers have probably heard the phrase "correlation is not causation." A scientific study showing that more neighborhood trees is correlated with less stress, for example, may at first seem like enough evidence to recommend the million-trees-planted initiatives that the former mayors of Los Angeles and New York City issued in 2006 and 2007. By 2015 New York City accomplished its goal in planting the millionth tree.[10] But what if a lack of trees is simply a proxy for blight or poverty that also affects stress? The standard counter to this criticism is to include a statistical model that adjusts for neighborhood differences. This is often done through multiple regression equations, which is just a way to make a clear (linear) relationship between an outcome measure (e.g., stress) and a set of other variables (e.g., trees, blight, poverty). This approach is a good practice to account for correlational differences between neighborhoods, such as poverty and blight, that are associated with both stress and lack of trees. But what if stressed people are more likely to move into neighborhoods with fewer trees? Since one hasn't actually observed differences before and after trees were planted, one can't really say in the end that trees reduce stress; it may be the other way around. Can one really recommend to policy makers that a city plant trees in its neighborhoods to combat stress? In fact, this hypothetical study has not even really studied individual stress, but groups of people living in the same neighborhoods.[11] Maybe there is a subset of individuals living in poverty-stricken neighborhoods that plant trees around their homes to help them reduce stress, but the vast majority of people living in the same neighborhoods receive no stress reduction because of trees. The potential for different groups of people in the same neighborhood to experience different sources of stress, referred to by social scientists as subgroup differences or treatment effect heterogeneity, may undermine any ability to say anything about effects on neighborhoods. In this way, trees might be correlated with stress, but it would be unclear from this study if planting trees was a useful prescription for reducing stress for neighborhoods or just a subset of people.

More rigorous scientific evidence forces us to critically question whether what one observes is actually a consequence of some action and not just a random occurrence. This is the much discussed idea of *causality*. Economist Josh Angrist notes that "empirical research is motivated by a belief that estimates for a particular context provide useful information about the likely effect" in some other similar context "or events in the future."[12] The basic idea of causality is that an input (cause) produced the effect.[13] Ultimately, if one can establish that a cause produced an effect, then predictions about the future can be made, and society can take corrective actions.

The very idea of causality has also led to heated debates in the social sciences and medicine, where some have argued that estimates of causal effects often have limited applicability to real-world policy contexts and that more emphasis should be placed on understanding general patterns and how different contexts impact human behavior.[14] In the quest for finding causal estimates, social scientists and epidemiologists may miss out on examining the importance of general patterns, which in some contexts provide sufficiently convincing evidence to demonstrate that something real has happened. The US crime drop in the 1990s, in New York City in particular, is a good case in point of an issue for which it has been difficult to isolate a cause. Victimization rates for robbery dropped by 28 percent between 1990 and 1994 and then dropped another 70 percent between 1994 and 2005. Between 2005 and 2014 robbery declined by another 36 percent. In total, robbery rates were nearly 86 percent lower in 2014 than in 1990. Criminal homicide followed a remarkably similar pattern.[15] As a number of scholars have documented, this trend was fairly widespread across the city and not isolated to specific NYC boroughs.

While such changes are illustrative of an important downward shift in crime in New York City, these shifts don't explain what caused the crime decline.[16] Scientifically demonstrating with certainty that one thing *causes* another is often viewed as the ultimate goal of research on crime, health, and other social factors. Because scientists are generally allergic to absolute certainty, few will actually use the word "cause" in a research paper. Many social scientists devote their entire career to proving causality, often with limited success. Indeed, the desire for causal conclusions can limit the scope of what researchers actually choose to study, often forcing them to pursue very narrow sets of research questions that can only be measured in highly controlled settings.

Proving causality in place-based programs can be quite challenging, due to the various effects that may be triggered from any one intervention. Being able to conceptually isolate the impact of the change, while also being able to accurately and consistently measure a specific input that caused a particular effect, is rarely possible. At best, what one can hope for is establishing relationships that clearly increase "the probability that an effect will occur."[17] Despite these challenges, social scientists have developed a hierarchy of evidence for determining when evidence is getting close to showing cause and effect.[18]

Although all levels of the hierarchy value causal evidence, studies that rely on experimental designs are given greater status. The best method for determining cause and effect is experimentation, or randomized controlled trials, as they are known in medical research. Randomized controlled trials are a fundamental method that scientists use to control biases, which are inherent to all scientific studies and that cloud our ability to explain cause-and-effect relationships. Bias here refers to the tendency to erroneously attribute the effect of an outcome as being caused by a treatment. For example, one may attribute a positive change in the average daily walking patterns of people in a neighborhood to the installation of a new sidewalk, when the real cause is that a set of new residents to the area, who moved there specifically due to the area's walkability, are driving this rate of change.

Experiments are often misunderstood by the public and policy makers, and even some scientists. In its most basic form, a study is labeled an experimental trial when the scientific investigator manipulates some treatment, exposure, or condition with the intent of seeing what happens next. The "what happens next" part is a key part of the experimental design. This is also referred to as time order, in that it allows one to see what occurs before and after the manipulation. In any experiment, the scientist should have the ability to control the timing of a treatment, who gets exposed to it, and, possibly, by how much, as well as the conditions under which the treatment is delivered. This unique opportunity to control exposure, dosage, and the environment of the treatment is the main tool of the scientific trade, used to ensure that any observed outcomes are based on the treatment, and not the normal, everyday things can affect a place over time. This process of regression to the mean, or the tendency of things to return to their normal state, is a common concern in scientific research, as it can lead one to erroneously attribute an intervention as the cause of a change when it fact it was just a coincidence. If John Snow could have timed the removal of the pump handle to the middle of the outbreak, he may have avoided skepticism that cholera was already going through its natural course of decline after killing hundreds of people.

In the previously mentioned example of trees and stress, one doesn't know for certain if the outcome of reduced stress is caused by trees being planted or if people with less stress in the first place are more likely to plant trees. Conducting a study that measures people's stress before and after trees were planted in their neighborhoods could avoid this problem of selection bias or reverse causality. While it's not always possible to guarantee that the problem of selection bias is completely eliminated, conducting an experiment is the best way to minimize it, as the investigator has direct control over the intervention and can observe changes in outcomes before and after the experiment was conducted.

Taking this idea a bit further, one can imagine that a scientist might want to see if aspirin reduces headaches or if people who view elements of nature, such as grass and trees, can reduce their stress level. Both are legitimate trial conditions manipulated by scientists in order to assess the impact of an intervention on human health. In both examples, people are exposed to treatments (aspirin or green views) and then subsequently followed to see if they experience changes in certain outcomes (headaches or stress). The time order—that the treatment precedes the measure of any outcome—is part of a well-controlled sequence. However, to know for certain if there is true cause and effect, scientists must also compare individuals to others that are not exposed to an experimental intervention, also known as the control group. A key factor for drawing some reasonable conclusion about cause and effect is to consider the condition of people or places absent any treatment exposure: in short, those possibly unlucky people who do not get a real aspirin, or those who do not get to gaze at that relaxing image of a green space outside of their window. Those groups outside of the experimental treatment are commonly referred to as a *counterfactual comparison*. This method of drawing conclusions about causes dates back to the eighteenth-century philosopher David Hume.[19] One cannot actually observe what would happen to a person or a place if it did not receive a treatment. After all, a treatment was received. However, one can draw this conclusion by comparing what happened in a similar set of comparison groups that could have received the treatment but did not.

In this way, another key advantage of trials is the ability to assign some treatment to an "experimental" group of people or places and directly compare another "control" group of people or places that did not receive the treatment. Control groups typically take the form of those who receive no treatment, get the usual care, or are given some form of a placebo condition that should have no impact on the theoretical outcome of the intervention. Comparing the outcomes of the control group to the experimental group contributes to the researcher's ability to assert whether a particular treatment causes a particular effect. Control groups should be thought of as counterfactual conditions. If one has ever thought, "What would happen if I didn't take my medicine?" they have in effect thought about their own counterfactual condition.

Counterfactuals provide a set of comparison conditions and are fundamental to helping establish causality. If getting treatment A produces outcome B, then the converse should also be true: not getting treatment A should not produce outcome B. If one really wants to know that a particular treatment or intervention works, it's just as important to know what happens if people or places don't get the treatment.

Control groups are valuable because they can disentangle tangential effects of a given treatment and allow us to more accurately detect if a true cause-and-effect relationship exists. Imagine that one thinks a room with a view of green space is thought to reduce stress. And, a study is run that has people sit in a room with a view of green space and measures their stress levels. For the people assigned to the room with a view of green space, stress reduces by 20 percent. But

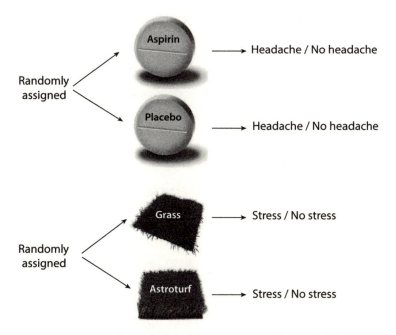

FIGURE 3.2. Logic of a causal analysis generated from an RCT.

then a control group of people are assigned to a similar room without such a view. For this group stress reduces by 19 percent. One might conclude from this study that views of green space do little to reduce stress. Without a control group this key finding is undetectable.

An advantageous way to reduce selection bias is to randomly assign people or places to experimental and control groups, as this assures that all people or places could have received the treatment and are otherwise similar. When this is done, the experiment is referred to as a randomized controlled trial (RCT). Figure 3.2 shows the causal logic of a RCT. Random assignment is the best experimental manipulation available to scientists to minimize selection bias.

It's a common misconception that random assignment defines an experimental trial. The manipulation into a treatment itself is what defines the trial, and many trials proceed with only an experimental group. These trials, however, don't meet the gold standard, since they cannot compare the conditions of a treatment group to a comparison group. They are simply a pre-post design that meets the average standard of evidence, as they cannot rule out the problem of regression to the mean or that changes may have occurred as a natural consequence.

Some basic principles follow for establishing causal relationships of treatments including: that the treatment *preceded* the observed effect; that the treatment is *related* to the effect observed; and that there are *no other likely explanations* for the change one observes other than the treatment.[20] Experimental trials are preferable because they meet these principles. Manipulating the treatment assures that it precedes the effect and allows us to observe how outcomes change for places or people receiving the treatment compared to those not receiving it. Through manipulation one can be confident that individuals or groups receiving treatment or the control condition are similar to each other in all other factors. When manipulation is done through a lottery or random assignment one can be assured that the experimental and control groups are "balanced." This means that the groups will ostensibly be the same in all factors, both measurable and unmeasurable, except for the treatment itself. That said, there might be things that are different between two groups that are unmeasured (unobservable), but could make subjects (person or place) respond differently to a treatment and bias evidence of its effectiveness. The random assignment ensures that every subject (person or place) has an equal chance of receiving the treatment.[21] By equal chance, then, the two groups will look similar on observable and unobservable factors. This balance allows us to much more confidently conclude that a treatment, exposure, or condition has actually caused some outcome in a way that is uncontaminated by other factors and competing explanations.

Consider an RCT where a group of people are randomly assigned to take aspirin or to take a placebo "sugar pill." The placebo is designed to look like aspirin, but is lacking its active ingredient, acetylsalicylic acid. Because of the random assignment, the people in the experimental and placebo control groups will be the same in terms of all factors (e.g., height, age, race, income, health conditions) except for the acetylsalicylic acid. If headaches decrease more in the experimental group than in the placebo group, one is on firmer ground in saying that it was really due to the aspirin. Consider a second RCT where a group is randomly assigned to spend time in an experimental room with a view of natural grass or to a placebo control-group room with a view of Astroturf. Again, the placebo is designed to look like natural grass, but is lacking the active ingredient of graminoids that creates the morphology in natural grass. The people in the experimental and placebo control groups will be the same in terms of all factors except the graminoids. If stress goes down more in the experimental group than in the placebo group, one is on firmer ground in saying that this reduction was due to the natural grass.

The two prior examples were fictitious, though there are similar experiments that have been conducted.[22] These examples also show that randomized controlled trials have application beyond the world of pharmaceuticals and are useful for the scientific testing of place-based treatments.

There are numerous RCT examples out there demonstrating that experiments with place are possible and can produce groundbreaking new knowledge that can inform policy. Perhaps the largest and best-known example of this to date is the Moving to Opportunity (MTO) study. The MTO study is a five-city RCT started by the Department of Housing and Urban Development in the 1990s. Some 4,600 very low-income families in Baltimore, Boston, Chicago, Los Angeles, and New York City were randomly assigned to one of three conditions: an experimental group that received rental housing vouchers to move into a low-poverty neighborhood; a comparison group that received rental housing vouchers and could move anywhere; and a control group that received no vouchers.[23] The study concluded with a number of landmark scientific findings, including that people in the experimental group had significantly less obesity, diabetes, and unhappiness after they had moved, compared with the control group.[24]

The MTO study's use of random assignment to achieve *balance* between its three trial conditions was a major advantage. The study cannot directly demonstrate balance for countless unmeasurable factors but, owing to the basic principle of random assignment from thousands of individuals, one can be sure that the groups are likely similar. One can also directly demonstrate balance with measures that show that the treatment and control groups are alike. The MTO reported that its three study arms were balanced in numerous factors, some of which we show here (see table 3.2). Looking closely one can see that the experimental and control groups never differ by more than a few decimal or percentage points. Balance like this is testament to random assignment, and the ensuing analyses of the MTO left little doubt that the changes experienced by the people in the study were due to the vouchers that caused them to move and not factors like age, education, or income that also play a role.

The MTO is a landmark piece of science in terms of place-based research. The randomized housing mobility experiment elegantly showed us that among adults moving out of high-poverty neighborhoods, measures of happiness, physical health, and perceptions of safety improved.[25] Adult women in the study that moved to the low-poverty neighborhoods were also significantly less likely to become morbidly obese or to have signs of diabetes.[26] For girls, the study also suggested some improvements in mental health and criminal behavior.[27]

TABLE 3.2. MTO Experiment Showing Similarity between Treatment and Control Groups

	2,134 people that got vouchers to move (experimental)	1,139 people that received no vouchers (control)
Age (average)	44.5 years old	44.6 years old
African American	66%	64%
Hispanic	30%	32%
Employed	25%	27%
High school diploma	36%	37%
Household income (average)	$12,439	$12,834
Very dissatisfied with their neighborhood	47%	48%

However, as with all scientific studies, the MTO had its limitations and showed tradeoffs with moving for some recipients of vouchers. Chief among these was the finding that moving out of high-poverty neighborhoods increased rates of depression, PTSD, conduct disorder, and criminal behavior for adolescent boys—a key piece of information suggesting that maybe relocation isn't for everyone.[28] However, other evidence suggests that children who moved before the age of thirteen benefited from leaving high-poverty neighborhoods, suggesting that if a move is going to benefit children it should occur before they are teenagers.[29] Another consideration is the excessive costs and global problems of relocating people as a policy compared to "in-situ" programs that try to change the built environments where people live. In-situ programs that change the surroundings people live in without moving them can compete with relocation strategies in terms of value and impact. Many people may have difficulty moving and decide to stay where they are, as is evident from the fact that over half of those in the MTO study that received a voucher stayed in public housing. The idea of mass relocation as a place-based policy solution also may not sit well with many people who've experienced historical discrimination in the form of forced relocation.[30]

Additionally, it is worth pointing out that the MTO study didn't actually manipulate the built environment of the places where people lived; it simply moved people to new places.[31] The MTO experiment does provide valuable insights about how place impacts the safety and health of the population, but it doesn't tell us what outcomes would look like if people had stayed in their neighborhoods and the blocks they lived on were redesigned.

One reason that place-based randomized controlled trials are so few and far between is that partnering with and then convincing community-based authorities to have a scientist dictate the timing and administration of a particular place-based program, including random assignment, is very difficult. This is the so-called "politics of randomization," and not all scientists are as convincing as John Snow was to the St. James's Parish Board of Guardians. On the contrary, local authorities may have the false idea that scientists are unethically experimenting on their communities and see random assignment as an unfair way to take away their control of when and where a program gets implemented.

Today, randomized controlled trials involving human subjects are highly monitored endeavors, subject to extensive ethical and operational checkpoints prior to launch and during commission. Moreover, random assignment is, in fact, the absolute fairest way to decide who gets some treatment or intervention in situations where it is unclear what treatments or interventions actually work.[32] And, in the context of limited resources, random assignment is arguably ethical, because it gives everyone an equal chance of receiving the treatment. People seem to feel more comfortable with random assignment when they think of it like playing the numbers in a lottery—that is, anyone can win by getting the treatment or intervention, but because not everyone wins there exists an opportunity to learn something new and potentially important. It's one of the reasons that a larger call has gone out for more widespread RCTs in business and government. In fact, companies like Google and Amazon already conduct tens of thousands of RCTs each year and about one in ten of these trials lead to actual changes in business practices.[33]

The time commitment, costs, and administrative challenges are enough to deter many scientists from even trying to complete a place-based RCT that seeks to change the built environment, the operational challenge of which is noteworthy. In one trial that we undertook, small parcels of land were randomly assigned to receive a place-based treatment and others were not.[34] We had successfully argued that a lottery was the fairest way to assign our treatment and had fully arranged both municipal and legal approval to implement it. However, when we were finally at the point where workers had to actually go out and make the changes to our randomly selected spaces, we hit a hurdle. Before making the changes, the workers had to designate each space with a small spray-paint marking on the adjacent sidewalk. However, all of the colors of the rainbow were already taken for other city business—red for electricity, orange for telecom, yellow for gas, green for sewers, blue for water. Without a color for science, we were at an impasse. How about purple? As luck would have it, purple had not been claimed, and a hardware store hundreds of miles away sold us their last case of purple temporary marking spray paint. Crisis averted, the trial proceeded, but not without some reflection that place-based trials are rife with challenges both big and small.

Even with the growing interest and technical capacity of place-focused scientists, many situations exist in which place-based randomized controlled trials are not possible. Prohibitive costs, time delays, logistical challenges, political aversion, and ethical constraints often make these trials more difficult to undertake than other types of scientific studies. Some place-based change advocates have argued that actual RCTs are not really viable if our goal is to make rapid decisions and implement policies within reasonable time frames.[35] One counterargument could be that big business does tens of thousands of randomized controlled trials each year as part of a rapid-cycle learning process—why can't policy decisions important to the public also be guided by RCTs?[36] But the point is well taken that in many situations randomized controlled trials may not be feasible.

When an RCT is not feasible, natural experiments or quasi-experiments can be used as a suitable second choice. Natural experiments involve random assignment to treatment or control conditions caused by nature or other factors, such as an idiosyncratic policy change, that are outside of the direct control of the scientist. Because the scientist does not control the timing of the random assignment in a "natural experiment," they must adapt their data collection schedule and analyses to document what conditions were like in the treatment and control groups before and after the change. A great example of a place-based natural experiment was captured in a recent study of the widespread destruction of ash trees caused by the emerald ash borer beetle across the Midwest. This beetle was discovered in southeastern Michigan in 2002 and was subsequently credited for the loss of one hundred million ash trees. Because the spread of the beetle in Midwestern counties is largely a result of the seemingly random spread of infected ash wood through the movement of firewood or construction materials, it created an ideal opportunity for scientists to study the effect of losing trees on the health of the surrounding population. We'll explore this natural experiment in greater detail in a later chapter.

Quasi-experiments are often controlled trials, but without random assignment. Even though the scientist is involved with administering the treatment as well as choosing the control groups, quasi-experiments remain limited by their inability to achieve balance, because the scientist cannot know for certain if the groups receiving the experimental and control condition are identical on all factors other than the treatment. For example, imagine a study that involves comparing changes in exposure to crime and stress among residents in a neighborhood that was selected by a scientist in collaboration with a city-housing and park agency to undergo a housing and park redevelopment with residents in a neighborhood that looks similar demographically but did not receive the redevelopment. The residents in the neighborhood that received the redevelopment would be the treatment group. But in this case we cannot know for certain if the neighborhood that did not receive the redevelopment and was selected to serve as the control group is truly similar on all factors. In this example, post hoc statistical adjustments for measured factors like socioeconomic status and preexisting levels of crime and stress would help better balance the treatment and control groups, but not to the same degree as a true RCT that assigned the groups randomly. In later chapters we will also present several place-based quasi-experiments in greater detail, including a study of the effect of vacant-lot greening on stress and crime outcomes; a study of the effect of installing cul-de-sacs to reduce drive-by shootings; a study of the effect of business improvement districts on crime; a study of improvements in housing designs and childhood asthma; and a study of the effect of abandoned-housing remediation on crime.

Even though natural experiments and quasi-experiments have less of an ability to establish cause-and-effect relationships when compared to RCTs, they remain important opportunities to learn a great deal about which place-based programs might be of value and which might not. In the end, it's important to realize that, no matter what type of scientific study is being undertaken, oftentimes the scientist conducting the study is thinking about it as an approximation of a RCT, even when randomization to treatment conditions or a non-treated control group is impossible. The question inevitably then becomes, Just how far off is the study from the gold standard of an RCT and what can be learned from the results? The answer lies in the basic characteristics of the place-based study in question.

One final comment on causality is warranted here. Recent innovations in statistical modeling have tended to outpace our basic understanding of a theory of action, and it is possible to find relationships that have no causal explanation. If one is simply interested in prediction, then having a causal explanation for the process is less important. Forecasts of weather or crime patterns using machine learning algorithms, for example, are made routinely with no theory.[37] This approach relies on complex algorithms, which learn patterns in the data that can more accurately predict where and when the next rainstorm or string of burglaries is likely to occur. The approach doesn't involve a theory—just a prediction. To offer a useful and rigorous notion of the actions that affect outcomes, there needs to be a fundamental theory explaining the dynamics at play. Focus groups or well-constructed ethnographic observations of places may provide insights for inductively developing a theory that explains the mechanisms at play. Biologists, anthropologists, ethnographers, and other scientists toiling to understand microprocesses are an immensely valuable complement to raw empiricists conducting place-based research. A qualitative understanding of a place may be needed to bring some depth to place-based research, and to provide a compelling explanation for statistically significant findings.

Generalizability and Place

Generalizability is the ability of scientific research to transcend the laboratory, whether that laboratory is one with pipettes and petri dishes, or a neighborhood trying out a new community program. It is a cornerstone of the research process and perhaps the primary reason that governments and other funders invest in science: so that what is born in a laboratory can be converted to products and processes that improve populations, organizations, and places in our society.

The US government defines research as "a systematic investigation, including development, testing and evaluation, designed to develop or contribute to generalizable knowledge."[38] This is, of course, no surprise, given that the US government and other funders want to maximize the impact of their investments and to see that whatever is found to work in the lab or a single community has a wider application to larger groups of people and multiple communities. This idea also squares well with our recommendation that place-based solutions be scalable, affecting more than a single location. For example, a $100,000 urban tree-planting program that is scientifically proven to reduce stress in one set of neighborhoods in a city holds promise for generalizability and subsequent application in other similar neighborhoods in another city. Even if shown to improve health and well-being, a very expensive medical device may still only be generalizable to hundreds of people with the same disease and access to the technology.

There is also an important differentiation between scientific research that is intended to test a particular place-based program for the purposes of generalizable knowledge, and a place-based program that is focused on improving a single location. Even if the intent is just to understand whether a program had an impact in that particular context, it is usually the case that there are similar contexts elsewhere. The fact that a place-based program is implemented in a field context outside of a laboratory means that we can study how it might apply to another similar setting.

One approach to increasing generalizability is to directly involve community members in research so that field applications have community buy-in and tackle real-world problems that other communities will similarly want to benefit from.[39] However, there are situations where researchers and community members deride generalizability. At multiple meetings with elected leaders, government administrators, and community groups, we have heard people say they only care about how the results are relevant to their city or neighborhood. This is problematic on a number of levels. First, it is anathema to the definition of research, as research should generate insights for other places. Second, it is simply uncharitable and impedes the development of best practices and the benefits of learning something in one place that may have application elsewhere. Third, there may be a reputational and resource return to a community if it becomes the model for a particular place-based program. Fundamentally, one has to have a control group to know that the community benefited relative to other similarly situated places.

Communities implement place-based programs all the time, yet seldom do they seek a research partner to evaluate whether the program actually improved conditions in the community. This is a major loss, since there is often the opportunity to learn about the relative success of a program to determine if it should be expanded or discontinued. In addition, there is the potential loss to other communities if no generalizable knowledge is produced. There is a lot that goes into designing a good experiment, and scientific partners should be involved early in the process so that place-based changes in communities can be evaluated. When the county executive, mayor's office, or local civic association are just forming their ideas, a scientific evaluator can be a useful addition, and their inclusion could also perhaps create important new connections to local universities and research groups. Those connections have the potential to grow, and sometimes researchers can even bring their own resources to the table when they see a place-based program that has particular merit and could be generalized to other locations.

Given that generalizability is a key aspect of place-based research and evidence, how do we formulate studies that have a higher likelihood of being generalizable beyond just the people or places that were in the studies themselves? Although effective at helping to build a case for causality, randomized controlled trials are famously *inadequate* for their generalizability. It's not that randomized controlled trials themselves are somehow inherently ungeneralizable. But the way they are conducted can make the trials themselves, and the very specific people and places that are part of the trials, often ungeneralizable.

Scientists who conduct trials are often much more focused on establishing cause and effect than they are on generalizability. In their enthusiasm they often end up enrolling highly restricted groups of places or people in order to isolate, as much as possible, the effect of some treatment or condition on some outcome (e.g., selecting only the only blocks with the highest levels of crime or individuals with the poorest health for an experimental intervention). These restrictions are often in addition to random assignment, which presumably is already doing its job in terms of helping to isolate the effects of given treatment, as opposed to other rival factors.

To generate knowledge that is generalizable to a population, *random sampling* is essential. Random sampling is a scientific process employed when one knows that it's impossible to measure every person or place in the population. In its most basic form, simple random sampling is a fair and accurate way of choosing a subset of places or people for study. This process is fair because random selection ensures that every person or place under consideration has an equal chance of being selected, just like a lottery. This process is also accurate if the scientist is able to enroll enough randomly sampled people or places that by the law of large numbers, this sample is sufficiently large to represent the larger population of people or places.

For instance, take the question of whether garbage cans on city street corners prevent or create trash. Sometimes people appropriately place their trash in a garbage can instead of throwing it on the street, but sometimes street-corner garbage cans overflow with illegally dumped trash that would otherwise have been properly disposed of. A researcher decides to investigate this question across five US cities and place time-lapse cameras to observe street corners to which trash cans have been randomly assigned (see figure 3.3). The five cities have a total of ten thousand trash cans scattered throughout their boundaries, making it impossible for even the most comprehensive study to observe them all; consequently, the scientist takes a random sample of five hundred (or a 5-percent sample) trash cans and then randomly assigns them to street corners. This amount is more than enough because the sample has been randomly selected and, as such, can be said to reasonably represent the experience of all ten thousand trash cans across all five cities.

FIGURE 3.3. Image of garbage cans creating more trash around them.

Random sampling is a fundamental concept that appears in the first few chapters of most any introductory statistics textbook. This concept is so basic that many controlled trials forget to include sampling design in their studies. For many medical trials this means that the sample being studied does not represent the population with the disease, but rather those willing to participate in an experimental trial of a new drug or form of surgery. For place-based research that is conducted in the field and outside the well-ordered confines of a laboratory, random sampling is often a necessity to generate generalizability. Biases come in many forms when trying to determine if a place-based change or program actually produces the outcomes it claims to in the real world. The people implementing the program may preferentially want to try it out in neighborhoods where they think it will succeed, which is referred to in evaluation science as "creaming."[40] If proven successful, will the program be generalizable to neighborhoods other than those already primed for success? Random sampling is a fair way of choosing which places to include (as every place that is eligible can in principle be selected) and is necessary to bolster generalizability and promote uptake of the program in places other than the few places studied. One of the difficulties of taking programs that appear to work in demonstration trials and expanding them to include other settings is that they aren't selected through random sampling. As a result, we don't know if the program worked because of the specific setting that was selected. This is one of the hurdles that planners face in attempting to draw conclusions about whether a specific place-based intervention will work elsewhere.

A few final thoughts on the idea of generalizable knowledge are worth mentioning. Just because a single study is deemed to be generalizable does not mean that it is the final say on whether the program will be successful. Any scientific study must be considered within the context of other, similar studies that have also been completed. This lets us discern reproducibility: to determine if the study findings were a one-off or if they can be applied other places and other times. For this reason, organizations that rank the quality of evidence often put a premium on studies that have been replicated in more than one setting.[41] Of course if a very large study is done in multiple places, this helps address the concern that the findings are not specific to a single place, but it still does not eliminate the need for replication by others. A good example is the research on "hot-spots" policing interventions. Here we have multiple randomized trials in different cities, all showing some evidence that putting extra police in a high crime area reduces crime compared to other high-crime areas that did not receive extra police.[42]

Scientists are pioneers at heart, and being first out of the gate to report a new finding is a highly prized achievement. Few scientists want to be second, fewer third, and so on. But reproducing the findings of a landmark study that has come before is important for demonstrating generalizability to another place at another time. Replicating studies in other settings is a big challenge and is one of the reasons why there are few programs or interventions that are proven effective in real-world policy contexts. Replication is also a challenge in many types of scientific endeavors. An article appearing in the *New Yorker* titled "The Truth Wears Off" notes the problems of replicating landmark studies.[43] There is now a field of emerging research focused on reproducing original research, noting that many studies suffer from the problem of false discovery. People have a tendency to write up results that confirm their preconceptions. In his famous paper "Why Most Published Research Findings Are False," epidemiologist John Ioannidis highlights how many research papers report findings that turn out not to be true, which is particularly a problem when there are only a few studies in a field that report large effects.[44] On the other hand, a scientific field with an abundance of reported effects that are small and come from nonexperimental research designs are more likely to be reporting evidence based on false discoveries. False discovery is most likely when scientists do not emphasize that their results could have occurred by chance. This is especially problematic when there are financial interests at stake and a desire to report a treatment's positive effects; the incentive to find a breakthrough can push researchers to emphasize one set of results over another. Similarly, entire fields can be convinced that a finding is true and fail to change their minds when confronted with conflicting evidence because it goes against conventional wisdom.

There is hope that, with the advent of open-source journals available on the internet (original drafts of scientific papers, sources of data, and comments), scientific transparency and reproducibility can improve. Moreover, it's now required that funded RCTs be registered online, *before they get started*. This is important so that the scientific investigators can state what their a-priori expectations are (hypotheses) and what outcomes they plan to test. This guards against scientists only reporting results that are significant and discounting the results from outcomes that show no difference between the treatment and control groups. Publications like the *Journal of Negative Results* are also emerging to capture the breadth of research on programs that have evidence of not working, helping to curb the tendency of journals and researchers to publish null findings or findings contrary to scientific consensus.[45]

As the information age matures, science has also now embraced research that is about summarizing findings from research fields. These "studies of studies" take two forms: systematic reviews and metaanalyses.

A systematic review involves providing a synthesis of studies based on clearly detailed criteria for selection that ensure that the review and the reported results can be replicated. Cochrane Review Groups, for example, provide systematic reviews each year of health research.[46] The Campbell Collaboration provides reviews every year of criminal justice, education, nutrition, social welfare, and other topics.[47] Each of these groups has explicit criteria for how to select and screen studies for review. Bogar and Beyer, for example, conducted a systematic view of the relationship between urban green space, violence, and crime. After using explicit search criteria for databases of research studies, they identified ten out of roughly three thousand studies that were quantitative examinations of the relationships between urban green space, crime, and violence. Their review indicated that crime and violence were twice as likely to be lower in urban areas with more green space. In terms of total crime they found only one study that suggested it was higher in urban areas with more green space compared to five studies that found crime was lower.[48]

However, it should be noted that eight out of ten of the studies selected did not observe these places before and after the greening remediation. Several of these studies examined trees, while others examined the impact of planting grass in vacant lots. In fact, only two studies reviewed involved a trial that manipulated greening. Only one of these studies provided suggestive evidence that greening lowers violent crime. From this review, we can say that, across ten studies, greening is associated with less violence. The authors of the systematic review note the differences in methodologies, but the details of study differences matter. This is an emblematic case where correlation is not causation. The study is still useful for generating testable hypotheses, but not for generating causal evidence that urban green space lowers violent crime.

A metaanalysis is a method of combining estimates from multiple studies into a single overall estimate of the causal effect of an intervention. The approach was developed and coined by psychologist Gene Glass in the social sciences as a way of combining a large collection of results "from individual studies for the purpose of integrating the findings."[49] The goal is to provide a clear estimate across a diverse set of studies. Since its development in the social sciences, it has been given a special place in the field of evidence-based medicine, as it is widely recognized as the top of the hierarchy of evidence.[50] However, this is in the context of a collection of randomized controlled trials, with the assumption that the summary of results across all studies is a better gauge of the effect of a treatment than a single study. In the social sciences, however, a metaanalysis often involves summarizing studies with different levels of evidence. In fact, the method is best applied when it involves aggregating similar studies in different contexts. This avoids an aggregation fallacy that suggests that multiple studies, all using less rigorous methods of inquiry, will trump the findings of one high-quality randomized controlled trial. It is important to underscore that a metaanalysis of ten correlational studies does not represent better evidence than a single randomized controlled trial.

An example of metaanalysis can be seen in a paper written by statistician Richard Berk and colleagues examining the effect of arrests for domestic violence on future partner violence that was conducted across four randomized controlled trials, each occurring in a different city.[51] In these study sites, police responding to the calls for domestic violence were given orders through random assignment to arrest a suspect, to issue an emergency protection order and counseling for the victim, or to restore order at the scene. At the time of the studies, domestic assault was not subject to mandatory arrest laws, as it is today, so police were allowed wide discretion in how to handle these incidents. All settings involved randomly assigning accused batterers to arrest or an alternative treatment, but the locations and study populations were different. As a result, we learned from this metaanalysis that making an arrest at the scene impacts future domestic violence among the affected parties. Berk and colleagues found that arrest on average increased the chance of subsequent arrests for violence, but the effect of arrest varied across study sites and the background characteristics of the accused abuser. For example, employed men who were arrested were significantly less likely to be arrested in the future for domestic violence. This example showcases that even when the aggregate effect of a program or intervention is beneficial it won't work for everyone. We shouldn't lose site of the fact that an overall treatment benefit is always estimated for the average case and does not mean that every person or place will benefit.

As the number of RCTs of place-based interventions grows, metaanalyses will provide evidence of the overall effectiveness of these interventions across multiple contexts. Although a number of place-based metaanalyses have been completed, they have almost exclusively synthesized studies that are low on the hierarchy of evidence. Unfortunately, ten studies of limited value don't produce one high-value metaanalysis estimate. Again, this underscores the need for place-based scientists to first focus on producing the highest-quality individual studies they can to produce a body of work worthy of a metaanalysis.

Another important aspect of place-based research is that it is fostering a basic science of policy implementation. Often the public is stalled in taking direct collective action in public-policy areas related to health and safety because of a belief that peoples' lives can only be improved by addressing the so-called "root causes," like persistent poverty and low human-capital skills.[52] This is a mistake; as we reveal in this book, lives can be changed to improve health and safety with strategic changes to places that don't directly address "root causes."

Levels of Evidence

There is no clear guidebook on what is the best level of evidence, but a useful framework is provided by the US Department of Education's What Works Clearinghouse,[53] as well as similar guides for understanding what works in crime prevention and medicine from the US Prevention Task Force.[54] There are a number of hierarchies of evidence that are useful for generating evidence-based policy. For the What Works Clearinghouse, the focus is on both the strength to which the cause and effect can be established (interval validity) and the size of the effect found.[55] For this discussion we will simply focus on hierarchy of evidence in terms of establishing cause and effect (see table 3.3).

TABLE 3.3. Ranking of Study Designs

Rank	WWC (B.2)	Crime solutions	USPSTF
1	RCT	RCT	RCT
2	Regression discontinuity or single case	Quasi-experimental with a control group	Quasi-experimental with a control group
3	Quasi-experimental design	Quasi-experimental with a nonequivalent control group	Cohort or case-control studies
4	None of above	Nonexperimental case studies	Time series (before and after) design
5	Not applicable	Not applicable	Expert opinion

All hierarchies of evidence established by government agencies and panels place RCTs at the top of the hierarchy for the reasons we've already discussed. As a brief recap, recall that randomization assures that the groups being compared are on average equivalent in all observable and unobservable factors. The differences between treatment and control groups are solely the experimental conditions that the scientists have manipulated and not self-selection. The manipulation by scientists of groups into experimental versus control conditions means that they can observe outcomes before and after the deliberate action, allowing them to attribute the changes in outcomes to the experimental condition. However, it is important to note that we are talking about probabilistic changes and not absolute certainty. RCTs rely on statistical methods to assign probabilistic differences because one cannot control for all possible extraneous influences.

The second-tier study design across the hierarchies from the WWC, Crime Solutions, and the USPSTF involve quasi-experiments. These types of studies involve designs where there was a direct manipulation by a program, policy, or a scientist, and there exists a control group that is arguably similar on observable factors. The main difference between quasi-experiments and RCTs is that the groups aren't randomly assigned, so one can't be certain that the groups are equivalent on all extraneous factors. In both types of designs one gets to understand the effect through a comparison of a control group. But the scientist has to be able to articulate why other candidate explanations are less likely than the treatment effect. The challenge is that the scientist has to be very convincing. However, as we will show, often this approach is sufficient to argue for more policy experimentation even if it does not provide definitive evidence of a causal effect. Also, quasi-experiments often have the advantage of happening on a large enough scale or in a relevant enough context that they can be useful guides for what to predict in another setting.

The third-tier study design involves a quasi-experiment where the control group is not equivalent on observable factors. Here, one can still draw some conclusions about effects but must recognize that the control group may not be sufficiently similar to provide a very strong counterfactual comparison of what would have occurred in the absence of the intervention. Statistical adjustments are often used to make the treatment and control groups comparable on observable factors, so that drawing implications about the likely causal effect is still reasonable, barring no other likely alternative explanation. However, we will not be emphasizing this method in the book, because it is more difficult to persuade making policy changes to how we design places based on comparisons of groups that are not equivalent on observable factors.

The fourth-tier study design involves an examination of a change over time with no comparison groups, and is often referred to as a time-series study. This is the classic study that involves examining what happened before and after an intervention. Here one can see that outcomes changed at the same time as the intervention was launched, but it is difficult to rule out other causes, such as historical changes that coincidentally were occurring, or perhaps the intervention was done in an area that was more susceptible to change in the first place.

The fifth tier involves studies that solely rely on statistical adjustments with no control group. This type of study is commonly referred to in epidemiology, public health, and the social sciences as a descriptive study. The goal is to examine how an outcome (e.g., crime, stress, obesity) varies in the population based on characteristics of people, place, and time. The approach is useful for generating ideas about likely sources of health and safety problems, or for forming questions that can be tested later in an experimental context. For example, a descriptive study that finds people living near trees experience less stress provides a basis for testing later whether in fact trees reduce stress. We will discuss several studies like this that provide likely explanations for the results observed from RCTs and quasi-experiments.

Evidence Matters

Evidence matters when it comes to changing places. Causality and generalizability matter when assessing the level of evidence we have to inform an investment in a program to make changes to places. The more rigorous the scientific evidence, the more defensible our predictions about the effects that are likely to occur from a program or policy change to a place. Arguably, resources are well spent when based on sound evidence. The best evidence is often that produced from real-world experiments that systematically change places and environments and then painstakingly measure the impact of these changes on people. The fact is, communities experiment all the time by changing places, but they can more definitively make conclusions about their impact when scientific collaborators document effects through a place-based experimental design.

This doesn't mean that only experimental evidence matters. Rather, it means we should at least look for the best evidence available and proceed accordingly. We should not let the perfect be the enemy of the good and end up in situations of inaction, paralyzed by our limitless appetite for ever-better research. Nonetheless, embarking on more carefully constructed place-based experiments, natural experiments, and quasi-experiments is a crucial next step in legitimizing the scientific study of place and in helping figure out which programs should be pursued or expanded and which should be abandoned or retooled.

Changing aspects of places can be done as part of an *evidence-generating policy* model.[56] Think of each decision to change the design of places as a series of trials with expected outcomes that can be tested. In this framework, changes can be implemented by policy makers and communities with an eye toward testing whether the changes indeed make people safer and healthier. Under an ideal model of evidence-generating policy, place-based programs that look like they may be successful in a few areas can be expanded and tested through randomized place-based trials. This model is similar to the concept of an efficacy trial in medicine that conducts a study on a small scale to see if a treatment works, before expanding into an effectiveness trial that tries out the new treatment in a real-world clinical trial.[57]

The next chapters will present some of the latest scientific evidence from real-world research on place-based initiatives. Many of these exemplars will be randomized controlled trials, natural experiments, or quasi-experiments applied to place-based issues in housing, land, transportation, and business. Many of these studies have their origins in collaborations between scientists and urban planners and showcase the power of early engagement, rigorous research designs, and open communication to learn something new and make beneficial changes to places that help reduce crime and improve health outcomes in communities.

4

Cities in Ruin

BUILDINGS ARE ONE of the most obvious features of the built environment to modify when it comes to making place-based changes. A recent artistic genre has made this point clear: "ruin photography," which uses the decline of the built environment as its subject and captures urban decay, raw and uncensored, as a critique of the decline of many blighted cities, such as Detroit, that were once thriving industrial zones for manufacturing, exporting goods, and generating local wealth.[1] Ruin photography looks at urban abandonment with an aesthetic eye, carefully documenting visual evidence of extreme dilapidation while insinuating a kind of nostalgia. By highlighting the decline of structures that are now so common in many postindustrial cities, ruin photographers show us why changes to these structures and their surrounding neighborhoods could make them beautiful again.

Figure 4.1 shows a great ruin image from Detroit: a collapsing house, built circa 1890, that was once a majestic mansion. Neglected urban spaces like this are, in effect, fodder for artistic expression as well as examples of the historic authenticity craved by the gentrification class that is so often at the leading edge of urban revitalization.

Alternatively, one might be less attracted to what the image shows, because this crumbling mansion gives us the sinking feeling that places and their built environment can become real eyesores if left to decompose. While some may see them as a basis for a massive teardown project, as is currently occurring in cities like Detroit and Baltimore, there remains an opportunity for rehabilitating these crumbling structures and creating healthy space.[2] Imagine what the block this house sits on would be like if this building and others around it were restored to their past glory, or even if they were restored much less ornately to structures that average working families could live in. Why did building structures—mansions of the wealthy and working-class homes alike—collapse

FIGURE 4.1. Ruin photography example from Detroit, Michigan.
Source: Yves Merchand and Romain Meffre, "The Ruins of Detroit: 2005–2010,"
http://www.marchandmeffre.com/detroit.

in so many postindustrial cities like Detroit, Baltimore, Chicago, and Philadelphia?

Evolution of Negative Housing

The US housing market is an evolving case of private market failure and suboptimal public policy intervention. Various crises have led to a highly regulated and subsidized housing market that helps shape demand though individual tax deductions on interest paid on mortgages, along with other forms of government subsidies. On the supply side, developers get subsidies for the construction of homes that meet specific government regulations, such as local quotas for affordable housing or low-income housing tax credit subsidies. Such affordable housing units are then built by developers for considerable profit.[3]

State policy interventions in the housing markets have historically focused on reducing substandard rental housing through the use of zoning and building codes to prevent overcrowding, ensure appropriate light and air quality in homes, and minimize exposure to noxious materials and fire hazards. However, little attention has been paid to the impact these massive public work projects have on the places where people live.

The story of the house shown in figure 4.1 is illustrative of the current crisis facing some of our most economically disadvantaged cities. This house, built before the passage of the National Housing Act of 1934, when the US government began to regulate home ownership loans, is located in a formerly affluent section of Detroit. It was probably financed by a balloon loan, and its original inhabitants were likely affluent industrialists or bankers. The house was built to convey social status, through its complicated design and expensive materials, and no doubt brought great joy to its original inhabitants. Over time, houses such as these started to become a major financial drain for their owners, as family sizes shrank, energy costs increased, maintenance costs rose, and the demand for large homes in urban cities dropped.

The larger economic forces that facilitated demand for opulent homes in urban cities shifted with the decline of industrial jobs in the United States and a movement of more individuals into service-sector employment and to homes in the suburbs.[4] The city of Detroit is in many ways an exemplar of the effects of deindustrialization on housing in the US. The rapid decline of the US auto industry, centered in Detroit, led to private and municipal fiscal stress in the 1960s and 1970s and impacted the provision of infrastructure maintenance, public education, and public safety services.[5] Those who could afford it vacated the city altogether. More attractive suburban developments were, then, like gasoline on a fire, wiping out any potential market for this kind of house. Chances are, this dwelling was eventually subdivided into apartments, as a result of the diminished market demand, and then abandoned altogether. At the same time, all over the country, the same story was playing out, as once-vigorous urban housing markets declined and large sections of city neighborhoods were hollowed out. This house is emblematic of the problems many cities face, which have been exacerbated with the recession of 2008 and the collapse of the housing market caused by subprime loans.[6] The degradation of housing has more consequences on the lives of individuals than housing values, as housing is fundamental to our safety and health.

Degraded Housing, Public Safety, and Health

There is an increasing body of research pointing out that housing quality is associated with poor mental and physical health. The public health challenge of poor-quality housing is not just a problem of the developing world. Exposures to unhealthy housing conditions are also common in poorly constructed and maintained housing stock in the United States and other developed countries. Exposure to lead, for example, has harmful consequences on brain development and is most likely to happen to children in and around their homes. Lack of safe drinking water, exposure to mold spores, infective waste disposal, and disease-carrying pests are contributing factors to many diseases. Mold, for instance, can be caused by leaks in roofs or water pipes. Disease-carrying insects are more likely to form colonies in damp homes. Such degraded housing has been found to be associated with increased risk of asthma, headaches, cardiovascular diseases, and other chronic health problems. Infectious diseases are also more likely to spread in crowded housing stock. [7] To put it simply, substandard housing is bad for human health. There are many examples of degraded housing stock that affect populations, but it is the poor that are the most impacted.

In the United States, perhaps the greatest symbol of degraded housing is the high-rise public housing stock in our cities. The development of high-rise public housing was advocated for in the 1930s as an efficient method of clearing out slums and improving the public health and safety of neighborhoods.[8] Figure 4.2 shows a poster from 1936 as part of the Depression-era Works Projects Administration, promoting public housing development as a way to reduce crime. One of the early drivers of high-rise housing development was the architectural preference to create open spaces, such as plazas and parks in formerly crowded cities.[9] Le Corbusier's Radiant City design plan, later derided by Jane Jacobs, became the model for US public housing development designers.[10] Local governments under the Housing Act of 1949 were provided authority and funds to clear slums and construct high-rise public housing. Federal policies encouraging slum clearance and high-rise public housing development continued into the 1960s as part of a national effort at urban renewal, subsidizing state and local governments to construct affordable housing and highways.[11] In the typical public housing design, slums would be cleared, high-rise developments would be constructed, and wide open roads would be built to make cities clean and attractive.[12]

By the end of the 1970s though, most US public housing developments that had been built in the 1950s were no longer viewed as desirable places to live.

FIGURE 4.2. Advertisement for New York City public housing development, New York Federal Art Project, 1936. *Source*: United States Library of Congress, Prints and Photographs Division, WPA Poster Collection, LC-DIG-ppmsca-52154.

During the 1960s and early 1970s, crime was on the rise and public housing structures had become more degraded than ever.[13] Alex Kotlowitz's bestselling book *There Are No Children Here* vividly details the miserable living conditions in high-rise public housing.[14] Following the lives of two brothers, Lafayette and Pharaoh, the book showcases the Henry Horner Homes in Chicago.[15] Surrounded by decrepit buildings, the brothers negotiate the chaos of living in spaces that were neglected by the Chicago Housing Authority.

High-rise public housing, while not uniformly awful, is not a place to safely raise children. In the final years of Chicago's Henry Horner Homes, residents were given flashlights during the day so they could find their way through the lobby. Residents often couldn't use their own mailboxes because of vandalism, and elevators often broke down, with long waiting times for repair. Broken elevators and unsupervised children have historically been a dangerous mix in high-rise public housing complexes in the United States. In New York City the number of injuries and deaths in elevator shafts have led a personal-injury law firm to develop it as a specialty area for litigation.[16]

Even the low-rise, "garden-style" public housing developments had their design flaws. The Richard Allen Homes, a notorious hot spot for crime in North Philadelphia, paved over all of its green space with blacktop after unmaintained lawns turned to dirt, and then to mud when it rained. The central courtyards of this garden-style development, which once included lawns and playgrounds, morphed into parking lots, trash dumps, and open-air drug markets. Scientific studies of places like Chicago's Ida Wells housing developments show that insensitive maintenance strategies, which reduce people's exposure to trees and vegetation, can increase crime and contribute to poor health.[17] Public housing developments were not uniformly horrible in the 1960s and 1970s, especially due to the close social connections that emerged among their long-time residents, but the general quality of life was much lower than it could have been if residents were living in reasonably maintained housing.

Oscar Newman's 1972 book *Defensible Space: Crime Prevention through Urban Design* is widely credited for illustrating how the design of public housing influenced criminal opportunity.[18] Newman focused his case studies on NYC public housing complexes, where, he pointed out, robbery rates were much greater in high-rise buildings, even when the actual population density was comparable to many low-rise developments.[19] Newman found that the majority of crimes occurred inside of public housing buildings, suggesting that the design of each building was important. He argued that natural surveillance was often impeded in places like lobbies and hallways.

Newman's classic point of comparison was the two housing projects of Brownsville and Van Dyke, both located in Brooklyn. These two housing complexes had similar residents and residential density, but differed on design. Brownsville was designed as a maximum six-story building, with a visible lobby from the street and a buffer zone from parking lot to smaller segmented street walkup stairways. All of these features increased the possibility that someone could be seen when walking around the complex. In contrast, Van Dyke was a high-rise development with isolated corridors, stairs, and elevators. Browns-ville had significantly fewer crimes in the building than Van Dyke.

Despite being a pioneering work that incorporated many important scien-tific features, including a counterfactual comparison case, Newman's analysis was based on a sample of only two housing complexes. We don't know if they are representative of actual differences in the population of residents in hous-ing complexes more generally, or if the differences observed are simply idio-syncratic and could occur by chance. Yet there are some interesting ideas and insights to be gleaned from Newman's work on the idea of defensible space and crime prevention through environmental design (CPTED). Newman argued for the creation of small, multifamily housing complexes where resi-dents share limited access and common areas, which would "allow residents to distinguish neighbor from intruder."[20] Despite its shortcomings, this was important work in establishing the use of systematic methods of comparison to question the planning decisions behind public housing construction projects that had occurred decades earlier.

Newman's work was also among the first to outline, in clear terms, how to design housing with an eye toward reducing criminal opportunities. While there is a body of research that suggests that public housing is correlated with crime, it remains unclear if it is the buildings' design, the social organization of public housing,[21] its mismanagement,[22] or the land-use patterns around these places that promotes crime.[23] Weighing the relative impact of these possible causal factors is important, as local planners and public housing agencies lack the broader resources to impact "root causes" of crime, like the concentration of poverty, but might have the wherewithal to implement design adaptions that could mitigate criminal-opportunity structures in the places they manage.

By the 1980s large public housing developments, and in particular high-rise public housing complexes, had developed a reputation for being centers of crime. Chicago's Mayor Jane Bryne famously moved into the Cabrini-Green public housing complex for three weeks in 1981 to an effort to draw attention to the rampant crime in the city's public housing.[24] Many cities in the 1980s sought funding to demolish and replace high-rise public housing, but federal law required a one-for-one replacement, making it financially difficult to tear it down. In 1992 Congress passed a new housing law that provided funding to local housing authorities to tear down distressed public housing complexes. These high-rise developments would be replaced with less dense developments that subscribed to Newman's defensible space design principles. Called HOPE VI, or "Housing Opportunity for People Everywhere," these new developments also sought to deconcentrate impoverished residents, as there would be fewer units in any single development than in the traditional high-rise building.[25]

The large-scale demolitions of public housing complexes was both expensive and disruptive to the people living in them, but it provided a unique opportunity to learn what happens to crime when these complexes are demolished. In the case of Chicago, the housing authority demolished nearly 22,000 units of high-rise public housing and relocated affected residents to either private market housing or to low-rise public housing developments. A study of this relocation process found that crime was reduced substantially in the former high-rise neighborhoods and produced only a small increase in crime in the neighborhoods where residents relocated.[26] The results from this study suggest that the design and management of such places creates criminal opportunity for people living in public housing.

While the evidence on the role of substandard housing and crime is complicated, the negative impact of poorly planned, designed, and constructed housing on health is clearer. Research shows that the exposure to known pathogens in substandard housing is associated with a higher risk of respiratory infections, asthma, and lead poisoning.[27] While this research is largely correlational, and we don't have measures of diseases before and after people move into substandard housing, it is still convincing, because the diseases observed are known to be triggered by specific harmful pathogens seen at higher rates in substandard homes. Housing is only one source of many health and safety issues. But the connections between substandard housing, crime, and health cannot be ignored, and they raise important questions about how to change housing in a way that improves population health and well-being.

Rebuild or Escape?

The general policy prescription of the past two decades for dealing with the failures of public housing has been to demolish high-rise complexes and to use rental vouchers to relocate residents to private market apartments or to rebuild public housing in the form of lower-density low-rise developments. Scattered-site housing development has been espoused as the model approach to public housing, as the concentration effects of poverty are less likely. Similarly, cities across the United States have seen demolition as a preferable option for dilapidated and abandoned housing in place of restoration. In both circumstances the preference has been for subsidizing private market housing developers to build affordable housing or to allow tenants to shop for their own rental units with government-issued vouchers that pay a market rent for qualified landlords. This leads to the natural question of whether to 1) rebuild or restore distressed housing, or 2) provide residents with relocation options.

To answer the relocation question, a series of studies have been conducted as part of the US Department of Housing and Urban Development's (HUD) Moving to Opportunity (MTO) for Fair Housing program, which used a unique experimental demonstration to examine the short- and long-term outcomes for roughly 4,600 residents of distressed public housing complexes in five cities (Baltimore, Boston, Chicago, Los Angeles, and New York) who participated in a lottery that allowed them to potentially win a voucher to relocate.[28] Because the program was run through a lottery, it qualified as a randomized controlled trial field experiment. Randomly drawn winners (the treatment group) received either unrestricted Section 8 housing vouchers to rental markets or vouchers that were for designated low-poverty areas and that included rental counseling. Lottery "losers" (the control group) stayed in their existing public housing units. A series of important scientific publications have been generated from the MTO experiment that examine crime, health, and employment outcomes for tenants and their children that received the vouchers as compared with those that did not.

The results from the MTO housing mobility experiment showed mixed results. In general, adults reported better measures of happiness and improvements in physical health and perceptions of safety.[29] Adult women that moved to the low-poverty neighborhoods were also significantly less likely to become morbidly obese and have signs of diabetes.[30] For girls, the results suggested some improvements in mental health and criminal behavior.[31] For boys, there was evidence that their family's relocation led to reductions in violent-crime arrests but increases in property-crime arrests among teenagers, although these effects appear to have attenuated over time as the boys became adults.[32] The results from a longer-term follow-up show that moving out of a high-poverty neighborhood did not lead to higher incomes for the adults, nor did it improve educational outcomes like math or reading test scores.[33] On the more positive side, when families were offered a housing voucher and their children were under the age of thirteen, these children were more likely to attend college, earn higher incomes, and live in wealthier neighborhoods as adults and less likely to become single parents.[34] These findings suggest that some of the mixed evidence for adolescent boys may have to do with the disruption caused by moving. We don't know why boys fared differently when they moved as teenagers, but the evidence from the MTO research suggesting that boys do better when they move at an earlier age is consistent with another study comparing siblings. This study shows that when families move out of poor neighborhoods, the benefits to life outcomes tend to be realized by the younger sibling.[35] Duration in a neighborhood of concentrated poverty may be more important than previously realized and explain the strong tendency for poverty to transfer from one generation to the next.[36] While these MTO studies provide some insight on what happens to people who are offered the opportunity to leave distressed public housing *and* who take advantage of this opportunity, they leave unaddressed the question of what would happen to people if we designed different housing for them and they stayed in the same neighborhood.

The landmark research that emerged from the MTO experiment is the best scientific evidence ever produced on the impact of place on human social, economic, and health outcomes. However, as we've previously mentioned, the costs of relocating people and the myriad of problems associated with mass relocations mean that the findings from this study largely offer us insights into changes from public housing to private markets. Over half of the participants in the MTO study who won the lottery and were offered a voucher to relocate decided to stay in their public housing complex. One can imagine that people are reluctant to move when they have come to depend on the social network of close friends and family living nearby in public housing. Furthermore, the idea of mass relocation as a solution to poverty does not sit well with people who have experienced historical discrimination in the form of relocation.[37] Moreover, the ultimate outcome of using relocation as a policy mechanism for the poor is to create more abandoned places. Relocation also runs counter to the main point of our work here: that places can be improved rather than abandoned.

In many older industrial cities in the United States, people see an abundance of vacancy and decay as part of their everyday urban experience. How do we tackle such ubiquitous blight? To some, it may seem intractably voluminous, leaving policy makers at the Department of Housing and Urban Development and other government agencies that oversee urban redevelopment to resort to approaches like property clearance and resident relocation as their primary options. However, there are potentially less expensive options that improve blight and permit people to stay in their existing neighborhoods. Urban planners and scientists are now beginning to identify low-cost opportunities that have been shown to be beneficial and cost effective through demonstration programs and field experiments.[38]

One option is to deal directly with vacant single-family homes. These properties are particularly problematic because they are large in number and are more likely to be neglected and vandalized, and therefore generate negative visual images of a neighborhood, which can stigmatize residents, especially children, and send the message that they live in an inferior place that no one seems to care about. For outsiders, these images send a message that such places should be feared and avoided, and worse—that the people who live in these places are damaged, and should be avoided, too.

Studies have examined the association between housing vacancy and property-value losses, crime, and health outcomes like sexually transmitted diseases, cardiovascular diseases, and diabetes.[39] But these studies don't actually observe changes to health and safety outcomes before and after properties became vacant, so they offer less evidence on whether outcomes were directly affected by home vacancies. There are also studies explaining how an area improved after an intervention to remediate abandoned properties.[40] But these studies include no control group, so we can't really know how things changed compared to another similarly situated area, and whether the change in question was really due to the intervention or just larger factors that were happening at the same time.

The economic costs of abandoned housing alone justifies the need for more insight into ways of addressing the problem. The Government Accountability Office reports that cities spend anywhere from $233 to $1,400 per property on temporary exterior maintenance costs, such as boarding up broken windows and otherwise securing these abandoned structures. These costs increase in cities where structures require demolition and significant remediation of the land on which they once stood.[41] There are a handful of scientific studies that give us sufficient evidence and guidance as to how the design and rehabilitation of housing impacts health and safety. In these examples, we can observe what happens to people or places before and after changes are made to housing structures, as compared to other places where structures are left in the same condition over the same time period. Dilapidated housing can impact both the safety of a neighborhood and the health of those living inside of it. Perhaps no topic is more poignant than what happens to the health of children living in poorly designed homes.

Breathe-Easy Homes

Asthma afflicts millions of children worldwide. In the United States, chronic asthma is particularly concentrated in poor neighborhoods with low-quality housing. Poor ventilation, leaky roofs, and other aspects of poorly built and maintained housing increases the exposure to microparticles and other triggers for children with asthma.[42] While there is a great deal of laboratory work on the actual triggers of asthma, there has been relatively little consideration of place-based solutions to this common childhood affliction. How much better would things be for children who have chronic asthma if they were living in a cleaner, better-designed home? It's a question that remains largely unanswered.

One public housing redevelopment project in Seattle, Washington, created a unique opportunity to scientifically answer this question. The Seattle Housing Authority's High Point area was awarded an initial grant in 2000 from the US Department of Housing and Urban Development (HUD) as part of its HOPE VI program to revitalize existing public housing.[43] High Point was originally developed in the 1940s to house families working for military contractors for the war effort and was converted into public housing in the 1950s. By the 1970s the community had fallen into disrepair and was overrun by gang activity, crime, and vacant housing units.[44] The housing that did still exist was often rundown, with leaking roofs and windows, which led to mold and pests.

The High Point revitalization grant in combination with other funding totaled over $550 million, and in 2004 the Seattle Housing Authority began the process of replacing 716 dilapidated public housing units with ones that were newly built. As part of this effort, housing in High Point was built according to certified "Built Green 3-star standard," which signifies high-quality construction materials that are sustainable and energy efficient and that promote improved indoor air quality. Taking a digital tour of the High Point neighborhood now reveals a wealth of amazing changes, including the addition of community gardens, walkways, and stormwater management. It should then come as no surprise that this redevelopment has won numerous design awards, including the Global Award for Excellence from the Urban Land Institute.[45]

The High Point revitalization stands in direct contrast to older forms of subsidized housing built in the 1940s and 1950s that tended to be made of the cheapest construction materials and from the most basic designs. The federal government in the 1930s was even lobbied by private real-estate interests against providing publicly funded housing, who saw this as a threat to the private market's ability to provide housing for the poor. Some didn't want the units to be too nice, as public housing was thought to be a temporary way station for families as they transitioned out of hard times and back into the private market. Having people live in these housing developments for a long time was not part of the original plan. Thus, environmental health and safety amenities were seldom considered in their design or construction.[46]

Understanding how much of a difference the condition of a home makes on someone's health has been an issue that community health workers have grappled with. For over a decade, a research team at the University of Washington explored the clinical effects of asthma control through an intervention with community health workers who would visit homes and provide guidance. The study team conducted a randomized controlled trial (RCT) where 274 children with asthma received a comprehensive intervention that involved an environmental audit of the home, an action plan for helping remediate the home that included the delivery of allergy and pest remediation materials, and four to eight additional visits by community health workers. This treatment was compared to houses where families received only a single environmental audit and action plan.

The study found that six months after the treatment intervention there was a substantial drop in the use of urgent health services. In the two months after the intervention there was a 17 percent drop in the use of urgent health services for children in housing that received a comprehensive treatment compared to only a 4.6 percent drop in the single audit action plan group. Parents and caregivers also reported a higher quality of life due to the reduction in the number of stressful hospital visits related to asthma attacks. While both groups appear to have received benefits, it is unclear how effective this program is, given that follow-up visits from the community health workers are relatively expensive to maintain, and, at the time, the services could not be reimbursed through health insurance.[47] In addition, it was clear from the clinical intervention that many of the asthma problems in these homes were associated with structural deficiencies, including the fact that the majority of them had moisture problems associated with leaks and dust-laden carpets that could not be addressed from the clinical intervention.[48] This RCT is a good example of the limits of behavioral modification programs that don't address structural conditions of the places where people live.

Fortunately, the same study team had the opportunity to explore what happened when children with asthma were able to move into structurally improved homes as part of the High Point revitalization effort. In addition to constructing "Built Green" homes, High Point pioneered the construction of sixty Breathe-Easy Homes (BEHs) to reduce the risk of asthma and its symptoms for children living in the community.[49] Figure 4.3 shows an example of a BEH and its special features targeted at reducing childhood asthma, including filtered

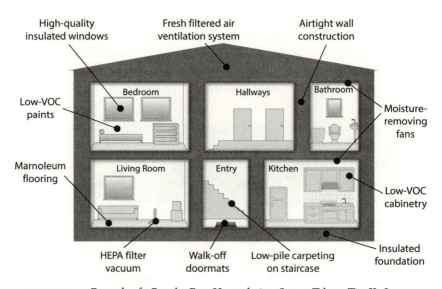

FIGURE 4.3. Example of a Breathe-Easy Home design. *Source*: Takaro, Tim K., James Krieger, Lin Song, Denise Sharify, and Nancy Beaudet, "The Breathe-Easy Home: The impact of asthma-friendly home construction on clinical outcomes and trigger exposure," *American Journal of Public Health* 101, no. 1 (2011): 55–62. © The American Public Health Association.

air intake in all living spaces, drywall construction that minimizes air pockets, organic compound paint, and sealed cabinet construction.[50] BEHs are designed in a way that minimizes particulates in the air, such as mold and dust.

The study involved an examination of thirty-four children who were diagnosed with persistent asthma, had been living in a public housing site, and were moved into the newly constructed BEH units.[51] Families moving into BEH units also received in-home asthma education, but not follow-up home visits from community health workers. Data were collected on BEH children immediately before they moved into the new homes and one year later. Data were also collected on dust allergens in homes before and after moving into the BEH units.

The study compared asthma-related triggers for children who moved into BEHs with a control group of children who had similar baseline asthma levels and whose parents were similar in age, employment, education, race, and ethnicity. The two groups looked much the same, although one group was exposed to their new BEH and the other was not. Recall that the earlier RCT of the clinical intervention on asthma remediation found improvements for the intensive treatment intervention of community health worker visits relative

TABLE 4.1. Impact of a Breathe-Easy Home Compared to Clinical Intervention

Change	Children that moved into BEH (experimental group)	Children that received general health intervention (control group)
Rescue medicine used	−4.1%	−2.0%
Asthma attacks	−5.1%	−2.1%
Nights with symptoms	−3.5%	−1.4%
Mold, smoking, pests, and other triggers	−1.3%	−0.6%

Source: Takaro, Tim K., James Krieger, Lin Song, Denise Sahrify, and Nancy Beaudet. "The Breathe-Easy home: The impact of asthma-friendly home construction on clinical outcomes and trigger exposure," *American Journal of Public Health* 101, no. 1 (2011): 55–62.

to a single assessment. This follow-up study found that the improvements in caregiver quality of life, urgent clinical care, and improvements in a breathing test were even greater for the BEH children than the intense clinical intervention. The study also showed that mold levels dropped to zero when residents moved into BEH units. There were greater improvements in BEH units in terms of water leaks and other moisture-related problems, as well as overall structural triggers for asthma. Also, an important side note is that twenty-two of the BEH residents had participated in the original health-worker home visits study, which improved outcomes for everyone, suggesting that the effects observed in this study are actually underestimating the additional value of a BEH home.

Table 4.1 shows some of the relative differences between the BEH and control groups. What is readily apparent is that both groups benefited and had less asthma, use of rescue medicine, nights with asthma symptoms, and asthma triggers in their homes. But the children in the BEH homes experienced substantial improvements due to these changes. This is evidence that place matters, as a clean and well-constructed home was better for these children's health in the long run than a clinical education intervention that required much greater maintenance and adherence to a medication schedule.

This study suggests that structural features of homes are central to health, especially for acute health problems like asthma that largely occur after some sort of an environmental trigger. What this study also suggests is that directly treating the structural deficits in places is at least as important as directly treating the people in those places with medical care.

This makes sense. After all, it's hard to imagine combatting chronic asthma for children in a home that is laden with moisture caused by a leaking roof, poorly constructed walls, and flooring that continuously collects dust mites. A more recent study using the same comparison group found that modest renovations add additional benefits in preventing asthma symptoms and home triggers.[52] Even basic weatherization, such as improving home venting and adding insulation, and simple changes to homes, like removing carpets, might significantly improve asthma symptoms for children. The takeaway message is that basic changes to the features of homes, whether through the building of more expensive BEH units or the renovation of existing structures, produces measurable changes in health. In both of these cases, asthma improvements occurred over and above the clinical interventions that require people to change their behavior. While changes in the built environment can impact chronic health issues like asthma, what do we know about their impact on crime and safety?

Fixing Doors and Windows

Housing abandonment is an increasing problem for many cities in the United States.[53] In 2010, Philadelphia alone had some forty thousand vacant properties, including over three thousand with abandoned buildings or other structures.[54] This number of vacant structures has remained steady over the past fifteen years, despite wide-scale revitalization efforts in many areas, as well as substantial public policy efforts such as Philadelphia's Neighborhood Transition Initiative in the mid-2000s and the more recent Land Bank effort directed at this issue.

There are a host of studies rooted in the "broken windows" theory, which suggests that neighborhoods with vacant or abandoned properties are associated with more crime.[55] Vacant properties are more likely to be neglected or vandalized, to lack curbside appeal, to suggest that no one is monitoring, and to serve as invitations to crime. But are these properties really *causing* crime to occur, or are they just part of a larger cycle of crime and urban depopulation? Conversely, perhaps it is crime that is causing the abandonment of buildings and other forms of community disorder and incivilities. The best way to answer this question is to see what would happen if we renovated abandoned buildings and measured the occurrence of crime. That is to say, what if we actually fixed the broken windows? This could serve as an empirical test of what had been simply theory and speculation based on associations between levels of crime and levels of vacancy.

A few years ago an opportunity presented itself to do just that. In 2011 Philadelphia passed a "Doors and Windows" ordinance requiring property owners

FIGURE 4.4. Photos of renovated vacant properties. *Source*: Kondo, Michelle C., Danya Keene, Bernadette C. Hohl, John M. MacDonald, and Charles C. Branas, "A difference-in-differences study of the effects of a new abandoned building remediation strategy on safety," *PloS One* 10, no. 7 (2015): e0129582. *Note*: This figure shows four properties that received doors-and-windows remediation. Pink posters on doors of properties shown in the upper-left- and lower-right-hand quadrants notify the owner of a date by which the structure must be in compliance or face penalty.

to install operating doors and windows in all vacant buildings on blocks that were more than 80 percent resident occupied. Fines of three hundred dollars per day for each opening were levied against those who failed to comply.[56] The ordinance also required property owners to have buildings sealed up by a licensed contractor—not just with unattractive, and in fact quite pervious, plywood boards—in an effort to make buildings more aesthetically appealing.

Figure 4.4 shows a comparison of houses that complied with the Philadelphia ordinance. The before-and-after contrasts are striking. Even though the properties are still vacant, the simple action of replacing broken doors and windows and removing graffiti completely changed the curbside appeal of these properties. This included residents who saw these buildings every day in their "before" states, and would-be criminals who might take advantage of an otherwise vacant home that lacked an effective guardian.

But what effect did this have on public safety? We found that remediating vacant properties in this way indeed makes a difference. The study compared crime around hundreds of buildings cited by the new ordinance that complied with the violation and installed working windows and doors (treated buildings), to hundreds of buildings cited by the ordinance that made no renovations (control buildings). These comparisons were made within the same sections of the city, and treated and control buildings experienced similar amounts of crime occurring around them before any renovations were done. In effect, this research design compared treated and control buildings and isolated whether the "Doors and Windows" treatment caused any changes in crime.[57]

Figure 4.5 shows a density map of abandoned buildings that were cited by the ordinance. What is striking is how many buildings were cited in such a relatively short period, dotting the landscape across much of Philadelphia. Close to 30 percent of the properties in violation complied with the ordinance and installed working doors and windows. In the year that followed, there were 20 percent fewer assaults, 39 percent fewer gun assaults, and 16 percent fewer nuisance crimes around the buildings that complied with the ordinance compared to those that did not. Narcotics arrests, on the other hand, went up around buildings that had been renovated, possibly reflecting the fact it was easier to detect drug sellers when they weren't able to hide so easily. These findings suggest there are substantial benefits to renovating abandoned buildings, even in very simple ways. And the study also showed that crime actually was prevented and not simply displaced around the corner to an adjacent block.

The "Doors and Windows" ordinance had a positive impact on both minor quality-of-life crimes and more serious crimes, which is a major driver of community stress and urban depopulation. New doors and windows and a freshly cleaned building facade likely signaled to potential criminals that the property was occupied, and that crime was not tolerated. Moreover, the dual challenge to potential criminals of being seen more easily from the outside through glass windows (as opposed to plywood coverings) and entering the openings of abandoned buildings through glass windows that make noise and leave an obvious, lasting visual sign of forced entry when shattered, may have also been the mechanism behind the reductions in crime. Here, however, we are speculating.

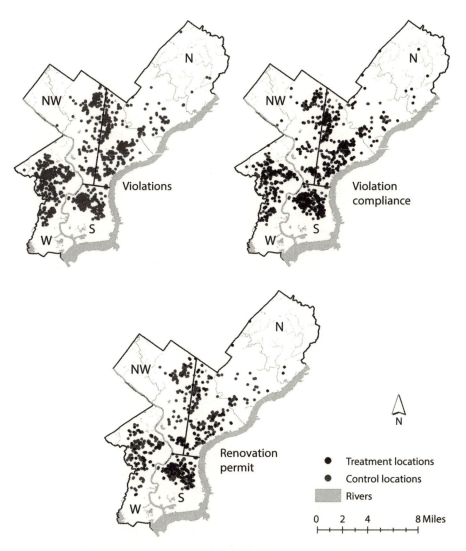

FIGURE 4.5. Location of violations, compliance, and renovation permits from Philadelphia Doors and Windows Ordinance. *Sources*: Philadelphia Department of Licensing and Inspection (2013), North (N), Northwest (NW), South (S) and West (W) sections are indicated; Kondo, Michelle C., Danya Keene, Bernadette C. Hohl, John M. MacDonald, and Charles C. Branas, "A difference-in-differences study of the effects of a new abandoned building remediation strategy on safety," *PLoS One* 10, no. 7 (2015): e0129582.

On its own, this intervention wouldn't make a considerable dent in the Philadelphia crime rate, but it should be considered within the context of only those blocks with abandoned buildings. If you took the estimates from the study and extrapolated, you'd find that there were almost five hundred fewer crimes per month in Philadelphia as a result of the building changes that were spurred by the ordinance. Thinking from the perspective of a resident living on a block in Philadelphia, this is a consequential difference.

But the fact that compliance with the ordinance was not randomized means we cannot know for sure if the effects observed were causal; thus, we launched a randomized controlled trial (RCT) of abandoned-housing remediation in Philadelphia. In this study, hundreds of abandoned houses are being selected and then randomly assigned to three groups: fully treated (facades cleaned including graffiti removal, doors and windows replaced, monthly trash removal); partly treated (graffiti removal and monthly trash removal); and not treated. This study will allow us to determine if fixing up abandoned buildings reduces crime because of the building renovations themselves, or if any realized impacts simply reflect the fact that people are showing up each month to pick up trash and maintain the property. Regardless of this study's ultimate findings, the RCT method will provide stronger evidence to city policy makers about the crime reduction benefits of remediating vacant housing with working windows and doors.

Better Homes for Our Health and Safety and Addressing Gentrification

According to housing inventory estimates from the 2010 census, there were 13.9 million vacant homes in the United States.[58] A problem of this scale suggests that any substantial housing remediation program could lead to widespread population health benefits. Importantly, these changes to places do not require massive economic restructuring or moving hundreds of thousands of people to new locations. An effective housing remediation program, however, would require a concerted effort to provide, rebuild, or remodel housing to meet basic health standards, including proper ventilation and minimizing roof and building leaks. Thanks to revised building codes, newer housing construction provides such assurances. A substantial remediation program would also require maintaining or repurposing buildings when they've become vacant. The few studies we've provided in this chapter make it clear that new home designs can improve children's asthma, and that remediating abandoned buildings can improve neighborhood crime.

The effects of housing design on childhood asthma are quite large. This makes intuitive sense. After all, children tend to spend a lot of time in their homes. A home with reduced dust, mold, and other triggers does more to improve symptoms than providing education services because it is treating one of the primary underlying causes of asthma. While restoring broken windows and doors is a more modest change to housing structures, there is rigorous evidence that even modest changes can reduce neighborhood crimes.

Scholars have noted that concentrated poverty in neighborhoods is a major reason why substandard housing exists, often in the form of public housing, and is associated with crime and health problems.[59] Reducing poverty is incredibly challenging, but we do have some tools to address substandard housing that we should use. In the poorest of settings, changes to the built environment of housing are even more influential on health and safety than in wealthier areas.[60]

A natural concern that is raised when talking about changes to housing in distressed neighborhoods is its potential to spur gentrification, or the migration of higher-income residents into working-class neighborhoods. Revitalization efforts in distressed neighborhoods could lead to an influx of higher-income residents that increase the demand for housing and push up housing prices, rents, and property taxes. An influx of higher-income residents may in turn displace long-term residents who are unable to pay the changes in monthly rents or property-tax increases that result from higher assessed home values. While there are clear examples of individuals that have undergone involuntary moves as a result of gentrification, these tend to be focused on individuals living in downtown neighborhoods with increasing housing values in places like Boston, Chicago, Los Angeles, New York, San Francisco, Seattle, and Washington, DC.[61] There is evidence that gentrification is occurring in formerly distressed downtown neighborhoods in a few large US cities where residential populations have grown slightly and average incomes of residents have risen by more than 25 percent between 2000 and 2010.[62] But these trends are happening in only a handful of cities on the East and West Coasts, and even in those cities gentrifying neighborhoods reflect only a small share (10 percent) of the total available residential housing. In the vast majority of large US cities with an ample stock of distressed housing (e.g., Baltimore, Columbus, Charlotte, Dallas, Detroit, Houston, Indianapolis, St. Louis), gentrification is not occurring on any notable scale.

Anyone who has spent time in these cities will recognize the signs of gentrification, including the construction of condominiums and the opening of coffee shops and restaurants catering to a higher-income class. The evidence from studies that examine out-migration rates tend to find that residents who own homes are just as likely to stay in a neighborhood after it has undergone some gentrification than to leave.[63] Some of this may be due to limits in their choices of places to move. If there are fewer places to move within a neighborhood because housing prices have risen, it's reasonable to suspect that households with limited income will stay put. But property-tax increases are unlikely to displace homeowners, as it is rare for cities to dynamically reassess property values. Many cities take years to change them, or only reassess at the point of sale. Yet there is evidence from a number of studies that examine the movement patterns of renters before and after a neighborhood has shown signs of rising income relative to surrounding neighborhoods and finds evidence of outmigration, suggesting that gentrification does lead to the displacement of lower-income renters.[64] But studies that examined population-level migration using national samples in the 1990s find that lower-income residents are not more likely to move in a gentrifying neighborhood than one that is not gentrifying, and that when gentrification occurs to predominately minority neighborhoods, it is primarily middle-class households moving in of the same race.[65]

Evidence also suggests that when average incomes tend to rise in a neighborhood relative to its surrounding areas, the racial demographics of the areas are slower to change. Sociologist Patrick Sharkey, for example, finds that the lessening of poverty in US neighborhoods between 1970 and 2000 is not associated with white residents displacing blacks.[66] Rather, the evidence suggests areas become more ethnically diverse.[67] This also fits the patterns of gentrification in this time period due to the influx of Asian and Hispanic residents to lower-income, mostly black center-city neighborhoods.[68]

However, in the last ten years we have seen a rise in gentrification in center city neighborhoods of a different form, as higher-income white professionals move into working-class neighborhoods that are either predominately black or ethnic enclaves.[69] These facts suggest that gentrification in inner-city neighborhoods is increasingly a possibility when successful urban renewal happens. While there is little chance that place-based efforts to remediate or stabilize vacant housing stock will on its own spur gentrification in neighborhoods of concentrated poverty, place-based interventions in housing should be mindful of signs of gentrification after an evaluation has been conducted. For example,

Rene Goodwin, a resident of South Philadelphia undergoing gentrification, saw her assessed home value jump from $90,000 to $250,000 in a single year. She noted that "to keep an urban area vital, there has to be an infusion of new people and buildings, but that doesn't mean you destroy people who have kept up the neighborhood, who've swept the sidewalk," she said. "It's that commitment that has made developers interested in the neighborhood—and then you're going to penalize the people who've stayed?"[70]

Area-specific policies can be put in place to buttress against the negative effects that gentrification can have on longer-term poor residents. Inclusionary zoning, for example, is an approach that requires developers to set aside 10 to 20 percent of residential units for lower-income people, or to pay a fee that gets placed into an affordable-housing trust in the municipality to help the local housing authority or nonprofits to build newer units.[71] There is some evidence such policies can produce a sizable amount of affordable housing that is also more resistant to busts in the housing market,[72] though more careful analysis is certainly warranted as spikes in the value of housing in some cities will make place-based policies like inclusionary zoning insufficient on their own.[73] Another policy response to curb the dislocation of lower-income residents due to gentrification is to create homestead exemptions that reduce the value that a city can tax a house that is someone's primary residence. Longtime owner provisions and senior-citizen property-tax freezes are also being implemented in cities facing gentrification pressures. To incentivize the construction and maintenance of affordable housing in gentrifying neighborhoods, cities can also create tax abatement policies or provide bond funding to property developers. Finally, cities can also require property developers to enter into community benefits agreements for neighborhoods. Community benefits agreements typically require developers to build a share of affordable housing and add other environmental improvements to a neighborhood, like building parks or community centers.[74] It is important that these agreements are done transparently and truly represent the stated interests of the impacted community, rather than an interest group that is trying exploit the development process for its own financial gain.[75]

At the same time, we need to recognize that some gentrification can lead to potential benefits, including greater economic vibrancy, improvements in public safety, greater attention from public service agencies, and greater investments in neighborhood institutions like schools and parks.[76] Jacy Webster, a fifty-six-year-old long-time resident of a working-class South Philadelphia neighborhood that has recently undergone an influx of higher-income young families, noted that, while he now feels like a stranger to his new neighbors, "it's actually safer than it's ever been."[77]

There is no easy fix to larger systemic issues that generate inequalities in the price of housing. But the type of place-based housing interventions we are advocating for, including breathe-easy homes and abandoned-housing repairs, are not going to be the sources for generating larger market changes in the housing values of entire cities. Rather, they are intended to showcase examples of place-based interventions that can be done in ways that are relatively cheap, sustainable, and scalable to entire populations in the most disadvantaged neighborhoods of cities.

What we've presented here is some preliminary evidence to convince you that there are solutions emerging that are actionable and that have been scientifically shown to improve health and safety. We hope this evidence convinces readers that the apocalyptic ruin photography images filling urban art galleries from Sydney to Detroit are not reflective of an inevitable state of urban cities, and that positive changes can occur.[78] While signaling a great movement forward, what's been done to date on this issue is only a first set of modest scientific tests. More substantive programs need to be advanced to address decrepit buildings and structures that exist throughout many cities in the world. More scientific testing of these efforts is needed to wade through actions that work and those that do not.

In looking at the case studies we've presented from Seattle, Philadelphia, and other cities, it is striking just how much the condition of the buildings around us impacts our health and safety. Despite serving as inspiration for ruin photographers, abandoned and dilapidated buildings are clearly bad for us. Fixing them, even in small ways, may lead to transformational benefits. But buildings are just one piece in a larger puzzle of place-based initiatives. The next chapter looks at land as a second important opportunity to change places and improve lives.

5

The Nature Cure

ON A LONG LIST of issues for which people report that they are "not willing to listen to the other side," gun rights is near the top. Scientific discussion over the impact of gun availability on rates of violent crime has led to contentious debate.[1] Now, imagine what would happen if someone said they advocated for ways to reduce crime that had nothing to do with regulating gun ownership. What if policy discussions were also focused on adding green space, trees, and vegetation to cities as ways to combat gun violence and improve population health more generally? This policy debate would surely be less contentious—but, you may ask, would that actually make a difference?

The idea of greening spaces, especially in cities, as a solution to a host of problems has increasingly captivated public conversation. Many people feel a clear visceral connection between trees and other natural vegetation and their own health. In fact, talk of "therapeutic landscapes" has been around for centuries. The first-choice solutions to health problems like tuberculosis were back-to-nature interventions that reintroduced city dwellers to the clean air of the country. Some even argue that merely seeing the color green has therapeutic benefit. But does actual greening—such as infusing concrete cityscapes with grass and trees—positively impact our health and safety? Lack of natural vegetation has long been thought of as a component cause of crime and poor health, but only a few scientific studies rigorously examine how changes in trees or greening might actually lead to observable changes in crime and health.

The late comedian George Carlin once joked, "Why do we park on driveways and drive on parkways?" The answer goes back to the 1800s, when the verb "parking" referred to the action of creating park land for recreational or other purposes, and "a park" was a noun. "Parking" had nothing to do with stopping and disembarking from a form of transportation. The change in idiom came about when people started using park areas to tie up their horses and carriages.

The term stuck, and when the automobile took over as the dominant form of transportation, it made sense that we would be driving on parkways.[2]

Parking thus originally came into use as city planners sought to interject parcels, pockets, and strips of nature into the urban landscape. A "parkway" often refers to the strip of land between a property and the curbline of a street. After the massive fire that destroyed nearly the entire city of Chicago in 1871, city planners developed a uniform street grid system where street widths and lengths were standardized, along with the amount of space required between property and curblines.[3] The minimum area of green space for parking was four feet between the sidewalk and the curb on both sides of a street. In some street layouts the green space was set to be wider, especially near larger roadways. Visitors to Chicago often marvel at how many trees and gardens adorn the public right-of-way on residential streets, especially since this space is technically owned by the city, but maintained by adjacent property owners.

Chicago also designated twenty-six miles of boulevards to receive extra green space, commonly referred to as the city's "emerald necklace."[4] These boulevards serve as a continuous street network that links the city's eight large parks. These planned green spaces, which were laid out at the same time as the larger park system, were designed to serve multiple purposes. First, they interjected healthy green spaces and trees into the urban hardscape. Second, the emerald necklace provided a median between roads and residences. Originally the concern was a buffer from horse manure, but now this green space functions to keep cars separated from people's houses, kids playing outside, and street traffic. Third, these green spaces were regulated and maintained to assist in stormwater management.

When they first emerged, urban stormwater systems of the 1800s were incredibly innovative, but they often combined sewer and stormwater into the same drain system with little insight into the likely occurrence of major rainstorms. When stormwater exceeded the capacity of the drain systems, the overflow would spill into streets and fresh waterways. This polluted rainwater could then back up into the surrounding watershed and lead to a host of environmental health issues, including contaminated drinking water.

Stormwater management has become even more important as climate-change trends have wrought more major heavy rainfall events in the United States, especially in the Northeast and Midwest.[5] Philadelphia, a city with a dearth of parkways in its urbanized core neighborhoods, has wrestled with stormwater management over the past few decades. Rainstorms have increasingly caused serious flooding, resulting in sewage backups into houses. This has led to large-scale coordinated efforts to introduce "green infrastructure" into many Philadelphia neighborhoods—using parkways, pocket parks, swales, underground cisterns, and other forms of green space to absorb stormwater runoff.[6]

Due to prior land-use planning decisions, space for these sorts of green infrastructure installations is at a premium in older colonial cities like Philadelphia, Boston, New York, and Baltimore. If you look at a satellite map of their residential neighborhoods, much of the landscape is really hardscape—rooftops, parking lots, asphalt streets, and concrete sidewalks: prime locations for stormwater runoff. By contrast, cities like Chicago, Washington, DC, and Kansas City were designed with a green infrastructure. For example, civil engineers in Chicago in 1900 had to figure out how to reverse the flow of the Chicago River to prevent industrial pollutants from running into Lake Michigan, the city's main drinking-water source. George Kessler's redesign of Kansas City in the 1890s transformed a poorly designed boom town once defined by dirt streets and random, ramshackle buildings into a City Beautiful masterpiece. Not surprisingly, many neighborhoods in older colonial cities like Philadelphia that were designed without sufficient attention to green space are the most acutely at risk in the event of combined sewer-stormwater system mishaps during rainstorms and the health crises that may follow. Green infrastructure may also produce other benefits to neighborhoods that face stormwater runoff, including mitigating crime.

A good demonstration of the environmental health and safety benefits of interventions is Philadelphia's green stormwater infrastructure program. The program was designed to mitigate the consequences of major flooding events by allowing water to collect in catchment areas that had natural vegetation in place of pavement. While the environmental benefits of stormwater mitigation was clear, was it possible that the greening program could have other public benefits? One study in Philadelphia showed that nuisance crimes were reduced after the installation of new stormwater basins, planters, rain gardens, swales, and tree trenches as part of Philadelphia's green stormwater infrastructure program.[7] This remains one of the first scientifically documented success stories of greening water infrastructure in any city.

There are also the health and safety benefits of trees and other initiatives to increasing green space in cities. The use of trees in city planning was part of the larger parks movement that took off after the design and construction of New York's Central Park. Most city dwellers of the mid-to-late 1800s had come from rural farms in the United States and abroad. The mass urbanization movement of the industrial era led many city leaders to long for the reinsertion of nature into their built environments.

In many ways, today's urban greening activities, while small by comparison, are a lot like those that began over a century ago. As the concept of environmental sustainability has grown within the context of the larger climate-change and urban-resilience narrative, cities and regions in the United States have increasingly taken policy leadership positions on environmental issues. This is due in part to their progressive leanings, but also to a general sense of frustration with the contentious national political discussion over climate change and other issues affecting cities. Many urban leaders and residents are problem solvers by nature and are faced with big problems that other levels of government simply cannot solve. Urban leaders have now begun to take matters into their own hands, sometimes with great success.[8]

Cities have carved out local plans that augment larger mandates to reduce their carbon footprints and become more energy efficient.[9] The metaphor of the city as a "metabolic system" developed by Abe Wolman in 1965 has undergone a resurgence in urban planning and environmental science.[10] If the city is a metabolic system, then its trees are a potential source of carbon digestion coming from the emission of fossil fuels from cars and buildings. Cities like Pittsburgh and Chattanooga went through decades of pollution so thick that cars drove with their lights on during the day and luncheonettes closed because businessmen went home at midday to change their shirts, soiled each morning simply by sitting at their desks. Something had to be done. The very design of dense, hardscaped urban populations prompted the need for natural solutions to counterbalance their increasingly gloomy feel and obvious obstacles to economic success, like air pollution.

Among numerous other urban revitalization programs, tree planting thus became a major policy goal for US cities. In 2006, Los Angeles, a city with 1.5 million trees, set a goal of planting a million more. They also sought to replace the iconic non-native environmentally underperforming palm tree with native shade trees.[11] In cities like Pittsburgh, fiscal pressures and a quickly declining tree canopy led to the creation of citywide nonprofit agencies focused on trees. Tree Pittsburgh, which was established in 2006 to serve as a planning and advocacy organization, has published an Urban Forest Master Plan. In Philadelphia, a sustainability plan called Greenworks set a goal of increasing neighborhood tree coverage by 30 percent by adding 300,000 new trees over twenty years.[12] The city has managed to plant over 120,000 new trees in less than half its target time. Of course, a reasonable question to then ask is, Do these new

urban forest initiatives really make a difference in these cities? After all, planting trees and maintaining them is expensive.

Cities have difficult choices to make in terms of budget allocations. The path
of least resistance often prevails and budgets are formed each year based on past
years and what the city feels it needs to be responsive to its citizens' short-term
needs. A quick glance at almost any major city's budget will show that the investment in law enforcement is one of the highest public expenditures. If there
is a choice to add funds either to the police department or the forestry division,
law enforcement often wins. This of course makes some sense, and we are not
advocating against investments in law enforcement. However, there may be
major benefits to place-based strategies that involve natural spaces in land use,
such as the planting of trees. Some cities, like Chicago, have protected their parks
budget from the politics of city-wide budget challenges. A separate property
tax assessment is dedicated to funding parks in the city and its surrounding
county.

A recent estimate of the number of trees on earth—three trillion, or roughly
four hundred trees for every human—seems an impressive number, unless you
consider that over the past twelve thousand years the earth has lost over half
of its trees.[13] While it is a laudable goal for cities to plant a million new trees,
this is only small gesture toward restoring the earth's tree population. The
strength of urban tree-planting programs, however, is their potential impact on
crime, health, and economic development. A closer look at some scientific programs that have either studied urban greening interventions or implemented
their own urban greening interventions provides additional proof of these connections. Planting trees in cities may actually be an investment in both safety
and environmental health. In fact, these efforts may serve as a form of "soft policing" that produces the environmental benefits for which they were initially
introduced while improving the health and safety of the city population.[14]

Crime-Fighting Trees

There are a few noteworthy studies that examine in detail the influence of natural vegetation and trees on housing values and crime rates. One study by a
team from the US Forest Service considered the question of trees and crime
by looking at over two thousand single-family homes in Portland, Oregon.[15]
The research group measured tree coverage from aerial photographs around
each home and collected land-use data from the city assessor's office, including
the age of the house, lot size, and the number of commercial properties nearby.

They even conducted an on-site observation of each house, much like Google Street View, and measured the presence of garages, driveways, and bars placed on the windows, as well as visibility from the road, among other factors.[16]

Their statistical analysis found that larger trees in front of a house, especially those with a crown of leaves on top, reduced the risk of property crime over a three-year period—even after taking into account crime on that property during the previous three years. In contrast, having lots of low-lying trees around a house increased the risk of crimes. The researchers argued that it was the height of trees and foliage that really mattered—trees that were at least forty-two feet high were associated with fewer crimes. What explains this mechanism? Apparently trees at least forty-two feet high tend to generate foliage at around nine feet, which may shield a home's second story from view, making it hard for a burglar to see if someone is home, but is also too high for anyone to hide near a tree at the ground level. These results suggest that the form of trees may matter: trees that obstruct the view of the second floor of a house but do not provide a hiding place for criminals on the ground may help reduce crime on blocks. But, again, because the scientists weren't observing changes to trees, just comparing places with different types and amounts of trees, the study left some questions unanswered.

A similar approach to this question was taken by researchers in Chicago who looked at trees and grass around public housing apartment buildings and their effect on crime. Their study area was ninety-eight buildings within Chicago's Ida B. Wells public housing development. The researchers found that crime was significantly lower around apartment buildings where there were more trees and grass, when compared to other buildings with distinctly more barren surroundings, which had been largely paved over as a result of the city housing authority's desire to "keep dust down" and save on ground maintenance costs.[17] The study's findings suggest that differences in crime were likely attributable to differences in the amount of trees and grass around the buildings.

However, much like the Portland study, this Chicago study of crime was only a comparison of differences after any changes in green space had occurred; therefore, we are unable to clearly see what effect grass and trees really had on crime. What if the buildings with more grass and trees had renters that were less likely to engage in crime? What if the barren buildings had more criminals living in them beforehand? With these unanswered questions in mind, the researchers sought to refine their approach.

A second study by the same group of scientists at the University of Illinois took advantage of a natural experiment,[18] this time at the nearby Robert Taylor

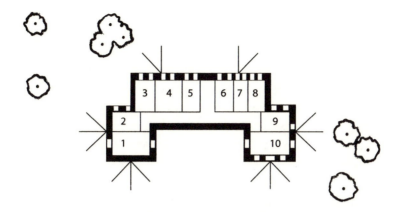

FIGURE 5.1. Plan view of an apartment building and trees nearby. *Source*: Kuo, Frances E., and William C. Sullivan, "Aggression and violence in the inner city: Effects of environment via mental fatigue," *Environment and Behavior* 33, no. 4 (2001): 553. Copyright © 2001 by SAGE Publications. Reprinted by Permission of SAGE Publications, Inc.

Homes, an area that the Chicago Housing Authority referred to as "the worst slum in the United States."[19] At that time, Chicago public housing residency was randomly determined. Through a lottery system, residents were assigned to various homes within the Robert Taylor Homes' twenty-eight high-rise buildings—a situation that presented researchers with an ideal opportunity to learn about what residents in different homes were experiencing. More specifically, some of these homes had preexisting trees and grass, and some had little if any as a result of being paved over long before. The random assignment of who got to live in which building should mean that the families are similar on characteristics such as income, education, life circumstances, violent tendencies, and other observable factors. Due to the lottery, people living in buildings close to trees and grass should be similar on many characteristics to those living next to paved areas, thereby giving the researchers the ability to look at the true effect of living near greener space in public housing.

This natural experiment was focused on two main outcome variables, levels of aggression and mental fatigue, for 145 urban public housing residents living close to varying levels of nearby grass and trees. To measure nature, pictures were taken of the space around each building and trained field observers rated each building they visited (see fig. 51). As we discussed, the use of random assignment here bolstered the strength of its findings. The differences in green space around each building were ultimately compared to questionnaire responses from adult tenants in each of the buildings.

Residents living in buildings with more trees and grass nearby reported committing fewer acts of aggression in the previous year than residents living in buildings surrounded by barren land and pavement. Reported levels of fighting, pushing, grabbing, shoving, slapping, or throwing something at a family member were lower for those living in housing projects close to trees and grass. The same pattern was also seen for measures of psychological aggression like threatening others, throwing objects, and hurling insults. Residents who lived in buildings surrounded by more green space also scored significantly higher on attention span, which was measured by a procedure that asked respondents to repeat back numbers read to them in reverse.

The relationship between buildings with more green space nearby and lower aggression was no longer apparent when the researchers controlled for attention span. These findings suggest that barren buildings may lead to deficits in attention span, which in turn increase aggression. They also found that measures of stress were not highly correlated with green space near buildings. So it appeared to them that the lack of vegetation around buildings may lead to reduced attention span and increased aggression.

While the exact mechanisms remain unclear, maybe there's some sort of a bioevolutionary or psychologically embedded unconscious understanding of green space and vegetation inherent to human well-being. Maybe these scientists learned something from Chicago's "worst slum" that reflects our fundamental need as human beings to have the natural world in our daily lives if we are to remain calm, happy, and healthy. But of course this is only one study, and we didn't get to see residents before and after these locations changed their green space. A rival explanation for the findings could be that less aggressive and mentally acute residents over time were able to find their way into the buildings with green space nearby. This seems implausible, given that the assignment of rental units is done by a lottery. But not being able to observe the actual change in behavior means that the evidence is less convincing than if it were an actual randomized controlled trial.

Philadelphia's Experiment with Greening

Is the evidence on crime fighting grass and trees compelling? Should cities really start planting green space to prevent crime? In the 1990s, a handful of citizens in Philadelphia's Kensington neighborhood were fed up with its disheveled look, the drug dealers milling around, and the ubiquitous violence they were seeing every day. They were going to do something about it.

Portions of the iconic 1976 *Rocky* movie were filmed in Kensington and showed the hardscrabble alleys and corners, replete with "creeps on every other block." The Lucky Seven Tavern was on one of these corners and the setting of several scenes in the movie, which paints a bleak picture of Kensington and of the Lucky Tavern as a dark, abandoned place. The Lucky Seven was demolished in the years after the movie, probably as the unoccupied building became decrepit. Unfortunately, demolition wasn't a great solution to the abandoned property, as what was left in its place was a vacant lot full of trash and demolition debris. Images of the Lucky Seven lot taken from Google Street View show some of this detritus from the early 2000s. Around 2010, however, this vacant lot took on a new look—cleaned, greened, and nicely fenced through a new community program started by a group of Kensington residents a decade earlier.

These residents of Kensington originally hatched their vacant-lot greening program both to deal with the abundance of blighted spaces they saw each day as well as to increase the value of their homes. In 1996, the New Kensington Community Development Corporation teamed up with the Pennsylvania Horticultural Society, and later the Philadelphia Office of Housing and Community Development, to create a public-private venture to revitalize the neighborhood through what they called "land care"—now named LandCare. This early pilot version of the land care program was intended to use basic greening to clean up vacant lots in the hopes that it would stimulate development and increase property values.[20]

The Philadelphia LandCare program was purposely designed as a basic and low-cost treatment for vacant plots of land that were about one thousand square feet each, like the site where the Lucky Seven once stood. It was set up to be scalable so that it could be applied to the many small vacant lots across the neighborhood and be an easily reproducible script for implementation. The process was to remove the trash and debris, grade the land, and plant some grass and a few trees to create a park-like setting, then to install a low wooden post-and-rail fence, with easily accessible entrances, to invite people to use the space while also preventing the illegal dumping of trash and construction materials. The maintenance of these lots simply required a monthly trash cleanup, grass mowing, and a check on the health of trees. A before-and-after visual of the vacant-lot greening treatment is shown in figure 5.2.

The vacant-lot greening treatment costs a little more than a dollar per square foot to install and about a nickel per square foot to maintain each year.[21] The grass planting takes only an hour and is in the form of a seed mixture of

FIGURE 5.2. Vacant lot greening produces rapid and noticeable change.

resilient grass applied with leaf blowers. The trees selected for these lots are the heartiest species to survive urban spaces. The wooden post-and-rail fence was chosen to be inviting and more durable than the tall metal hurricane fences that were meant to keep people out and often ended up rusted, torn down, or cut through. Despite some early concerns, these wooden post-and-rail fences were only infrequently torn down or subject to graffiti. The whole installation process typically took a week or two, to clean and green a half dozen vacant lots on the average abandoned city block. Visually, the change on such blocks was rapid and dramatic.

To be sure, the Philadelphia LandCare program is not a luxury park-making initiative, nor an attempt to create some sort of destination amenity for wealthier residents from other neighborhoods. It was not envisioned as a luxury greening installation program like those in San Francisco's Golden Gate Park or the High Line in New York City. The LandCare program was designed to improve conditions for people right where they lived. You didn't need to sell your house and move somewhere else, or take the bus across town to get some green space in your life. New park-like spaces were now right next door and often in large numbers. One reporter described the program as the beginnings of a "park of a thousand pieces" that would launch in a single Philadelphia neighborhood and grow to cover over 10 million total square feet (almost 250 acres) throughout the city.[22] And, perhaps because of its simplicity, it would also grow to generate interest and even implementation in multiple other cities across the United States and around the world.[23]

Did these vacant-lot greened spaces actually achieve what they were supposed to? Although they did spur some redevelopment, only about 5 to 10 percent of the properties that were greened subsequently had homes or other structures built on them. However, nearly all the Philadelphia LandCare greened lots have been diligently maintained, many for as long as a decade or more. The economic benefits have been clearly documented in multiple natural experiments. In Kensington, newly greened and maintained lots were shown to enhance the value of adjacent properties by as much as 30 percent.[24] A more detailed citywide analysis by researchers at Temple University later corroborated this smaller neighborhood pilot study by showing that homes near newly greened vacant lots had significantly greater increases in value than those near vacant lots that were not greened.[25]

This leads to new questions: If many of these interim greening treatments are really semipermanent, and if we know they are improving economic conditions, what else might they be improving? By chance, our team at the University of Pennsylvania met the director of the Philadelphia LandCare program at a meeting of the Federal Reserve Bank. The director had heard stories from residents that LandCare's greening of thousands of vacant lots across Philadelphia was making neighborhoods safer. He asked if it was possible to study their program and see if the stories lined up with empirical evidence. As epidemiologists and criminologists, we were familiar with using quasi-experimental methods to test drugs and other compounds or to evaluate the effect of a new court program, so we looked at this as an opportunity to apply the same value-neutral scientific approaches to vacant-lot greening. With some pilot funds from the Centers for Disease Control, we set out on our research task.

Because the LandCare program had already greened thousands of vacant lots, we started by considering these. In total, over 4,000 lots had been greened in the decade from 1999 to 2008, and we chose these for study. These lots represented about 8 percent of all vacant lots in the city and some 7 million square feet (over 150 acres) of land.[26] To best answer our research question, we examined before-and-after changes in crime and people's health around vacant lots that were greened as compared to a random sample of over 13,000 vacant lots that were not greened but, very importantly, could have been (1 greened lot for every 3 not greened). These control lots were matched to the greened lots in terms of city section (Northwest, North, West, and South), square footage, date of installation, and important neighborhood indicators such as unemployment, education, and income.

The control lots were the key to disentangling the effects of countless other phenomena that could have biased the results and made it look like the greening was having an impact when it was not. For instance, crime was going down citywide over our decade of study. Any crime reductions around the greened lots might really be due to this larger phenomenon and not the greening itself. By using the control lots for comparison, we were able to avoid this problem of a historical effect, as it would be happening to the control lots as well.

The map on the left in figure 5.3 shows the vast amount of space that had been greened in Philadelphia as part of the LandCare program. The map on the right shows the breadth of our study's control lots, which, again, were a random representative sample of all vacant lots in Philadelphia. It is striking how much of the city is covered by vacant lots. The widespread scale of these lots reinforced for us the importance of testing this form of land remediation, especially since, if it worked, it could have implications for the health and safety of many residents.

What impact did greening these vacant spaces have on people's safety and health? In this first study most of the outcome measures we considered were

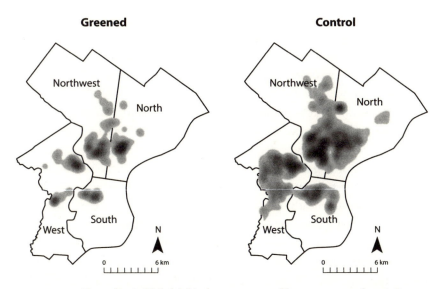

FIGURE 5.3. Vacant lots in Philadelphia that were greened between 1999 and 2008. *Source:* Branas, Charles C., Rose A. Cheney, John M. MacDonald, Vicky W. Tam, Tara D. Jackson, and Thomas R. Ten Have, "A difference-in-differences analysis of health, safety, and greening vacant urban space," *American Journal of Epidemiology* 174, no. 11 (2011): 1296–306.

unchanged by the greening. However, a few key crime and health outcomes changed that affected our understanding of the LandCare program and the broader notion that changing places could really change people's lives.

Chief among these was the finding that gun violence dropped significantly near the newly greened lots, much more than it did near the vacant control lots. This drop was over 8 percent per year and had been sustained for four years, until the end of our study. These were unexpected findings, as our previous research on urban gun violence and crime generally found few examples of efforts that work. The findings seemed reasonable, given theories like "broken windows" that suggest that crime is deterred by reducing visible signs of blight and disorder, but now this finding on gun violence was evident regardless of what metrics or statistical models we chose. We heard from some of the people doing the greening that they would find guns on the lots and from the police that Philadelphia's vacant lots were "storage lockers" for illegal guns. It seemed that people intent on shooting others could no longer use vacant lots to store their weapons once they were greened and free of overgrown weeds and trash.

In addition to this finding, we also found that residents who lived near the newly greened lots were more likely to call the police and complain about smaller nuisances. After a space was cleaned and greened, people seemed to want to keep it that way, stepping up to protect it more often than before. Residents living near newly greened lots also reported significantly less stress and more exercise when compared to residents living near vacant lots that remained overgrown and untended.

This first study in Philadelphia suggests some promise for reducing crime and improving health by remediating vacant land. However, even though we did everything possible in our quasi-experiment to make vacant lots that were greened as similar as possible to those that weren't greened, the lack of random assignment suggests that rival explanations are plausible. Maybe lots were chosen for greening because nearby residents more actively lobbied for them; or maybe lots were chosen for greening because they were in locations that were seen as likely to produce economic or quality of life benefits. Although these explanations are unlikely, due to what we observed to be an equitable selection process by the city groups that did the greening over the decade we studied, the possibility of a less-than-random selection process, witting or not, still remained.

The concerns with the self-selected nature of the vacant-lot remediation process led us to pursue funding from the Centers for Disease Control and the National Institutes of Health to conduct a three-year randomized controlled trial (RCT) of vacant-lot greening in Philadelphia. This study is one of the few true experiments of place-based change, with 541 randomly selected vacant lots from across the city. These lots were randomly assigned into three groups: one that gets the full cleaning, greening, and maintenance; one that receives a cleaning and maintenance treatment; and one that gets no intervention—this is the control group. The greening intervention involved removing trash and debris, grading land, planting new grass and a small number of trees, erecting a low wooden perimeter fence, and regularly maintaining the lot. The cleaning and maintenance intervention involved removed trash and debris, mowing the existing grass and weeds, and maintaining the lot. By creating two intervention groups (full greening and maintenance) we got to examine if any impact on crime and health would emerge from the greening itself, or from the fact that people were showing up every month to maintain the lot.

A side benefit of the project is that the local community also gets hundreds of newly greened vacant lots through a federal government subsidy to study their impact. Our preliminary results showed that simply being in view of a newly greened vacant lot significantly reduces people's heart rate and their stress, one of the first such biological findings tied to a place-based change as part of an actual experiment.[27]

Our primary results also confirmed the findings of our earlier quasi-experimental study. Interviews of households living near the different lots and an analysis of crime data before and after the interventions showed that those living near remediated lots (either fully greened or just cleaned and maintained) were less concerned about their personal safety when leaving their homes and reported increased use of outside space for relaxing and socializing. The analysis of crime data showed that gun assaults were significantly reduced due to vacant-lot remediation.[28] And actual shootings that resulted in serious injury or death dropped significantly by remediating a vacant lot with the greening or maintenance intervention.[29]

While crime reduction and reduced fear are important improvements, an ethnographic team involved in the study also witnessed tensions develop in one of the sites of the experiment, as some residents thought the vacant-lot greening was tied to a recent increase in the construction of new row homes and associated property-tax increases for the area. But in another neighborhood that was also part of the experiment, residents consistently viewed greening of vacant lots in a positive light and wanted to see more work being done to remediate abandoned housing. This section of Philadelphia is more economically distressed and has not had any gentrification, and is marked by visible signs of drug trafficking, gun violence, and street crime. The differences in the experience of greening vacant lots also speaks to the importance of understanding the community context in which a field experiment can apply. It suggests that the benefits of greening vacant lots may be most beneficial to reducing crime in particularly distressed areas and is less likely to be perceived as an encroachment by outsiders.

Following up on our work in Philadelphia, scientists at the University of Michigan and Tulane University, with funding from the Centers for Disease Control, have recently launched a four-city RCT of vacant-lot greening in Flint, Michigan; Youngstown, Ohio; Camden, New Jersey; and New Orleans, Louisiana. We are rapidly accumulating enough scientific evidence to support a broader public policy agenda to pursue the widespread use of vacant-lot greening as a cost-effective approach to producing a lasting impact on the health and safety of cities.

Seeing Green Space and Trees to Improve Health

The general idea that trees and green space are good for our health makes intuitive sense, but we've lacked convincing evidence that adding trees or green space actually improves health outcomes. Although there are studies suggesting that trees are good for cardiovascular, psychological, and respiratory health, most of the research compares people living near trees or green space to those living in more barren surroundings. Clearly, these two groups are likely to differ in many factors—such as income, education, and employment—that we can measure. The two groups are also likely to be different in factors that aren't typically measured; for example, individuals with healthier lifestyles may seek to live in areas with more trees and green space. The few natural experiments and randomized controlled trials we've discussed, though, suggest that greening space may indeed reduce crime, aggression, and even produce some health benefits. But what do we really know about the mechanisms? Is it that greening spaces produces other social amenities, like more invested neighbors, a positive shift in social norms, increased sense of ownership of spaces, or perhaps better natural surveillance? Are the mechanisms whereby greening spaces improve health and safety largely from group social processes, or are there individual physiological changes that occur in people when they are exposed to more nature? Or, most likely, a blend of both?

Some studies suggest that when areas are given more trees and grass, residents rate them as safer.[30] Others have found that stress measured by heart rate, brain electrical activity, and reported measures of emotional states are at healthier levels when subjects are viewing pictures with green vegetation versus urban scenes devoid of it.[31] Again, a stronger test of the relationships between green space and our health would be some form of an experiment that randomized people to different areas with more or less vegetation. The prior experiment with vacant-lot greening in Philadelphia is but one example, and we need more.

One of the most compelling studies of the effects of trees on health recovery comes from a small clinical study conducted over three decades ago. This study examined the records of hospital patients assigned to second- and third-floor rooms. One set of rooms looked at a brick wall whereas the others looked at a grove of trees. The researcher collected data on a sample of patients that had undergone the same gallbladder surgery with no postsurgical complications during the spring through fall months and matched them based on sex (e.g., males compared only with males), age (within five years), smoking, obesity, room color, and other factors.

In comparing patients the study showed that recovery from surgery, as measured by nurses' records, was substantially quicker for those with a tree-view room. Discharge was likely to occur a day earlier if a patient had a room with a view of trees. There were also significantly more negative notes in the files of patients who had a room with a view of a brick wall, and patients with a brick-wall view took more painkillers after their surgery.

A similarly designed study completed at around the same time found that inmates assigned to prison cells facing farmland were significantly less likely to make sick calls to the infirmary compared to those assigned cells that faced a prison courtyard.[32] While the results from these studies are limited to select outcomes, they do point to the psychological power of green views on our physical health.

We had the benefit of measuring physical and mental health as part of the vacant-lot experiment in Philadelphia. At the beginning of the experiment, one of our collaborators recruited twelve people who lived near two of the study sites to participate in a walking and stress study. These people were asked to take two prescribed walks of roughly a half-mile in their neighborhoods. In one study site, vacant lots received the full greening intervention, while in the other the vacant lots received no remediation and were part of the control condition. One walk occurred in the spring before the greening of vacant lots and the other in the summer after the lots were remediated. The study participants wore heart monitors during their walks to provide a dynamic marker of the human body's response to stress. Seven participants walked in a location that was greened and five in a location that was a control site. The study participants' heart rates dropped when they were in the view of a newly greened lot, whereas those of the participants who walked by vacant lots that remained blighted had significant increases, indicating a strong link between green views and stress. These findings are only suggestive of larger population benefits as the sample was only twelve people in only two neighborhoods.[33]

Fortunately, for the larger experiment we did measure other factors associated with stress, including mental health. Residents living near vacant lots that were part of the experiment were asked about often they felt nervous, hopeless, restless, depressed, and worthless in the past thirty days. These questions were asked two times before the intervention and two times after. Compared to residents living near vacant lots that received no remediation, residents living near vacant lots that were cleaned and greened showed a 42-percent reduction in feelings of depression and a 51-percent reduction in feeling worthless.[34] The same benefits were not evident in the lots that were only cleaned and maintained, suggesting that seeing fully remediated lots and green space near one's home provides psychological benefits.

The studies we have highlighted on the health benefits of seeing green space and trees were reasonably well-conducted natural experiments and a single RCT. But what happens if we take those trees and green views away? Will people get sick?

Beetles That Kill Trees Are Bad for Our Health and Safety

Trees are one of the biggest sources of oxygen for humans. It is reasonable to suspect that they may be one of the more important contributors to our health. But how much difference does a tree really make to a place, and what if that place suddenly lost most of its trees? The infestation of the emerald ash borer beetle in the Midwest provided a natural experiment to more concretely answer these questions.[35]

The emerald ash borer is a green beetle that is native to East Asia. When outside of its native habitat this beetle becomes invasive and destroys ash trees by leaving behind eggs that feed on their inner bark, disrupting their ability to obtain nutrients.[36] The beetle was first discovered in the United States in Michigan in 2002. Since then it has killed more than one hundred million trees. Emerald ash borer beetle infestations have resulted in the quarantine of mass amounts of firewood, untreated lumber, and ash trees.[37] When the beetle infests urban neighborhoods that are covered by only ash tree species, the effects are particularly devastating. Figure 5.4 shows an example from Toledo, Ohio, of the devastation this beetle can bring to urban neighborhoods.

A research team from the US Forest Service had been tracking the ash borer beetle infestation for years.[38] However, instead of asking the usual questions about the environmental impact of the infestation in the fifteen states that lost nearly one hundred million ash trees, this team began to wonder what the death of all those trees did to people's health. It was a tragedy for the trees, but a great opportunity that turned out to be a massive natural experiment of tree loss on human health.

Ultimately, the US Forest Service team compared the mortality rates from cardiovascular and lower-respiratory diseases in counties that had been affected by the infestation and counties that had not, as the beetle spread across the Midwest and some parts of the East, as shown in figure 5.5. The basic comparison was the change in mortality rates from 1990 to 2007 across the 1,300 or so counties before and after the invasion of the ash borer. This approach takes advantage of the fact that the spread of this invasive pest is not related to social or economic factors that may influence a county's health patterns. By comparing the changes in mortality rates for lower-respiratory and cardiovascular diseases, the study could isolate deaths that could be partially attributable to air quality. The team also smartly compared these deaths to those caused by accidents, which shouldn't have been influenced by air quality.

FIGURE 5.4. Destruction of trees caused by Emerald Ash Borer in Ohio. Street lined with ash trees in Toledo in 2006 and 2009. Photos by Dan Herms, Ohio State University.

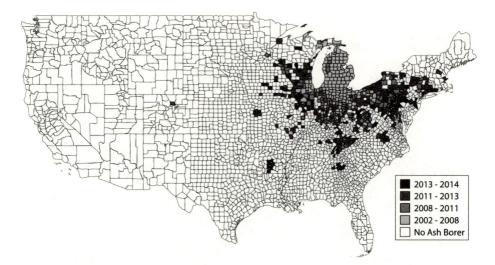

FIGURE 5.5. Timeline of the emerald ash borer beetle infestation, U.S. counties, years 2002–14. Data provided by Geoffrey Donovan, U.S. Forest Service.

Their analysis focused on the impact of the invasion of the emerald ash borer beetle on mortality rates in counties affected relative to those yet to be affected. This method removes the influence of any factors that are always different between counties, such as poverty or population size. The study also included measures of the age distribution of each county, poverty rates, income, and race, to remove these factors from influencing their estimates.

In the end they estimated that the "nasty pest," as they called it, caused at least an additional seven respiratory and seventeen cardiovascular deaths per year for every 100,000 adults in the affected counties. This translated into roughly 21,000 additional deaths per year—a staggeringly high number. The study team found no relationship between ash borer infestation and accidental deaths, a good check that what they found for respiratory and cardiovascular deaths held true. The largest effects were observed for counties that had more than four years of infestation, suggesting that the length of infestation increased the number of deaths and that the extended loss of trees wasn't something that these counties easily recovered from over time. The effect of the emerald ash borer beetle was also found to be most pronounced in wealthy counties that had greater amounts of ash tree coverage before the infestation began, suggesting that resources should be placed into planting more diverse trees that aren't susceptible to this invasive pest.

The emerald ash borer infestation also provided a natural experiment to examine the impact of tree destruction on crime. We collaborated with researchers from the US Forest Service to consider the question of whether losing trees in neighborhoods impacted crime by looking at blocks in Cincinnati, Ohio.[39] Between 2007 and 2014 Cincinnati removed over six hundred ash trees adjacent to streets and other public right-of ways that had been devastated by the ash borer infestation. We examined what happened to crime on blocks that lost right-of-way ash trees removed compared to blocks that didn't lose ash trees. The emerald ash borer clearly doesn't pick blocks to infest based on levels of crime, poverty, or other factors. Poverty and other indicators of social disadvantage are generally lower on blocks with more tree coverage. Therefore, we compared blocks with ash trees removed to those that didn't have ash trees removed but were similar in age, education, employment, poverty, and racial makeup. We found that crime significantly increased across all categories (excluding rape) when blocks lost trees due to the ash borer compared to those not impacted by the infestation. Blocks in the top 10 percent of trees removed experienced six more property crimes and two more violent crimes per year. We also found that blocks losing trees had rising levels of crime while blocks with healthy, maintained trees saw reductions in crime. The results suggest that preventing tree destruction is good for population health and crime prevention.

Green Space and Our Health and Safety

While it might seem plausible to argue that the green space around us impacts our health and safety, we should also look at this through the lens of how green space shapes our willingness to use these spaces and the quality of the spaces being used. Tree coverage provides shade, better air quality, and a nice neighborhood aesthetic, and it may make an area more attractive for outdoor exercise.[40] It may also diminish a burglar's inclination to break into a home if the canopy from trees blocks upstairs windows. On the other hand, overgrown bushes and weeds may provide natural cover for selling drugs and engaging in other vices like prostitution, while also providing a nice place for muggers to hide and wait for a passing victim or a drop spot for illegal guns, as we've shown. Indeed, not all green spaces are uniformly positive on health and safety outcomes. The context in which green space is used and maintained, especially in cities, seems fundamental to understanding how the built environment impacts our health and safety.

In this chapter we presented multiple case studies that used rigorous quasi-experimental and experimental designs to examine a variety of place-based changes, including the effects of public-housing tree cover on aggression, the cleaning and greening of vacant lots on crime and stress, and the loss of trees on health. None of these case studies settles the matter. But they provide excellent examples of how relatively straightforward place-based changes to our natural environments can significantly promote the health and safety of our communities.

6

Driving Ambivalence

TODAY, young adults in the United States and other countries are increasingly avoiding obtaining a driving license and buying a car. For millennials and post-millennials who are driving age (sixteen and above), this trend has been labeled "driving ambivalence" by academics and the press.[1] There are many reasons for this new driving ambivalence, including a recent increase in mixed-use urban development, the development of new or expanded public transportation systems, and a greater acceptance of alternative personal forms of transportation like bicycles. Driving less also has numerous health benefits, such as increased opportunities for regular exercise and neighborly interactions on the street. Regular exercise from walking and biking helps reduce our sedentary lifestyles, which are a main source of obesity. Walking and biking means there are more "eyes upon the street," reducing the risks for neighborhood crime and promoting more positive social interactions. In this chapter we will review some evidence on why moving away from cars is good for our safety and health, and how these facts provide additional justification for redesigning cities.

Every day, automobile crashes serve as reminders of the dangers of driving. Yet most people are probably unaware that over the past several decades driving has become increasingly less deadly. Figure 6.1 shows the basic trends of fatal motor vehicle deaths per 100,000 licensed drivers since 1994, collected by the National Highway Traffic Safety Administration. What may be surprising to some is how much safer it has become to drive.

One clear reason that driving has gotten safer is that we have made significant changes in how we design cars and regulate driving. Safety advocates, including Ralph Nader, have successfully lobbied the government to require the automobile industry to redesign cars to include seatbelts, airbags, roll bars, stabilization systems, and reinforced side doors.[2] Early critics of safety standards suggested that their benefits would be offset by increased risk-taking among

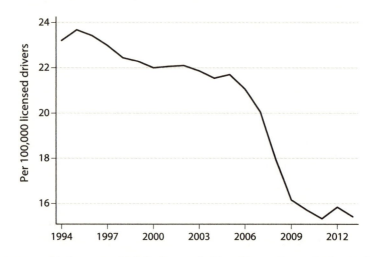

FIGURE 6.1. Yearly motor vehicle fatalities in the United States. *Source*: Fatality Analysis Reporting System (FARS) Encyclopedia, NCSA Data Resource Website, National Highway Traffic Safety Administration, http://www-fars.nhtsa.dot.gov/Main/index.aspx.

drivers. If you know your car has a seatbelt, maybe you'll just drive faster.[3] But public health experts herald the changes in government safety standards as one of the leading causes for the dramatic reduction in driving fatalities. Analyses in the 1990s suggest that the timing of government standards, such as requiring that manufacturers install seatbelts in all cars, and the adoption of mandatory seat belt laws, is closely tied to the reduction in deaths from crashes.[4] And there doesn't appear to be an offsetting behavior of riskier driving in the 1990s, or any greater level of fatalities for pedestrians or bikers.[5]

Independent of the improvements in traffic safety, it is clear that driving automobiles is not good for one's overall health. There are lessons from the success in redesigning cars for how we can design our cities to reduce car dependency. Cities with denser road networks and narrower roadways have fewer traffic accidents per mile of vehicle driven.[6] And neighborhoods with more foot traffic have less crime.

Figuring out ways to design cities in order to reduce driving also means helping tackle the obesity epidemic. More time driving means less time walking and engaging in other physical activities that promote health. Since 1950, the United States has paved as much roadway as the square footage of the entire state of Georgia.[7] Given this extreme growth, personal cars are more ubiquitous than homes and some commentators are now arguing that they have become "the new tobacco" in terms of their threats to health and safety. While the causes of the obesity epidemic are numerous, our reliance on automobiles is a major contributor.[8] Small reductions in physical activity over a sustained period of time, which can occur from a daily use of cars for short trips in place of walking, can lead to significant weight gain.

The health and economic costs associated with obesity in the United States are enormous and provide another justification for thinking about how to design cities that promote regular exercise.[9] The United States spends at least $140 billion a year in obesity-related health expenditures, accounting for roughly 10 percent of all medical costs.[10] Some research suggests that this may be a low estimate and that obesity accounts for as much as 20 percent of illness-related expenditure, most of which is paid for by private and public insurance programs.[11]

Urban development in the United States since the 1950s was the main contributor to our overreliance on cars, as cities and suburbs typically emphasized separating commercial, residential, and recreational land uses.[12] In less densely developed cities, trips are more likely to involve using an automobile.[13] Low residential density and the desire to build fully detached homes is characteristic of American suburban development.[14]

Cities across the country are now thinking about different ways to make walking safer in cities and more attractive for routine daily trips. Vision Zero, a larger pedestrian safety plan with the goal of zero traffic fatalities, is underway. As pedestrian deaths are largely the result of being struck by an automobile, efforts to promote and enforce safer vehicle operation is the key to this plan. Tactics include so-called "road diets," where lanes are removed from street segments and replaced by lined or barrier-enhanced bike lanes. Improved lighting and signage at intersections, speed bumps, longer street crossing times for pedestrians, increased enforcement at problem intersections, lower speed limits, and extended sidewalk or medians to shorten street crossing are the preferred safety strategies. After one year, New York City reported modest improvements in their Vision Zero efforts with a current year-over-year decline of 10 percent for traffic fatalities. In a city that averages almost one hundred traffic fatalities a year, it has a long way to go to achieve the goal.[15]

What is more interesting about this program, however, is the growth of a street safety advocacy alliance of city residents, bikers, and young people who have largely avoided cars as a means of transportation.[16] Rallies are being held to support pedestrian safety plans, which points to the growing understanding that large-scale changes in planning practices often start with a vocal and organized advocacy group who can articulate a clear and sympathetic message.

Pedestrians and bikers are a growing political constituency in many cities, demanding safety, infrastructure provision, and connectivity from urban governments.

Walking off the Pounds by Choosing the Train

There appears to be reasonably good evidence that designing ways to reduce our reliance on cars can improve population health. Modifications in the built environment, including increasing the availability of public transportation systems and more pedestrian-friendly urban designs, offer some promise of increased opportunities for physical activity and reduced reliance on automobiles. The availability of walking paths, the proximity to commercial establishments and public transit, and the relative attractiveness of a neighborhood's environment are associated with an increased likelihood that individuals will meet basic walking recommendations.[17] Research points to the health benefits of moderate physical activity, such as walking or biking.[18] The American College of Sports Medicine and the American Heart Association recommend either thirty minutes of moderate exercise five times a week, or twenty minutes of vigorous exercise three times a week, in order to reap the health benefits of physical activity.[19] Moderate forms of walking or biking are easier to sustain over long periods of time, and sustainable physical activity is likely a more effective method of weight control than vigorous physical activity, such as attending a daily exercise class.[20]

Increasingly, scientists have sought to examine whether increasing access to and use of public transit can be one way to reverse our reliance on cars and encourage daily walking.[21] People who walk to and from public transit obtain significantly more daily physical activity than those who do not.[22] Importantly, the same groups at the greatest risk for obesity, like minorities and the poor, are more likely to use transit and receive the benefits of daily walking. Despite these benefits, many people report that they would prefer to drive than take transit—because of a lack of adequate sidewalks, extended commuting time required, and perceptions that taking transit will expose them to crime. The promotion of walking to transit then involves both increasing access and the desirability of this mode of transportation.

Walking to transit as part of one's daily routine offers some promise for meeting recommended physical activity levels. But does this really boost health? After all, many people choose to live near transit because they like walking and are already inclined to do it. As a result, it is unclear how much a benefit transit

use actually delivers. Studies of individuals living near rail transit systems before and after they opened in Salt Lake City, Utah, and Seattle, Washington, find
that transit users are less likely to be obese prior to the opening. In Salt Lake
City, for example, researchers found that almost half of the study's participants
that lived within a half-mile of a future planned transit stop were previously taking transit by making a significant walk to a station that was farther away. They
did find that a group of new riders who started taking transit after the opening
reduced their use of car trips. But there were only eleven individuals studied
that were new riders, making the sample size too small to generate enough
meaningful variation and to detect differences over time.[23] In Seattle, research
on a sample of almost seven hundred people living near a transit line suggests
that transit users engaged in more physical activity and walking than individuals living in the same neighborhoods that did not use transit. Researchers
found that the difference in physical activity measured over a seven-day period
was solely attributed to transit use, suggesting that differences in walking to transit is what makes transit riders more physically active than nontransit
riders.[24]

As we can see, selection bias is a problem with most studies investigating the
link between transit use and health outcomes. People who like to walk to work
are more inclined to take transit. They probably are also likely to eat healthier.
In fact, research suggests that transit users look different than nontransit users
on such health dimensions as exercise and general physical activity. While the
study in Seattle suggests that transit users and nonusers exhibit similar exercise
patterns on the days that they do not take transit, we don't get to observe how
they would behave if they didn't have transit as an option. People predisposed
to being physically active choose to live in urban environments more suitably
designed for healthy lifestyles. This means that studies may overestimate the
benefits of transit use on health. But we can look at natural experiments that
add transit to places to address this problem. If people living in an area start
walking more frequently after a transit stop opens, this would suggest that there
are health benefits to expanding transit options.

A number of cities have recently developed or expanded light rail systems
in an effort to reduce road congestion.[25] Planners have promoted light rail transit
(LRT) along with mixed land use: transit-oriented developments that embed
higher density residential developments with retail and entertainment uses near
transit stops. LRT transit may encourage more exercise than transit systems like
buses, because fixed rail stations, often spaced a moderate distance apart, can
require riders to walk further from their residence or workplace to the stop.

Research that tracks people before and after the installation of LRT would be a natural approach to seeing if transit can induce more daily physical activity while reducing obesity and our reliance on cars for commuting to work. Fortunately, several studies have taken advantage of the expansion of LRT systems to examine their health benefits.

Riding Light Rail in Charlotte to Lose Weight

In 1998, voters in Charlotte, North Carolina, approved a half-percent sales tax dedicated to developing a fixed rail public transit system. The Charlotte Area Transit System first built the South Corridor LRT, a 9.6-mile, fifteen-station system that originates in Uptown Charlotte and extends southward to Interstate 485. The LRT line parallels Interstate 77 and South Boulevard, the most heavily traveled roadways for commuters living in the city's southern area and working in downtown Charlotte.

The LTR that serves the South Boulevard area was part of a larger comprehensive plan in Charlotte that sought to direct future population growth in and around designated development centers and transit corridors. Unfettered growth in Charlotte has caused stifling traffic congestion and related economic, environmental, and social impacts. Charlotte is served by two interstate highways (I-77 and I-85) that facilitated suburban low residential density development. As the population exploded in the region, these roads have become virtual parking lots during rush hour. The average commuting time rose 20 percent from 1995 to 2007 and is currently at around twenty-five minutes per average trip to work. Close to 80 percent of Charlotte workers commute to work alone in an automobile.[26]

Since its opening in 2007, the South Line has exceeded its ridership estimates substantially. The capital and operating costs of the project have likewise exceeded their estimates, which have led some analysts to question the economic logic of the fixed rail system over more inexpensive and flexible bus rapid transit systems. Despite some anti–light rail resistance, Charlotte has doubled down on its investment in LRT and extended the line to north Charlotte, connecting the city's urban core to its main university district at UNCC at a cost of just over $1 billion.[27] This expansion, completed in 2018, has extended what is now known as the Lynx Blue Line to just over nineteen miles and twenty-six station stops.

Charlotte also adopted development principles and a pedestrian overlay district plan around the half-mile buffer near LRT stations that emphasized more pedestrian-friendly street designs and sidewalk projects to encourage biking and

FIGURE 6.2. CATS Lynx Bland Street station in Charlotte, North Carolina. Photo by Patriarca12, used under the CC BY-SA 2.5 and GNU Free Documentation licenses.

walking to rail. Therefore, this LRT system offered a viable alternative to commuters in southern Charlotte neighborhoods.[28] The LRT stations opened in November 2007.[29] Figure 6.2 shows a visual of the pedestrian-friendly design near a LRT station at one of the station stops.

The opening of new LRT stations provided the opportunity for a natural experiment to study the health benefits of transit. With funding from the National Institutes of Health, we conducted a study that examined the impact of this rail transit system on obesity and physical activity levels among local residents.[30] Data for the study were collected on a sample of individual household members living near the site of the South Corridor LRT. Just over eight hundred adults were recruited through phone sampling, based on addresses that were within a one-mile radius of the light rail line, to participate in a survey in the year before the opening of the LRT, and around 60 percent were reinterviewed six to eight months after the LRT system started operating. Subjects dropped out of the study if they moved out of the area. The telephone survey measured perceptions of the physical and social environment of neighborhoods, social demographic factors, and respondents' daily travel and exercise patterns. Body mass index (BMI) was calculated using self-reported height and weight. Following agreed-upon metrics, individuals with a BMI equal to or greater than thirty were considered to be obese. Physical activity was examined according to whether or not the person surveyed engaged in vigorous activity three times a week for twenty minutes or more at a time, or whether they walked five times a week for thirty minutes or more. The survey also asked people about their plans to use LRT in the future. In the follow-up survey, individuals were asked the same questions and whether they used LRT to commute to work on a daily basis.

By comparing responses before and after the opening of the light rail line, we were able to control for residential location choice in examining the effect of light rail use on BMI, obesity, and the meeting of weekly recommended levels of physical activity.[31] This approach helps control for characteristics that might explain why individuals who use the LRT would experience a significant increase over time in physical activity levels and reductions in BMI compared to similarly situated individuals who did not use it.

About 5 percent of those surveyed used LRT to commute to work daily. This group was compared to respondents who were also working but used cars to commute and were statistically comparable on all but two factors (their racial group and their plans to use LRT in future).[32] These two remaining factors were included in the analysis to control for their potential influence on outcomes. In short, the study involved individuals that were very similar in their predispositions for residential location but were choosing different commuting options.

A basic analysis of the changes in BMI and physical activity before and after the opening of the transit line found that using LRT was associated with reductions in BMI. Light rail users reduced their BMI by an average of $1.18 \, \text{kg/m}^2$ compared to similarly situated car commuters over a twelve-to-eighteen-month follow-up period. For a person who is 5'5", that is equivalent to a relative weight loss of around 6.45 pounds. A graph of this change is represented in figure 6.3. Here, one can see that car commuters gained weight while the LRT users on average lost a few pounds. The key insight is that the two groups diverged from each other.

Light rail users were also 81 percent less likely to become obese over the follow-up period of roughly two years, suggesting that LRT use is helpful in preventing weight gain. About 11 percent of the LRT users qualified as obese at the time of the follow-up interview compared to 26 percent of individuals that didn't use LRT to commute to work on a regular basis.

A basic calculation of the average distances from home and work to the nearest LRT station stop suggests that using rail would add about 1.2 miles a day of walking. The yearly amount of walking this would generate is close to what one

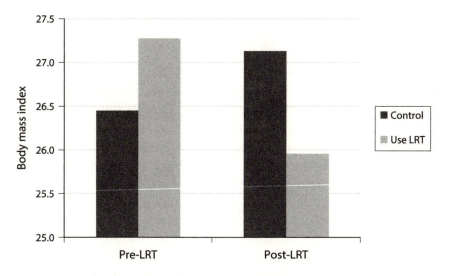

FIGURE 6.3. LRT use versus comparison group and changes in body mass index.

would expect for someone to burn an extra twenty thousand calories a year—what is needed to lose roughly six pounds. The findings from this study suggest that increasing the access to LRT for individuals to commute to work may help overcome some of the barriers to engaging in daily exercise.

The biggest limitation to this study is that measures were self-reported by study subjects. We don't get to actually observe an increase in physical activity and weight loss. People who use LRT could be underreporting their weight. While the sample size was large enough to generate meaningful statistical variation, it was still small relative to what one would want to know for how it applies to an entire population. As a result, the range of estimates reported in the study is rather large. We also don't know what the long-term results suggest for using LRT. Evidence is emerging in other settings to corroborate that, at least in the short term, LRT use substantially increases walking for sedentary populations. But we need more evidence about ways to encourage a reduced reliance on automobiles and the health benefits of transit use, especially in cities designed for cars. Fortunately, such a study was conducted in one of the United States' most iconic automobile cities.

More Walking in Los Angeles,
Fewer Trips in Cars

Arguably, no place embodies sprawling city design and car culture more than Los Angeles (LA). Its sprawling nature was not an accident, as the metropolitan area was originally a series of small towns connected by railway lines. During the first half of the twentieth century LA County had an extensive public transit system of railways and trolley lines that were designed hand in hand with real-estate developers looking to cash in on the desire of people who worked in central city business districts and industrial areas to escape to a suburban destination after work. Los Angeles had one of the nation's premier private rail systems, run by Pacific Electric, that connected the city to the beach towns of LA and Orange Counties, the San Fernando Valley, and the Inland Empire. Agriculture and oil fields existed between these locations, which the rail system connected, enabling fast commutes. Someone could catch a trolley line in the ocean front city of Santa Monica and be in downtown Los Angeles in forty minutes.

A massive federal investment in highway infrastructure after World War II meant that real-estate developers in the LA area no longer needed to rely on partnerships with Pacific Electric. The increasing desire of LA residents to purchase and drive cars also meant that fewer people were taking transit. These two factors effectively killed the ability of Pacific Electric to make a profit. By 1961, the city's metro transit system ended service of the last remaining Pacific Electric rail lines. Unlike other major cities that decided to maintain rail transit through taxpayer subsidies, Los Angeles abandoned its rail transit system. For more than thirty years Los Angeles was the nation's largest city with no commuter rail system. Calls for bringing one back went unheeded until the 1980s, when several sales taxes dedicated to transit development were passed. In the 1990s, LA Metro opened five rail lines (Blue, Red/Purple, Green, and Gold).[33] This trend continued in the past decade, with the development and expansion of the Expo light rail line. Service again exists from downtown Los Angeles to the city of Santa Monica, and Los Angeles now has an extensive rail service covering over one hundred miles and carrying more than 350,000 daily riders.[34] These are small numbers, however, when one considers the size of the LA metro area. A natural question, then, is whether the transit system actually takes cars off the street and generates the health and safety benefits we've been espousing.

Two labor disputes and subsequent strikes caused a month of service disruption to rail transit in Los Angeles in 2000 and 2003. Transit workers went on strike, resulting in complete system shutdowns. These two strikes provide natural experiments to examine the effect of transit on traffic congestion and safety in Los Angeles. At the time of the strikes, four of the major Metro Rail lines were operating and carried an estimated 220,000 passengers on an average weekday.[35]

Research studies by two separate teams of investigators showed that the strikes produced significantly more traffic congestion, as measured by reduced freeway speeds and length of commutes during peak commuting hours. These studies indicate that transit systems were significantly reducing the number of drivers on roads, suggesting that transit is more important to relieving traffic congestion in Los Angeles than most people would imagine.

Even when transit is available, people are less willing to use it when they are concerned about their personal safety.[36] When the effort to travel to transit seems daunting because of fear of danger, people will default to the easier decision to drive. But research suggests that transit isn't dangerous. One of our own studies examined what happened to crime before and after Los Angeles built its Metro Rail lines and during the LA transit strikes. We found that crime did not change substantively in neighborhoods that received Metro Rail transit stops. During the LA transit strike there was also no crime reduction in neighborhoods with transit stops.[37] Both findings suggest that transit doesn't generate crime in neighborhoods, which is compelling evidence that transit in Los Angeles has no impact on crime. After all, the location of transit lines was planned without any consideration of crime, and the strikes were a result of a labor dispute that had nothing to do with neighborhood crime patterns. These findings suggest few active offenders in Los Angeles use transit as their mode of travel, and that people shouldn't avoid transit use for personal safety fears.

These studies don't address, however, whether LA residents are willing to switch from driving to using public transit over a longer term. We are fortunate that a team of investigators at the University of Southern California sought to examine this issue when they realized that LA Metro was planning to expand the Expo LRT from central Los Angeles westward to Culver City. The team set out to study the impact that the LRT expansion had on travel behavior and health outcomes. Following a similar design as the Charlotte LRT study, the team surveyed nearly three hundred residents: those who lived within a half-mile of a future station (experimental group) as compared to those living further away (control group). During the baseline survey, the team collected data on travel behavior, walking, and driving, using travel logs that measured where respondents went and odometer readings from their cars for seven days. Additionally, most of the survey respondents wore accelerometers, which

FIGURE 6.4. Expo Line stop at Crenshaw, Los Angeles. Photo by METRO96, used under the CC BY-SA 3.0 license.

measured their actual walking behaviors based on GPS calculations of the distances they covered. The residents were surveyed before the Expo LRT expansion and again six and eighteen months after it opened.

An important point is that the two groups looked similar on income, length of residence, age, and other demographics. This isn't surprising, because the areas within a half-mile of the Expo line and those slightly further away are similar in house prices, land uses, and other factors. The primary difference is that one set of neighborhoods is close to Crenshaw Boulevard, a major thoroughfare with enough right-of-way to allow for the easy construction of a light rail line.

Figure 6.4 shows a picture of the Crenshaw stops for the Expo LRT. A key feature of the Expo LRT plan, like the one in Charlotte, was the development of bike lanes and improved sidewalks to encourage walking or biking to the transit line. In short, there was a clear design to get people to make this LRT an attractive line to use commuting around west and downtown Los Angeles.

An analysis by the study team found that average vehicle miles traveled per day were reduced by eleven miles for the group that lived near the LRT eighteen months after it opened, compared to those that lived further away. The entire difference between the two groups was a result of the increase in LRT use, suggesting that LA residents were willing to trade mass transit for their cars. Further, the reduction in vehicle miles was realized among the respondents that were not transit users in the past and appears to be a result of shorter car trips, rather than a complete substitution of mass transit for cars. Shorter car trips also meant a significant reduction in carbon emissions for the experimental group, who lived within a half-mile of the Expo LRT.[38] Individuals that lived more than a half-mile from transit were unaffected by the Expo LRT opening, underscoring the importance of transit-oriented developments that provide denser connected street and sidewalk designs and access to transit.[39]

In terms of health outcomes, the study found that the experimental group of respondents significantly increased their walking trips after the LRT opened compared to those who lived further away. Analysis of accelerometer data showed that those who were the least physically active were more likely to get significant increases in moderate to vigorous physical activity.[40] These results are consistent with those found in Charlotte and suggest direct health benefits to transit for those who are exposed to it and use it in place of car trips.

In consideration of the historic car culture of Los Angeles, the success of the LRT in reducing vehicle miles travel should be a hopeful case for other cities looking to encourage their residents to use transit. The good news is that studies in other settings show that when individuals switch from commuting in cars to public transit their energy expenditure increases an average of 124 calories a day,[41] which translates into just over 28,000 extra calories burned during the average number of working days in a year.[42] Similar research in Seattle is consistent with this study in Los Angeles and shows that the increase in physical activity among transit users occurs on the days they commute. These facts together give us some optimism for thinking that mass transit availability, especially fixed rail LRT systems, can lead to real improvements in physical activity levels that can be scaled to the population to generate health benefits.

Designing Out Cars to Reduce Crime

There are benefits beyond health when people are physically active in communities—walking and biking—there is crime reduction and reduced community disorder. When people are out on the street walking or biking they are more likely to interact with their neighbors, detect crime, and call the police. One approach to increasing walking is to design street segments to reduce automobile traffic and encourage walking and biking. Cul-de-sacs are an example of a street design that encourages walking and neighborly interaction.

One may think that it follows that neighborhoods with cul-de-sacs should be safer. But telling someone that neighborhoods with cul-de-sacs have lower crime than neighborhoods with drive-through streets isn't particularly compelling. After all, cul-de-sacs are often constructed in single-family neighborhoods that are more affluent. Researchers in England tried to address this issue by examining street networks and burglary on blocks in the same police district in Merseyside.[43] Characterizing roads based on whether they are major, minor, local, or private, and whether they are segments off of major roadways, researchers found that burglary rates on a street segment are significantly lower when located on cul-de-sacs or private roadways. In contrast, burglary rates on street segments are significantly higher on major roadways. An advantage of this study is that it controls for differences within the same census areas, such that the street segments being compared have largely similar housing stock and demographics. In addition, the sample size of street segments is sufficiently large to generate meaningful statistical variation. Yet we still don't get to observe what happens to crime on street segments before and after their design changes. Fortunately, a natural experiment in Los Angeles offered an opportunity to examine what happens when a high-crime neighborhood is redesigned from having street segments that allow cars to easily pass through to one with cul-de-sacs that encourage walking, neighborly interaction, and reduced car traffic.

The LAPD's Operation Cul-De-Sac

Yvonne Soublet used to awake in "the middle of the night to the sound of gunfire or the screeching wheels of a speeding car. One night she watched in horror as two rival gangs battled in an intersection near her South-Central Los Angeles home."[44] Times changed near Yvonne's home after the police erected barricades and began Operation Cul-De-Sac (OCDS)—an intervention designed by the Los Angeles Police Department (LAPD) to reduce drive-by-shootings in a ten block area of the Newton Police Division in South Central Los Angeles. "It is safer, and I sleep better," said Soublet, who was captain of her neighborhood block club. "I still hear gunshots, but they are two or three blocks away, not next door. We are finally coming together and trying to solve our problems."[45]

The LAPD designed this intervention after finding that 80 to 90 percent of drive-by shootings in Newton were occurring on street segments that connected two major roadways.[46] They decided to install traffic barriers in February 1990, by first imposing temporary concrete barriers and then permanent metal gates that could be opened for emergency access. The police commander in charge of the intervention noted that he "wanted to give the socially disadvantaged neighborhoods what the middle-class neighborhoods already had; that is, a physical characteristic something like cul-de-sacs that naturally deters gangs and drive-by shootings."[47] In this intervention the LAPD also assigned fifteen officers working on foot, bicycle, and mounted patrol for the first year of the operation.[48]

A professor at California State University, Fullerton, evaluated the impact of OCDS. Homicides and assaults dropped significantly in the two years after the installation of cul-de-sacs compared to the year before. A similar reduction did not occur in contiguous areas. Figure 6.5 shows the average number of violent crimes and assaults in the two years prior (1989–90) and two years after the installation of the cul-de-sacs compared to contiguous blocks in the same neighborhoods.[49] The main drop occurred in aggravated assaults—crimes emblematic of gang battles. After the barriers were broken and removed at the

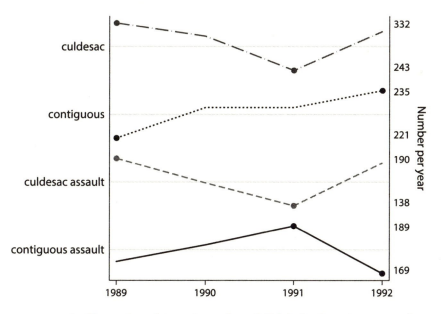

FIGURE 6.5. Changes in predatory crime and assault Cul-de-Sac Operation compared to contiguous areas.

end of 1991, the homicide and assault rates in 1992 climbed back to their pre-intervention levels in 1989. This suggests that the barriers were responsible for the reduction in violence. However, the study found no discernible change in property crime, suggesting that the cul-de-sac design was particular to the form of gang violence observed in Los Angeles and not general criminal offending.

This study provides useful evidence, with both an intervention area and a control group, that street access may influence violent crime involving gangs. However, the short time frame and relatively small size of the intervention limits how much we can generalize from this study to other contexts. But the study does suggest the powerful impact of a relatively simple intervention to reduce the use of cars and violent crime in areas plagued by gang violence. Whether such an approach could also be used to reduce burglaries in less crime-ridden neighborhoods is surely worthy of experiment. After all, the installation of the barriers themselves was relatively cheap, averaging only around $3,600 in 2014 dollars for a more elaborate barrier.[50] These barriers were taken away in the aftermath of the Rodney King Riots because they were criticized by the Christopher Commission as an example of the overreach by the LAPD.

Designing Out Cars to Promote Health and Safety

In this chapter, we presented evidence that LRT systems—when coordinated with other planning efforts that improve the physical design of areas focused on creating walking destinations that are safe and appealing—may be the real key to improved health outcomes. There are currently twenty-seven separate LRT systems operating in major US metropolitan areas, generating over five hundred million passenger trips a year. [51] While LRT is usually promoted for its help in reducing traffic congestion and environmental benefits related to reduced tailpipe emissions, we have found significant health advantages that have been largely neglected in the cost-benefit impact studies of these systems.

When the effort to travel to transit seems daunting because of distance or fear of danger, people will default to the easier decision to drive. The physical environment goes hand in hand with people's perceptions of the difficulty of tasks. Research shows people are more willing to walk and use transit when streets are more connected, block lengths are shorter, and there are easier pedestrian crossings.[52] Transit-oriented developments may impact exercise patterns by encouraging residents to live in areas closer to rail transit stations, where they can shop and use the train to commute to work. The Charlotte and LA studies we showcased, as well as others, suggest that taking transit generates real health benefits in the population. Cul-de-sacs and other strategies that reduce automobile use are worthy of more expansion and of investigation as a crime prevention tool. Designing our way to fewer cars is a sensible strategy for changing places to be healthier and safer.

Reducing our dependence on cars is not the only reason to redesign places. We should also consider the health and quality-of-life impacts of fun and recreation. In the next chapter, we will examine how science-informed placemaking and management can improve commercial and recreational areas such as parks and playgrounds.

7

Good Clean Fun

WHILE MOST PEOPLE understand the impact of parks and open space on human health, the relationship with commercial environments is less clear. In this chapter, we seek to explore recent place-based interventions in both park and commercial spaces with an eye toward how these environments impact health and safety. As noted throughout this book, crime and health are directly impacted by place.

In our mobile society, we have choices to make as to how and where we decide to work, shop, eat, and play. Research into business location decisions has determined that the presence of amenities like parks, trails, and waterways has a greater impact today than it did in the past.[1] During the industrial era, businesses wished to be located adjacent to rivers to facilitate the easy dumping of industrial waste. Today, businesses are more likely to seek a riverfront location so their employees have a nice view and access to riverfront jogging and bike trails. However, most commercial areas are near residential areas, to support the needs of the local residents.

In cities across the United States, commercial districts that were once planned as a support system for community life are struggling.[2] The declining investment in commercial areas in cities creates a self-reinforcing dynamic, where reduced population and incomes of remaining residents leads to business failures and commercial property abandonment. These derelict business strips, often located in highly visible areas on main streets and near transit system stops, lead to higher levels of crime with the presence of bars and late-night businesses that provide greater criminal opportunity due to reduced surveillance on streets by shoppers.[3] Crime is bad for business. Businesses located in commercial districts have a strong interest in assuring the safety of their employees and attracting customers. Successful business districts create jobs, so community viability is linked to business viability.

FIGURE 7.1. Abandoned and blighted commercial strip in Philadelphia. *Source*: Photo taken by author in February 2019.

The importance of neighborhood commercial development has risen over the past twenty years as city leaders, civic groups, and community development organizations have all come to realize the importance of vibrant and well-managed business districts. Healthy commercial areas reinforce local residential real-estate markets, improve the larger city tax base, offer a walkable community context for goods and services, reduce the need for multiple automobile trips, and provide community identity and a place to gather for civic events. Such districts also provide local employment opportunities for youth and an example of the benefits of entrepreneurship and hard work. In our focus groups and interviews with residents in impoverished and underserved areas, we tend to hear a consistent lament: poor city neighborhoods do not have enough businesses to meet local needs, and the businesses they do have are exploitative, do not hire residents, and are not in line with the broader economic goals of the community.[4]

Place-based interventions that seek to improve commercial and recreational areas have played an important part of the urban policy agenda for over a century. These interventions have become especially relevant in US downtowns.

As compared to neighborhood-based commercial districts, downtowns possess a larger place in the policy agenda of state and local governments. Many are the primary source for a city's job base, the hub of commerce generated by entertainment and tourism, and possess a city's higher-end real-estate values. The decline of downtown business districts that accompanied suburbanization is well documented in the urban planning literature. Over the past ten years, however, downtown business districts have witnessed a rebirth, as places for college graduates and empty nesters to live and work.[5] They have also become the center of tourism in many cities. This trend isn't random and is likely the result of transformations that many downtown districts have made to make themselves more attractive for business and for residential living.

Making Commercial Districts Safe

One approach that has been developed and is likely responsible for the turn-around of many downtown districts is the community economic development model of the business improvement district (BID), which is shown to reduce crime in business areas and improve real estate.[6] The BID model relies on special assessments levied on commercial properties located within designated business areas to augment services typically provided by public agencies, including sanitation, public safety, place marketing, and planning efforts. BID services typically take place in common-area spaces and are similar to home-owners associations in that they charge fees for maintaining general communal spaces. The creation and operation of effective BIDs requires a legal infrastructure that helps business owners or merchants to raise the money to pay for private security guards, trash collectors, and other individuals to serve as community ambassadors that provide local visitors with directions. While the legal arrangements for their creation, operation, and oversight differs across states and localities, BIDs all share a common mission of changing the places they are situated to make them more attractive and safe. BIDs have grown in popularity, as evident from their growth from around four hundred in 1999 to over one thousand in 2014.[7]

The main value added of the BID innovation was to offer a locally vested private nonprofit organization the ability to focus on coordinating fragmented public services in a business area, while also raising the money to direct specialized services in commercial areas. These organizations—at least the larger ones located in central business districts—have become the leading place-making organizations for the cities that they serve. They also have been shown to have a significant impact on public policy outcomes related to health and crime reduction. Los Angeles is one of the many cities that over the past twenty years has invested in this place-based model, and this case provides evidence that BIDs can be an effective strategy to reducing crime and the decline of neighborhood business districts.

Business Improvement Districts Reduce Crime in Los Angeles

In Los Angeles BIDs have grown from the two that were formed in 1996 to forty-one in 2019.[8] BIDs are managed and operated by private nonprofit organizations, but they are chartered and regulated by the city government.[9] Many of the BIDs in Los Angeles focus their services on sidewalk cleaning and graffiti removal, private security, place promotion through marketing, special events, and the maintenance of improvements made to the districts as part of redevelopment efforts.[10] Terms like "clean" and "safe" are commonly used in LA BIDs located in busy commercial districts—for example, the Figueroa Corridor, Hollywood Entertainment, and Historic Core BIDs. The Figueroa Corridor BID was formed in 1998 by business owners in response to economic decline and crime concerns.[11] Since its beginning, this BID has employed uniformed private security workers they call "Safety Ambassadors" who patrol the district. The BID also employs a "Clean Team" that cleans sidewalks, removes graffiti and trash, and conducts basic landscape maintenance to common areas.[12] The Clean Team, for example, in the last quarter of 2014 removed more than three thousand bags of trash and two thousand square feet of graffiti on a monthly basis.[13]

The Hollywood Entertainment BID, formed in 1996, employs armed private security officers who patrol Monday through Saturday from 6 a.m. to 8 p.m. and on Sunday from 10 a.m. to 6 p.m. These security officers are mostly retired or off-duty law enforcement officers. They work closely with the local police. This BID spends nearly 50 percent of its annual budget (just over $1 million a year) on private security.[14] These private security officers also initiate citizen's arrests when they see criminal violations occurring in public. Most of these arrests, nearly six out of ten, are the result of public intoxication offenses.[15] The BID has also hired unarmed BID security officers called BID Guides to provide an extra set of eyes and ears on the street that can report to the armed officers if they see issues that require their attention, like someone threatening people on the street.[16] In addition, BID private security engage in substantial order maintenance in the area; it also devotes almost a third of its budget to maintaining

FIGURE 7.2. Hollywood Entertainment BID clean team.

clean, graffiti-free sidewalks and streetscapes in Hollywood. The BID employs a private company Street Clean that provides these services on a contract basis, as shown in figure 7.2.[17]

The Historic Core BID is located in downtown Los Angeles. The mission of this BID is "to improve the quality of life of residents, property and business owners in Downtown LA's Historic Core through clean, safe, and enterprise programs."[18] For public safety this BID hires private security guards through Universal Protection Services, the nation's fifth largest private security company, who patrol the streets on bike, foot, and Segway vehicles seven days a week.[19] This BID also devotes substantial resources to street cleaning and trash pickup, employing a nonprofit company, Chrysalis, that hires homeless individuals, in an effort to link their direct service business to a broader social goal of improving the economic conditions of local residents.

BIDs tend to report on their outputs by focusing on the direct services they provide in their areas, rather than larger community outcomes like health and safety. For various political and legal reasons, BIDs neither study nor advertise their impacts on crime or health. If BIDs claim to have a general public benefit, they can run into legal troubles, as state tax laws limit BID services, fees, and their presumed benefits to the geography of the BID boundaries. BIDs may also be hesitant to claim that a place is now safe due to their services, as this could lead to a legal obligation.[20] Because they are authorized by property owners or merchants in commercial areas that pay for their services, it makes sense that BIDs focus on reporting on these services.

But what impact do all of these BID activities actually have on crime and safety? Two studies we conducted using crime data from Los Angeles found significant declines in robbery and violent crimes in areas that adopted BIDs,[21] as well as a comparison of overall crime in BID areas to other areas that did not adopt BIDs.[22] Between 1996 and 2003 a total of thirty separate BIDs were implemented in Los Angeles.

The focus of our first study was violent crime—in particular, robbery, given that a number of BIDs in Los Angeles spent considerable resources on private security and cleaning, to convey a message to potential criminals that an area is well cared for and thus off limits for nefarious behavior. Violent crime, compared to property crime, is also more likely to occur in public spaces. Thus, "street crimes" like robberies and simple assaults, as well as disorder offenses like public intoxication, are more likely than property crimes to be reduced by BID operations.[23]

We found that, over time, BID areas experienced greater annual reductions in robbery and violent crime than non-BID areas. Robbery dropped by 7 percent a year in BID areas compared to 5.7 percent in non-BID areas. Given that BID areas are likely different from non-BID areas in a number of factors, such as the willingness of businesses to pay an assessment fee for special services, we conducted an analysis of the change in outcomes for only those areas that eventually adopted a BID, and we found that robberies were reduced by an average of 12 percent greater than one would project by chance. In fourteen of the thirty BID areas, the drop in robbery observed was larger than one would predict based on the general trends in Los Angeles, suggesting BID formation can be credited for increasing the reduction in these offenses in these areas. Some specific examples include a 20-percent reduction in robberies in the Figueroa Corridor BID and a 15-percent drop in the Hollywood BID area. Figure 7.3 shows the reductions in robberies in each BID area.

However, the analytic approach in this first study has limitations. For one, the study assumes that BIDs don't fundamentally change the reporting of crime to the police. If BIDs lead to greater cooperation with the police, their adoption could actually increase crime reporting. This would push against finding any BID effect. At the same time, this study offers little insight into the various ways in which BIDs might impact violent crime, such as their adoption of private

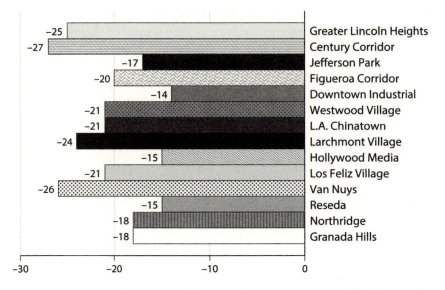

FIGURE 7.3. Percent Reduction in Robbery in Each BID. *Source*: MacDonald, John, Daniela Golinelli, Robert J. Stokes, and Ricky Bluthenthal, "The effect of business improvement districts on the incidence of violent crimes," *Injury Prevention* 16, no. 5 (2010): 327–32.

security officers, street cleaning, and environmental redesign to increase a sense of cleanliness and safety.

To address the questions of the actual mechanisms that might lead to crime reductions, in a second study we examined the connection between BID security spending and crime in Los Angeles after comparing what happened in BID areas and nearby neighborhoods. This is similar to a matched control design seen in other case studies discussed, including Operation Cul-De Sac. The advantage to this study is that BIDs form in about 6 percent of all LA neighborhoods. As a result, there are many areas from which to generate comparisons. The study found a 44-to-45-percent greater reduction in crime and arrests in BID areas compared to neighboring areas. BIDs are also associated with a significantly higher drop in police arrests: about ten fewer arrests per year in a neighborhood, or a 32-percent yearly decline.

In our examination of actual BID private security expenditures, the evidence suggests substantial returns for hiring individuals to patrol the street, which occurred in Figueroa Corridor, Hollywood, and Historic Core. An additional $10,000 spent by BIDs on private security per neighborhood is associated with fewer total crimes and arrests. What does an extra $10,000 look like for the average BID? For the twenty-one BIDs that devote resources to private security,

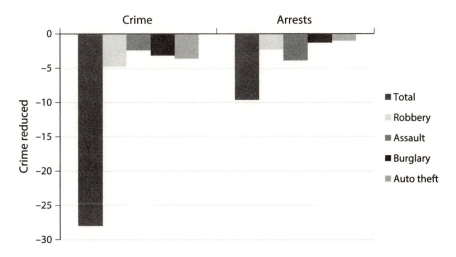

FIGURE 7.4. Percent Reduction in Crime and Arrests in BIDs.

this is about a 19-percent increase in their budget. The Figueroa Corridor BID spends about $43,335 for each of the roughly six neighborhoods it services with private security, whereas Historic Core spends about $66,182 and Hollywood Entertainment BID about $190,000 per neighborhood. For Hollywood, a $10,000 increase is a small percentage of the overall budget. Overall, the results suggest that private security spending leads to substantial reductions in crime that are cost-effective.

Given that it is possible that BIDs may displace crime to their adjacent areas, this study compared changes in crime in those areas close to BIDs before and after the BID started operations. The results suggested that BIDs had no meaningful effect on displacing crime to nearby areas. This is likely because crimes that are typically committed in commercial areas are not easily transferable to other areas—for example, preventing the armed robbery of a moderately inebriated person walking to her car from a restaurant. When famed bank robber Willie Sutton was famously asked why he chose such a vocation, he was reported to reply, "I rob banks because that's where the money is." This logic holds true for many types of crime: it happens because it is more or less likely based on the opportunity structure. As place is a prime element of that opportunity structure, it stands to reason that improving place management capacity through enhanced surveillance by means of better lighting, assigned human or electronic surveillance, or the enticement of more legitimate users to act as deterrents in a commercial area will not merely displace crime to another area.

Another way to estimate the value of crimes not committed due to BID operations is to either apply cost estimates using tort awards in jury cases that have elements similar to crimes like robbery and assault, or to survey individuals to find out how much they would be willing to pay to avoid such a crime. Utilizing these methods, we found that $10,000 spent by BIDs on private security produced a sizable $150,000 in benefits for averted robberies. The total social benefit of the crime reduction impacts was also rather impressive, coming in at twenty times more than the cost of BID security operations.

While crime victimization produces myriad economic and health costs for the victim, it also incurs sizable public costs related to the criminal justice system. Arresting, prosecuting, and imprisoning criminal offenders is expensive for state and local governments. Including the public costs deferred for every $10,000 spent by BIDs on private security translated into $4,863 in savings to Los Angeles in police- and court-related costs for prosecutions.

The BID model in Los Angeles appears to be one approach to reducing crime that focuses on special services areas that spend considerable resources on private security. Whether such a model would work in other special services arrangements, such as neighborhood improvement districts and homeowners associations, is worthy of further study. What is particularly striking of the BID evaluation in Los Angeles is that many of the successful areas, like Hollywood, Figueroa, and Historic Core, have now become major areas of economic redevelopment, suggesting that reducing crime is good for business.

Many other cities have also experimented with BIDs, and there is a growing body of evidence suggesting they help in reducing crime.[24] In New York City, areas that formed BIDs also had significant rises in their commercial property values relative to their surrounding neighborhoods.[25] BIDs have been noted in a number of academic studies and media reports for contributing to New York City's massive reduction in crime in the 1990s, though the evidence for these claims remains fairly thin.[26]

Beyond seeking to improve public safety, retail planning models like the BID design have long sought to create a sense of place to attract people. BIDs are largely placemaking and management organizations that plan retail environments to draw pedestrian traffic. In some ways, BIDs act like park districts in deciding ways to govern the use of public space. The fact that some BIDs have also taken on park management and design functions (Bryant Park in New York City and Dilworth Park in Philadelphia are two examples) suggests there is a connected logic between the management and design of commercial and recreational space.

Making Parks Places for Physical Activity

Remember when you liked playing tag with your friends as a child? How often did you walk to your neighborhood park or playground to play basketball or engage in any other physical activity? For many of us, parks and playgrounds were places for playing that also generated exercise. What would it take to get people to spend more time outside and maintain a healthier lifestyle? Clearly, parks offer one urban amenity that the public has invested in for over a hundred years. Parks were originally developed in Europe in the mid-1800s as a place to give people living in crowded slums near manufacturing a clean place to gather.[27]

The concept of the American urban park has evolved since its initial design and development. At first, parks in the United States were designed after the European model. They were located on the urban periphery and were largely inaccessible to poor immigrants and working-class populations. Parks were also often designed to protect a city's water supply; Fairmount Park in Philadelphia, for instance, was placed around the Schuylkill River, the city's primary source of drinking water. By designating large swaths of city territory around a public park, this prevented industrial development from encroaching upon and spoiling the city's drinking water supply.

The development of Central Park in New York led to widespread calls among other US cities for public park systems. Parks were seen as an answer to the growing social and physical problems related to mass urbanization. Decreasing levels of clean air, water, and the absence of light in densely populated residential districts led local newspaper editorial writers to equate public parks with public health.[28] Parks in the nineteenth century were also seen as a place where everyone could enjoy the benefits of clean air and open space, regardless of one's social class. Early park advocates made many of the same arguments regarding public health improvement and crime reduction that we are making in this book. After the Great Chicago Fire of 1872, some cities even promoted parks as fire breaks.

The development of the park system in the United States was part and parcel of the development of urban planning itself. Proponents of parks, like the advocates of urban planning, struggled to articulate a rationale for what was a rather novel political idea in the laissez-faire era of politics in the United States. Developing parks required all the tactics we currently use in our modern urban planning apparatus: the condemnation and taking of private property for public use; the development of a land-use regulation that would set aside a portion

of all land for parks and open space; the creation of a public funding mechanism to pay for land and its improvements; and the development of a system
for governing park management. Many park systems administrators, including
those who planned and managed New York's Central Park, created special tax-
ing districts in park buffer zones to capture the increased values of the park
and to pay off its expenses and debts.[29] This sort of "value capture" mechanism
is now utilized in many cities in the form of tax increment financing districts,
or TIFs. Thus, park promoters added economic and tax benefits to earlier health
and environmental claims, noting that well-placed parks would more than pay
for themselves in increased property tax revenues from those wanting to purchase expensive homes and apartments adjacent to them.

Another movement focused on parks as a source for physical activity, fitness,
and socialization for immigrant children. This movement led to the creation of
neighborhood parks as safe places for kids to play and exercise. In effect, this
was the start of the playground movement in the United States. The Hull House
in Chicago, an early social service organization, was a pioneer in the design and
provision of children's playgrounds in the 1880s. Engaging children in active
recreation and organized play was seen as a way to deflect them from the many
illicit temptations of the city.[30] In 1887, New York became the first state in the
United States to allow local governments to take private property for the
provision of playgrounds. The Olmstead Company in 1892 developed a model
playground in Boston's Charlesbank Gymnasium that contained playground
equipment for children and gymnastics and fitness equipment for men.

Soon every city had to have playgrounds as well as parks. Planning for small
parks and playgrounds became part of city and community planning, and rules
of thumb were developed. One suggested, early on, that each child should be
provided thirty square feet for park and playground space; another recommended that there should be ten acres of parks developed for every one thousand people. A standard like this could work in many places, but in the case of
large densely populated cities like New York, it was not possible without a major
appropriation of land by the government. Cities like Chicago set distance guide-
lines for different park facilities that would incorporate playgrounds.

From 1934 to 1939, the New York Park Commission built over four hundred
playgrounds. This was largely the result of the iconic and powerful Commissioner Robert Moses.[31] Moses's prolific development of urban playgrounds
was assisted by the standardization of design, materials, and equipment. Soon
blacktop, swing sets, basketball hoops, slides, monkey bars, and jungle gyms
defined the American playground.

Population and economic shifts in the 1960s and growth in street crime put parks and playgrounds under great stress. In many cities, there was insufficient municipal financial support for their maintenance, and police were also not effectively being allocated to keep parks safe. Even great parks like Central Park became feared spaces in the 1960s and 1970s, especially at night. Many city parks morphed from community amenities into feared eyesores. The lack of management of parks meant that playgrounds turned into sites of crime rather than a healthy place for kids to play.

Over the past fifteen years, many city neighborhoods in the United States have seen population growth and a resettlement of urban residents with kids. While public budgets are still strained, college graduates and empty nesters that have migrated to cities have an interest in park investment and civic groups devoted to parks have formed. Friends of the Park groups have proliferated, led by the example of the Central Park Conservancy, a private nonprofit organization with annual revenues over $150 million. Since 1980, the conservancy has raised almost a billion dollars for park restoration and maintenance.[32] While most Friends of the Park systems' resources pale when compared to Central Park's, increasing engagement with public, philanthropic, and civil society groups have reenergized many of these spaces around the country.

Public parks are part of the community planning model in most cities, and 70 to 75 percent of Americans report that they live within a short walk of a park.[33] Parks are even plentiful in some of the most disadvantaged cities, like Detroit, Michigan, where 74 percent of the population lives within a ten-minute walk of a park.[34] In Los Angeles, by contrast, only 54 percent of the population lives within a ten-minute walk of a park, but low-income neighborhoods are, on average, located closer to parks than high-income neighborhoods.[35] Given that parks are often plentiful in cities, the natural question, then, is to how to get the most stress-reducing recreation and active exercise out of this investment.

Yet the idea of using parks as places for physical activity is relatively new. The US obesity epidemic has multiple causes, with inactive lifestyles related to a reduction in physical labor being one of them, as we discussed earlier. While early US parks were designed to offer a respite from hard work, they are now needed to address the lack of structured physical activity in the modern lifestyle. As noted in our earlier chapter on the impact of greening on health outcomes, parks also offer a safe place where humans can interact with nature, which is known to reduce stress. It is easy to see the appeal of parks as an area to encourage more physical activity, since they are a common feature of most communities and are located in close proximity to where many urban residents live and work. Parks are already available on such a scale that they could offer considerable exercised-related health benefits for a city's entire population. But how do we actually promote physical activity in parks?

It isn't sufficient to expect that living close to a park means using the park for exercise. One commonly held assumption is that people don't use parks because of fear for their safety.[36] While this factor may hold true in very high-crime areas, research generally shows little correlation between public safety and park use.[37] Rather, studies suggest that a greater number of parks in a city, with more amenities, increases physical activity in the population.[38] People who live closer to parks are more likely to visit them and use them for exercise.[39] However, part of the relationship between proximity to a park and use may be explained by individual preference. After all, individuals who like using parks for exercise may be more likely to choose to live near parks. But there is stronger evidence that park size and amenities matter more than simply the distance from a park.[40] Amenities at parks will naturally draw people who are seeking out sports, jogging, swimming, and other recreational activities that require the expense of physical energy. If amenities are important, then the natural question is whether making structural changes to parks can improve the health of the population.

The evidence of the effects of park improvement on park use and physical activity is not terribly encouraging. One careful study conducted by public health scholar Deborah Cohen and colleagues at the RAND Corporation charted what happened after five parks were significantly upgraded, for over $1 million, as part of larger scheduled improvements by the Los Angeles City Department of Recreation and Parks (LARAP), including the refurbishing and the construction of new gyms, improvements to playgrounds, landscaping, and upgrades to walking paths. Each park spent its resources on a different set of upgrades, but all five parks made substantial improvements. The researchers compared these parks to five others that were in similar in size and amenities and had a comparable demographic makeup of their surrounding neighborhoods. The research team systematically observed and recorded data on park users seven days a week in different areas of the park to gauge how many people were using the parks and what activities they engaged in. In total they observed about two thousand people using each park in the week before the upgrades occurred. They also surveyed park users and residents who lived within two miles of each park. The same procedures were used to observe and survey park users and residents after the park improvements were made. A comparison of the changes in park use for the five parks that underwent upgrades showed no difference from the comparison parks in observed usage or reported use among park users and local residents. In both groups overall park use went down during the follow-up period. The only improvement noted for the five parks that underwent upgrades was in first-time park use and perceptions of park safety.[41]

A complementary study by Cohen's team looked specifically at a comparison of upgrades to a park with skating ramps that served young people and a park with a senior citizen's center. Both parks received over $3 million in renovation funds. For the park with skate ramps, this included improved skate surfaces, while the senior center underwent a number of structural improvements, including adding a gymnasium with exercise equipment. In short, both parks underwent major public works investments to increase their use for physical activity. These two parks were compared to another senior center and skate park in somewhat comparable neighborhoods in Los Angeles. A comparison of systematic observations of the four parks before and after the renovations showed a significant increase in the number of users only in the remodeled skate park relative to its comparison park. For the remodeled senior center the number of users engaged in physical activity declined relative to its comparison senior center. And very few people were observed using the newly installed exercise machines. In a total of twenty-eight observations of the senior center, only fifteen people were recorded using the equipment.[42]

However, one issue that impacted these studies of the effect of park improvements on use and physical activity was the fact that the LA park service reduced the number of scheduled organized activities in all parks as a result of budget cuts. Additionally, renovations to these parks took considerable time, which may have resulted in people who lived nearby changing their routines. The parks also did very little advertising to let local residents know that the upgrades had occurred, which is understandable, since park services generally have meager advertising budgets. Even with these limitations in mind, the results of the study suggest that upgrading the infrastructure of parks alone is not the key to improving park use for physical activity.

What, then, can be done to increase park use for exercise? Research based on interviews with park users and local residents around fifty LA parks suggests that some of the strongest predictors of park use are the number of organized activities, supervised activities, and accessible areas in a park.[43] A recent analysis combining over five studies that used systematic observations of parks as well as surveys of LA park users and nearby residents suggests that the average

neighborhood park has around fifty users for each hour of the day and generates 1,850 total hours of moderate-to-vigorous physical activity in a week. This
suggests that parks are, on average, operating on the scale of a large exercise class.
With an average of ten acres of space, a large exercise class does not seem like
a large amount of use. Additionally, estimates from this study show that only
36 percent of those who live within a half-mile of a park use it regularly for vigorous exercise, compared to an even fewer 16 percent of those who live one mile
away.[44] What can we do to make parks part and parcel of routine physical activity, given that the research suggests that park programs are the big draw and
that park infrastructure investment alone has minimal effect? Is it possible to
get people to use parks for more physical activity without devoting major sums
to programming?

Rather than expecting large-scale upgrades to encourage physical activity
in parks, we might look toward behavioral nudges that make exercising in a park
the default decision. A literature has emerged on the benefits of low-cost signs
for increasing the use of stairs over escalators and elevators. Several studies that
examine before and after the placement of motivational posters or signs next
to stairs and escalators find that they increase stair use. Figure 7.5 shows an example from a motivational sign used in New York City.

Studies from around the world, including Australia, England, Scotland, and
the United States, show that prompts or nudges near a staircase can increase
stair use over escalators and elevators. One of the first studies to examine the
benefits of simple prompts in a shopping mall, train station, and bus terminal
found that exposure to signs significantly increased the chance that people
would take the stairs instead of an elevator. Another study compared the benefits of two different types of signs to encourage stair use in a shopping mall.
In the first phase of the study a sign was installed next to the stairs with a figure
of a heart that said, "Your heart needs exercise, use the stairs." During the second phase another sign was installed that stated, "Improve your waistline, use
the stairs." An observation of the staircase by trained observers found that a
greater percentage of people took the stairs when either sign was present, though
the change was greater for people judged to be overweight when the sign noted
they could improve "their waistline."[45]

A review of published studies on stair use found that eleven had a comparison of stair use before and after the signs were installed.[46] The most convincing
evidence of the effect of signs on stair use comes from studies that examine what
happens before, during, and after a sign is placed next to a staircase. A stylized
example of this is portrayed in figure 7.6; the image shows what happened after

FIGURE 7.5. Example of a motivation sign. *Source*: Department of Health and Human Services, New York City.

the signs that said "Stay Healthy, Save Time, Use the Stairs" were installed for a three-week period in a subway station where a set of stairs and escalators were adjacent to each other.[47] Here one can see that stair use nearly doubled during those three weeks. After the sign was removed the use of stairs returned to its previous levels.

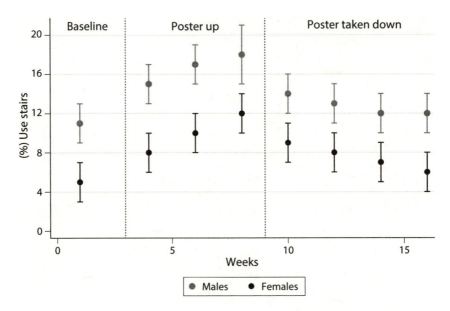

FIGURE 7.6. Example of weekly stair use during study of health motivation sign.

Under this design we have more convincing evidence that the sign itself plays a powerful role, because people being observed in public tend to go back to their previous stair use once the sign is removed. This pattern has also been observed in other studies with the same design.[48] The body of evidence regarding these simple behavior-modification prompts not only suggests that individuals are indeed motivated by a simple low-cost sign, but is more conclusive than studies that seek to make major changes to the design of recreational environments in order to encourage exercise—which, we noted earlier in the park example, failed to show any significant change in park usage or physical activity in parks through either direct observation or interviews.[49] We aren't arguing that infrastructure improvements and amenities in parks aren't helpful for increasing their use for exercise, but that in some circumstances people need to be nudged into making a health decision.

Simple Signs Increase Physical Activity in Parks

Drawing on the evidence from studies of the effects of simple signs on increasing stair use, and due to the lack of resources for major programming enhancements in the LA park system in general, Deborah Cohen and her colleagues at the RAND Corporation studied whether small changes in park management and infrastructure could increase the usage of parks for exercise. The primary aim was to examine if parks could increase usage with a small sum of $4,000 spent on outreach and small adjustments in park facilities to include signage. This study involved a randomized community trial that randomized fifty-one neighborhood parks in Los Angeles into three groups: a park-director intervention, a park-director and community advisory board intervention, and a control group that received no changes. Parks were first selected based on the one-mile radius of neighborhoods around them being sufficiently diverse in ethnicity and race. Because one park site voted not to participate in the study, the final study was based on fifty locations. Parks were randomized based on size; number of facilities and programs; and the racial, ethnic, and economic makeup of the surrounding residential population to ensure that groups were as comparable as possible in their setting.[50]

Each of these fifty parks was then observed seven days a week between spring 2008 and spring 2010 before the intervention started, and then again after the intervention, in spring 2010 and spring 2012. A total of twenty-eight observations were made in each park. Park users were observed in targeted areas and counted by gender, race, age, and level of physical activity. Park users were also surveyed in each park before and after the intervention. A survey of randomly selected households within one mile of each park was conducted before and after the intervention. While the study initially hoped to look at the effects of park advisory boards (PAB), who would in principle have more community input on the upgrades, the main investment of the additional $4,000 in each park was substantively the same, so the two groups were combined into one treatment group for point of comparison. About half of the funds were spent on the signage; the rest were primarily spent on increasing group activities and giveaway incentives for using the park (e.g., free key chains or water bottles).

The results from the study showed that the control parks saw a small decline in the number of observed and self-reported users on the order of 6 to 10 percent, as well as declines in physical activity. In contrast, parks in the treatment group that received the additional $4,000 saw a 7-to-12-percent increase in observed and self-reported park usage. For the park observations, there were an additional 192 more hourly users a week and an estimated extra 610 hours of energy expended.[51] There were no differences between treatment and control parks in staffing or facilities, so the effects appear to be attributable to the efforts to increase signage and outreach. The biggest observed changed in use was for children, and for whites and blacks (compared to Hispanics and Asians) who reported using the parks. Frequency of park use increased for those surveyed at parks after the intervention. Surveyed residents within one mile of the parks as well as park users both indicated more weekly exercise—about a relative increase of 19 to 34 percent in daily use of parks for exercise relative to individuals surveyed at and living near control parks. Signage was the single best predictor for the difference between the treatment and control parks.

The headline of the *Los Angeles Times* newspaper article report on this study sums it up: "Better Park Signs Can Spur More People to Exercise."[52] The study also shows that that if one takes the small investment of $4,000 in park purchases for signs and outreach, it equates to $0.28 per energy hour expended, which is a considerably cost-effective social investment in physical activity.

Whether the signs were placed in strategic locations as points of motivation was not directly addressed by this study. Yet the study builds on the existing staircase studies in showing that relatively low-cost signs that motivate people to use a space can increase physical activity. We need more examples of studies that add signs to trails, playgrounds, and sports and recreation areas in parks and remind park users of the benefits of physical activity. Apparently, seeing a sign in a park may motivate us all to do a few pull-ups or jog a half-mile.

Motivating People to Use Commercial and Recreational Spaces

The zoning and provision of park space and retail districts have been part of city planning since the mid-1800s in the desire to create places for leisure and physical activity. Today, this trend continues with cities developing parks for both recreation and business interests. The Highline park development in New York City is a good example, where an old railroad line traversing lower Manhattan was reconfigured as an above-street park.[53] The concept of designing business areas to be attractive and safe is taking hold all around us in the form of business improvement districts and related downtown associations. Parks are also seeing a similar transformation, but on a more limited scale. When places are safe, people are more likely to use them for entertainment and recreation.

The business improvement district model appears to be a particularly salient one for making places safer, and their successful expansion suggests that they do indeed spur commerce. However, the benefit of creating a BID in a poor, low-valuation commercial district in many cities has not been clear.[54] For parks, we see some evidence that they can be more effective at generating more physical activity when strategic investments are made to signage.

Imagine a downtown area with small-scale parks, nice shops, clean and safe streets, and signage that encourages exercise. This is the kind of place where a family wants to bring kids, where retirees and college students alike want to socialize, and where street entertainers naturally gravitate to perform and get paid. These places exist in many cities. Clark Street in Chicago; Bryant Park in New York City; and Rittenhouse Square in Philadelphia are three good examples. In these places, you will see live music, impromptu street dancers, kids climbing on virtual playgrounds of sculptures, groups of retirees talking on park benches, and local coffee shops and restaurants with sidewalk seating, creating a vibrant urban street life in the same spirit advocated for by Jane Jacobs. Some of these places remain attractive because they are designed with the idea of multiple uses. When they are well-managed and safe, they generate commerce and economic development. Small-scale parks and public spaces like these should be experimented with as part of a general place-based effort to design safer and healthier places to live.

8

Embracing Change

SCIENCE IS ABOUT uncovering the causes of phenomena and providing a clearer explanation of the world around us. Sometimes scientific discoveries come as a surprise. This makes it sound like science produces knowledge by accident; nothing is further from the truth. Most scientific discoveries occur as a result of a series of incremental studies that lead to a "new discovery," but scientific activity is often about dispelling presumptive truths. Recall the earlier discussion of John Snow and the cholera epidemic in London: his effort to address the source of the cholera outbreak was really an effort to reduce the deaths and dispel the miasma theory of "bad air" that prevailed during the 1800s.

In the quest to design healthier and safer places to live, work, and play, we have to recognize that we don't know all the answers. Sometimes interventions can bring about consequences they weren't intended to provoke, and, as sociologist Robert Merton has noted, science plays an important role in explaining the unanticipated consequences of purposive action.[1] Unintended consequences that are the result of place-based interventions might include increasing property values that spur gentrification or out-migration of the economically challenged. Thus, a place-based intervention to increase transit and associated development and encourage the formation of a business improvement district may lead to an increased demand to live in a particular area, which will inevitably drive up the costs of land. Rent and housing prices will rise and there may be some longer-term increase in the economic diversity of an area. If such interventions, however, simply lead to the displacement of those living in poverty to other areas, then there will be a reduction in economic diversity, and the benefits of the intervention will not address the population-level problems related to health and safety we've discussed. On the other hand, the potential for unintended consequences shouldn't prevent us from experimenting with place-based interventions to determine which models generate benefits for the greatest number of people. Urban planning policy is rife with examples of the unintended consequences of delayed action. Vacant land and abandoned housing in urban cities in the United States is just one example of the failures of federally financed urban revitalization policies in the 1950s, 1960s, and 1970s in the wake of deindustrialization and out-migration of residents. Just as we should acknowledge the potential for unintended consequences, we should also be prepared to see the unexpected positive benefits of interventions. Transportation planners, for example, didn't design their plans for installing light rail in Charlotte, North Carolina, with any sense that it would help individuals lose weight or even reduce crime by spurring economic development.

The Unintended Consequences of Positive Action

Sociologist Elijah Anderson's work on the "cosmopolitan canopy" showcases Rittenhouse Square and Reading Terminal Market in Philadelphia—places that foster civil interactions among people from very different backgrounds. In these places, individuals change their behavior, often acting differently than they would in their own neighborhoods. Something is harmonized in these multiuse areas that foster civility even in the face of race and class tensions.[2] The zones of cosmopolitan interactions Anderson refers to are similar to Robert Oldendburg's description of "third places," like coffee shops and main streets, where we suspend our race-and-class differences and interact civilly.[3]

In the most ideal cases, place-based interventions will lead to multiple uses that foster increased health, safety, and urban harmony. However, we shouldn't be naïve. It is also possible that some place-based interventions that foster economic development will also increase the homogenization of an area, which might lose the diversity of people and businesses that creates vibrant streets. A place-based intervention that leads to the greater desirability of a place—such as the expansion of transit, the greening of small park spaces, or the creating of a business improvement district—could also foster new housing or condominium developments, which would then increase the population in an area. Yet if an area doesn't have a school system prepared for the influx of new kids, the local public schools will be strained. And if the residential development is done with excessive tax breaks for developers and new homeowners, the local municipality won't receive sufficient tax revenue to provide adequate municipal services like emergency medical service, trash and waste management, and police and fire protection.

In this book we have provided many examples that suggest negative spillover is not inevitable. It is just as likely that there will be positive and unanticipated spillovers. Planners who implement place-based interventions and scientists who study them need to be looking for changes in multiple outcomes, not just the outcomes they are interested in assessing.

Not all scientific studies conclude in favor of their original hypotheses. If scientists mostly conducted experiments and research that matched their a priori hypotheses, one should begin to suspect the validity of their findings. Negative or even null findings are part of scientific discovery. We should recognize that many interventions planners try and scientists study may not make much of a difference; this is part and parcel of figuring out what works under which contexts.

Nevertheless, advocacy groups and the implementers of place-based interventions can sour on scientific study when it does not have a positive finding, an indication that their particular intervention or action is not having the desired impact. When presented with scientific findings that confirm what most people would expect, policy makers may question the need to invest money in something so obvious. When scientific studies run counter to what most people believe, or challenge conventional wisdom, there is often the impulse to say, "That just can't be true." However, science should challenge conventional wisdom when it doesn't fit the facts and provide the evidence to convince society to change a course of action. Suburbs weren't deliberately designed to make society dependent on cars and increase obesity. Transportation-oriented developments weren't initiated out of an interest in active living. But when we have high levels of scientific evidence that a place-based approach is bad for society's health and an alternative model is good for it, it is time to push for purposive action to change how we design our built environment.

In the following sections we discuss some examples of place-based interventions that were successful but produced unanticipated consequences.

University City District Success Leads
to Strain on Public School

Changes to populations are inevitable when an area becomes more desirable as a result of a place-based intervention. The University City District area of West Philadelphia provides an excellent example. This special service district was established in the 1990s under the leadership of University of Pennsylvania's President Judith Rodin as a way to promote residential and retail sectors in the neighborhood adjacent to campus; Rodin wanted to revitalize an area that was increasingly dangerous and in a state of urban decline.[4] In partnership with others, the university developed a five-pronged strategy in the two-square-mile area around the campus that involved: 1) increasing the safety and attractiveness of the neighborhood; 2) improving the housing market; 3) stimulating retail development as a neighborhood amenity; 4) directing university contracts toward economic development in the neighborhood; and 5) improving neighborhood public schools.

As part of this plan, the university created a housing subsidy program to induce faculty and staff to buy homes in the area, increased the size of the university police force, and established a business improvement district that invested in private security services for the entire neighborhood. The university also provided $24 million in capital financing and an annual student subsidy to create the public K-8 Penn Alexander School to serve the neighborhood.[5] All this effort was geared at making the University City neighborhood more safe and desirable.

In many respects, this initiative was a multipurpose place-based intervention. Across multiple measures, the University of Pennsylvania program appears to have been a success.[6] Nearly six thousand students now rent apartments or houses in the University City District neighborhood, and the number of faculty and staff homeowners has increased.[7] Multiple commercial strips have developed, replacing what were previously vacant properties and off-street parking lots. While this place-based initiative was established without an evaluation design in place and no set-aside control group, several studies have examined how housing prices rise and crime drops just across the borders of the University City initiative. Crime appears to lessen substantially just as one crosses into the area where the university police department provides extra police officers.[8] Home values also rise as one crosses into the catchment area of the Penn Alexander School.[9] Retail rents and property values in this area also have increased over time and outpaced general trends in the city.

All of these outcomes make it sound like there is nothing but positive outcomes to the University City District initiative. But the improvement in the local school and housing costs has resulted in a shortage of space for Penn Alexander students. As a result, parents line up days before kindergarten registration in the hopes of enrolling their children before the spaces are filled. One parent was reported in a local paper to have rented an RV to park near the school so they could camp out until registration opened.[10]

The result of the effort for parents to get their children into a highly regarded school, situated in a district largely characterized as low achieving, has been a sharp increase in housing prices and an increasing differentiation for the school environments for children who live in the area compared to those living in nearby neighborhoods. Clearly, the originators of the place-based initiative to improve the school did not envision it being at the cost of children in nearby neighborhoods. However, the improvements in education at the Penn Alexander School also benefited families who would have likely attended a school with considerably lower academic achievement. Recent data shows that 34 percent of Penn Alexander students are economically disadvantaged.[11] The school setting is clearly helping improve the lives of many children who remain poor and live in the neighborhood.

The success of the University City District and the resulting strain on the local elementary school is one example of an unintended consequence of the purposive action to reduce crime and spur economic development in the neighborhood adjacent to the University of Pennsylvania. In hindsight this strain may appear obvious, but at the time the University City District was launched and the Penn Alexander School was funded, no one was anticipating this success. President Rodin was simply trying to stop the downward spiral of decay in West Philadelphia, and the success of this place-based initiative generated the unintended consequence of an overenrolled school.

Successful Figueroa BID Impacts Infrastructure and Housing Options

Changes in rent prices and property values may also be a consequence of successful place-based initiatives that improve health and safety of an area. As researchers from the think tank the Urban Institute note, "Balancing the revitalization of neighborhoods while reducing the risk of displacement of low-income families poses a challenge for city officials and housing practitioners."[12] The place-based intervention of Figueroa Corridor BID in Los Angeles provides a good illustration. As we previously noted, business property owners established a BID in response to economic decline and crime concerns. By many measures the BID has been a successful place-based intervention. Following on the successful reduction in crime in this area, there has been considerable redevelopment of former vacant commercial properties into high-end mixed-used properties.[13] This area has gone through a noteworthy urban transformation in the past decade, spurred by the BID, the University of Southern California's

FIGURE 8.1. Proposed Figueroa redesign of street. *Source*: RELM Studio.

student body's interests in higher end off-campus residences, and an increase in the number of new residents seeking to restore the historic housing stock in this area. Figueroa now connects USC to a vibrant downtown Los Angeles, what the *Los Angeles Times* now refers to as a "dynamic innovation corridor."[14] The success of the Figueroa Corridor BID has spawned a major redesign plan to convert traffic lanes to bike lanes and pedestrian friendly sidewalks with tree coverage that will connect the BID to downtown Los Angeles (see fig. 8.1).

This dramatic change will come at a cost to traffic flow in this area, and opposition has emerged from the automobile dealers in the area that are key contributors to the BID. An innovative safe-streets design that connects residential, retail, employment, and education sectors while also facilitating greater use of bikes and walking to transit for commuting clearly fits the model espoused in this book, but it comes at a cost to local auto dealerships that depend on drivers who are car shopping. Ironically, this section of Los Angeles is also home to Southern California's Automobile Club headquarters and Felix Chevrolet's cat sign, which the LA Cultural Heritage Commission designated as a historic landmark in 2007.[15] Plans to remove car lanes are not popular among the driving culture and auto dealers. Ideally, dealers could move their facilities to a different part of Los Angeles and not stall the progress for a more integrated design of place that has the potential to improve the health of the neighborhood.[16]

The plans for redesigning the street corridor connecting Figueroa to downtown Los Angeles received support from the *Los Angeles Times* editorial board, who note the benefits of a "straight, safe route between two established biking communities—USC and downtown," that the city "should be replacing car lanes with cycle tracks and buffered bike lanes" and "not let fears of traffic congestion turn this transformative project into another incomplete street."[17] Similarly, the design has been noted as potential for a major Silicon Valley style innovation corridor, where businesses can establish themselves in the nearby downtown area and connect to the USC student population.[18] All of this change in the LA culture and the push for a less car-dependent downtown urban plan is a sign of change, as well as of the increasing demand for land in the Figueroa area and a resulting sharp increase in housing prices.

The change in the land value of this neighborhood has impacted poor residents who traditionally rented in Figueroa. While the city has set aside some land from a trust for the development of affordable housing and has a rent control law in place that stabilizes the prices for occupied rental units, the availability of newly created affordable housing in this location has been scarce. Additionally, the value of historic homes has increased and preservationists have pushed for stricter rules on renovations that also increase costs and push out the poor.[19] Gentrification and increasing prices have likely been major causes of the displacement of poor residents from this section of Los Angeles to nearby neighborhoods that are considerably more impoverished.

This underscores the need for place-based interventions to be cognizant of the unintended consequences of their purposive action. Set-aside parcels designated as affordable housing zones might be worthy of consideration in place-based planning efforts. Ideally, an experiment in set-aside parcels could be launched to determine the scale necessary to maximize urban renewal and minimize displacing the poor.

Light Rail Development Brings Boom to Neighborhood

In the case of light rail, the main policy goals of this costly infrastructure invest-ment are to increase transit as a modal choice for travel, reduce traffic conges-tion and pollution associated with crowded roadways during commuting times, and promote denser residential development around station stops. In Charlotte, zoning and transit-oriented developments (TOD) were tied to the planning and development of light rail stations stops. The recently expanded South Corridor light rail line has largely succeeded in increasing commuting via public transit and promoting denser development, while also showing a substantial public health benefit of increasing walking for those who choose to commute to work by rail. But this successful intervention has also spurred an increase in home prices and racial and economic homogenization of the area.

The South Boulevard corridor, which is adjacent to the light rail line, is now going through a rebirth. Real estate near the line and its fourteen station stops is selling at a premium. In the Starmount neighborhood near the line, realtor Julie McGee Sharpe notes that "I started in 2000 and Starmount wasn't even on the radar."[20] Now the neighborhood has seen sales up 25 percent and sig-nificant price increases. People love living just minutes away from the light rail line, as it brings easier access to downtown work and entertainment.

Research into the impact of the South Corridor light rail line on real-estate values compared properties along the light rail line (consider these treatment zones) with properties in areas that were initially considered for location near the light rail during the planning phase of the transit development (consider these control zones). After taking into account location and construction-related variables, the study found that there was an overall price premium of $97.2 mil-lion associated with being located near the light rail system. Condos were substantially more impacted, with an 11.3-percent premium versus single-family homes with a 4-percent premium.[21] This indicates that the light rail and zoning changes made around station stops generated more dense mixed-use urban de-velopment patterns in Charlotte.

While this all sounds positive, the demand for these areas means that more retail and apartment buildings are being developed and the availability of af-fordable housing has declined. One local resident notes that "in 1997, fixer up-pers in this neighborhood were going for probably about $95,000, and now a fixer upper is probably going to go in the high $200s." Ideally, this would mean that individuals who move to the areas around the light rail line will want to settle down and raise families and invest in the neighborhoods. But the potential for more homogeneous residents is a threat as prices for housing and land rise. As a local resident of the diverse neighborhood of NoDa Lori Penland notes, "I moved here because I wanted more diversity." Rising land prices mean higher rents for office and studio space, potentially pushing artists out as the area becomes more gentrified. Penland notes that this effort to redevelop should be done carefully so that it isn't just development for the sake of development and doesn't "push out the people that made this area."[22]

This example provides a key insight into the unintended consequences of transit development. The light rail design did involve zoning for transit-oriented developments along the line.[23] However, the zoning was designed for development around the catchment of each transit stop, not for a major redevelopment of neighborhoods nearby. Individuals who can't afford a car or who need to live close to downtown where they can access service jobs are being priced out of neighborhoods where light rail could benefit them the most.

Transit-oriented development follows a twentieth-century American planning model of the rail town, where commercial development was integrated into the area around transit stops for urban commuters who built weekend getaway homes. In a twist of irony, this model is spurring the gentrification of neighborhoods near transit lines with young professionals and the resettlement of suburbanites to urban city neighborhoods, causing an increasing homogenization of this area.

The Impact of Changes to Places on Services

Some analysts have argued that place-based infrastructure and built environment interventions put undue stress on municipal services because they often provide too many tax benefits for new development at the cost to existing residents and businesses. The use of tax increment financing districts (TIFs) to increase development in blighted urban neighborhoods is an example that some have argued creates problems for municipal financing. TIFs use tax abatement to get loans to pay for improving infrastructure, buying properties, and preparing land for development. The debt is secured and paid off through the estimated future property tax value of the improved area. This leads to a strain on general property and business tax revenues needed to pay for schools and other necessary municipal services like law enforcement, fire departments, and sanitation. The financing depends on a "but for" provision that claims that the development would not occur "but for" the subsidy. The city of Chicago, where TIFs are widespread in impoverished and downtown commercial areas, plans on retiring many of these locations because of the stress they cause for current needs.[24]

Other forms of development incentives, such as commercial and residential tax abatement programs, have similar impacts. Philadelphia has a program that sets the property and tax value of a vacant parcel or dilapidated structure at its current value, with the provision that the property owner can pay at that reduced rate for ten years. The idea is to give the owner a tax break for fixing up an abandoned structure or parcel of land. The city thus will not reap any property tax benefits from qualifying properties for at least a decade. This program adds service demands on the city, with new residents, some with children who will seek public school services, with no resultant increase in tax revenues. Additionally, there is an equity concern as the qualifying properties are valued well in excess of the median house value in the city and are largely occupied by high-income residents who pay little in taxes for a decade.[25] Proponents claim that "but for" this program, there would be very low or no demand for new construction in the city.[26] Some question this logic and see tax abatements as a give-away to developers and wealthier homeowners.

Embracing the unintended consequence of purposive action to change places is necessary. Clearly there are tradeoffs to some successes, including gentrification and the potential that planning efforts will affect real-estate prices and the demand for public schools and other municipal services. There is also the concern that when government provides tax abatements to generate economic development, they may in effect be crowding out what might have already been provided by the private sector and in the end provide less affordable housing and equity concerns from long-term residents.[27] These issues can be resolved through staggered tax abatement programs in areas where rehabilitating blighted space is needed, and even set-aside provisions that require developers to build a share of affordable housing. The key is to think through what unintended consequences may occur if a place-based intervention to improve safety and health is successful and to plan for them.

Successful place-based changes do not necessarily lead to gentrification or price increases that push out the poor from communities. In fact, there is little empirical evidence that shows that gentrification pushes out the poor at a faster rate. Several well-conducted studies show that working poor are less likely to leave a neighborhood when it is gentrifying than when it is stagnating—in other words, a poverty trap.[28] As we mentioned in chapter 4, this is less the case for long-term residents that rent houses and apartments. Here we see evidence that renters *are* more likely to be displaced when a neighborhood gentrifies.[29] There is evidence that when the working poor live in mixed-income neighborhoods, their children do substantially better later in life than if they raise their children in a poor neighborhood. While some claim that US cities are more economically and racially segregated than they were in the past, the evidence suggests that we've made substantial improvement to reduce racial segregation.[30] And yet upward mobility for the poor remains stunted.[31]

Rather than focus on the unintended consequences of purposive action as justification to stall the redesign of places, we should focus on the potential benefits spurred by redesign while proceeding with caution. Pilot experiments that field-test the redesign of places on a small scale can be done to see what works, what doesn't, and what is promising. We can also evaluate unintended consequences and put policies in place to minimize their impact. The only thing worse than experimenting is not experimenting and waiting for global forces of climate change, urbanization, and suburban sprawl to overwhelm cities across the world. There are ethical, financial, and political consequences of inertia. We have evidence for things that seem to work, and it is now time to discuss how to build that evidence-generating approach into a systemic model for changing places. We need to bring scientists to work with planners, developers, and the regulatory system that oversees the approval of efforts to design the places we live, work, and play.

Epilogue

Where Next?

STUART CHAPIN JR., a founding member of the American Planning Association, described planning as "a means for systematically anticipating and achieving adjustment in the physical environment of a city consistent with social and economic trends and sound principles of civic design."[1] We have effectively argued for this same goal, albeit based not only on sound principles, but also on sound science and empirical evidence, to really figure out how to design safer and healthier communities.

What has been missing from the planning lexicon is a true partnership with scientists to see what works, what doesn't work, and what is promising. The Robert Wood Johnson (RWJ) Foundation and the Centers for Disease Control and Prevention (CDC) both recognized the important intersections between urban planning and public health and have funded a number of studies and initiatives.[2] RWJ, for example, funded the Active Living by Design and Healthy Communities initiatives, espousing the same issues we have raised in this book.[3] RWJ notes the same basic principles on their website for Healthy Communities that the places where we live are "essential ingredients in a healthy life" and that the keys to this are "adequate housing and public transportation, quality health care, and safe places to exercise and play." They also note that, for too many people, healthy places to live "are either too far away or economically out of reach, creating major obstacles in the pursuit of better health and quality of life."[4] The CDC launched the Healthy Community Design Initiative (HCDI) that provided funding and technical assistance to local health departments to work with local community groups.[5] Most of the work has focused on conducting health impact assessments—a tool that allows one to predict potential future health benefits from a project.[6] Health impact assessments are a useful tool for planning public health projects, but they are not actual tests of whether a design change to a place improves health and safety. Randomized community trials and quasi-experiments should be also used as guideposts to help urban planners advocate for community designs that lead to improvements in the quality of housing for the poor, the abatement of blighted spaces, the greening of city streets and vacant land, streetscapes that help people to watch out for their neighbors, the use of public transit to promote physical activity, the design of commercial corridors that are clean and safe, and neighborhood parks that encourage children to play and adults to exercise.

While the evidence we've mounted doesn't tell us everything we need to know in order to design safer and healthier communities, it does point toward a growing wave of high-quality studies that show that the design of places is more fundamental to our health and safety than we think. When making a healthy choice is constrained by poverty and poorly designed communities, having a healthy lifestyle is more difficult, if not impossible. It has been argued that the neighborhood in which someone is born has as much to do with their health as their genes. We should be emphasizing place-based interventions as an important part of how we ensure safer and healthier populations for cities of the future.

The standard federal research and development model of science through the National Institutes of Health and the National Science Foundation focus on promoting research agendas and sustaining research laboratories over the long term. While federal science agencies have directly supported many of the studies that inform our understanding of how place impacts our health and safety, the model of investigator-supported scientific funding requires scientists to invest in the study of place through long-term partnerships that make incremental changes to places. As a result, there are few incentives for scientists to take risks and study a brand-new design idea. Academic and scientific careers are built on obtaining stable funding for research. Federal executive agencies that fund place-based research evaluations (e.g., the US Department of Housing and Urban Development) often do so with narrowly defined and prescriptive contract vehicles—again, making it risky for scientists to try something new.

In addition to the traditional public funding sources for place-based research, foundations are increasingly looking to partner researchers with practitioners around place-based policy interests and associated experimental evaluations. This is a good development, because foundations are willing to take risks; because they are not scientific funding agencies, they have less of a stake in investing in long-term research agendas and laboratories, and a greater interest in investing in research that takes direct action (e.g., Annie Casey, the Laura and John Arnold Foundation, Robert Wood Johnson). For example, the Laura and

John Arnold Foundation notes in their discussion of criminal justice funding that they seek scientists to "partner with local jurisdictions to pilot and test new policies and practices . . . to drive innovation and accelerate the adoption of proven reforms."[7] This is exactly the model we are espousing for place-based planning.

There is good news here. A new movement is afoot to rebuild communities with designs that encourage healthy and active living. Cities around the world are looking at many of the approaches outlined in this book, to redesign their roads, transit systems, open spaces, housing, and workplaces. The planned make-over of the South Los Angeles neighborhood of Watts is one such illustration.[8] Watts was the epicenter of a large urban riot in the 1960s and has remained a poor minority community characterized by sprawling public housing projects and commercial strip malls separated from residential land use. The "Watts Re:-Imagined" development plan will remake buildings and streetscapes so that they are inviting to pedestrians, connect to parks, and are accessible to rail transit. The plan also calls for mixed use of commercial, retail, and residential spaces, bringing businesses closer to residences. The Watts plan will also connect to the redevelopment of the Jordan Downs public housing project—once notorious for violence and gang problems—into a mixed-use, mixed-income design that includes tree-lined streets as part of a new urban village.[9]

Here is an ideal example where scientists could be on the ground to evaluate the impact of the Watts makeover. If the evidence shows that the redesign of the streetscape, parks, commercial space, and housing project leads to improvements in health and crime outcomes for residents in Watts, this model could be expanded to other impoverished neighborhoods in Los Angeles. Maybe other cities facing similar problems can consider experimenting with this same design. Changing places like Watts could have a greater positive impact on the life of residents than many other treatments and remedies in which the city of Los Angeles currently invests. But the change to Watts needs to be studied as part of an *evidence-generating policy* model of changing places.

New urbanism, active living by design, and crime prevention through environmental design are all theories that suggest that the habits of humans and their propensity for healthy activity can be shaped by the places within which they live, work, and play. The urban village design, with sidewalks that connect residential living to commercial destinations and transit hubs, are rooted in ideas espoused in new urbanism and active living by design. Street designs that connect people may also promote more guardianship and reduce crime. But do urban villages really work? A series of small-scale field experiments that randomly assign a sample of redevelopment efforts to the urban village design that also compare it to less comprehensive development projects—like fixing up housing stock, providing limited green space to vacant lots, or upgrading commercial corridors—would go a long way to providing cities with evidence of the extent to which creating a connected urban village produces superior life outcomes for residents. It is possible that lower-cost interventions that focus on improving building infrastructure and some form of clean green space are more than sufficient on their own in improving health and safety. But we need high-quality scientific study and experiments to tell us what really works.

Scientists need to be involved "early and often" in place-based projects. Cities have a better chance of choosing effective interventions when decisions or designs are carefully studied through pilot experiments that randomly assign the first set of places for study while putting other places on a waitlist. This is already happening in some communities, but it should become standard practice to assess place-based interventions based on which produces the greatest good for our health and safety. A partnership between practicing planners, real-estate developers, community residents, local nonprofit service providers, and scientists should be part and parcel of place-based changes.

Successful examples of such partnerships are now in existence. For example, in the field of social innovation there is now an effort to design and pilot studies as part of a research-practitioner partnership with communities to find scalable place-based programs that can lead to economic development improvements. The University of Southern California has such a center for social innovation.[10] It is focused on developing ideas with community stakeholders, pilot-testing them, and changing policies and practices to improve the quality of life for low-income urban communities. While the design and evaluation of pilot efforts are still in the infancy, this center provides an ideal model of creating change through science.

Many of the field experiments discussed in this book involved partnerships with city planning agencies and nonprofits. In the case of abandoned lots, the evaluation was based on Philadelphia's existing vacant land policy, and not on direct changes to place-based policies in the city. The actual design of place-based policy is often happening outside of the direct line of experimental evidence. However, this is now starting to change as cities and universities have adopted policy labs that try and conduct field experiments within agencies to test out what works in specific contexts.

Washington, DC, for example, created a policy lab out of the mayor's office (The Lab @ DC) with support from the John and Linda Arnold Foundation.

The Lab @ DC works to design policy and program interventions that are "tailored" to the context of the District of Columbia. The lab has focused its efforts in recent years on pilot testing and evaluating through randomized controlled trials the effectiveness of different policies and programs. For example, they have evaluated the impact of placing messages on garbage cans to reduce litter; targeted email messages to increase registration and participation in the Department of Regulatory Affairs educational programs; the effect of a rent subsidy program in reducing the chance of homelessness for low-income families; and the effects of body-worn cameras on police conduct. Noticeably absent from the lab are place-based experiments. But the basic model of designing policies and programs in partnership with the community and city agencies, testing those policies and programs through a field experiment, and using that evidence to guide future DC policy decisions is an ideal model for creating and testing place-based initiatives.

The University of Chicago organized five "Urban Labs" focused on crime, education, health, poverty, and the environment. Each lab partners with community groups to identify policies and programs to improve outcomes in their domain area, rigorously evaluate those policies or programs through experimental or quasi-experimental designs, and assess the ability to take the policies or programs to scale. One approach they have used to help overcome the potential cost barrier of trying out an idea is to use their innovation challenge—Design Chicago. Here, community groups or agencies propose a policy intervention to a pressing urban challenge. If selected, the staff from the university's Urban Labs work with local agencies or nonprofits to secure funding. In receiving the funding the agency or nonprofit collaborates on the design, implementation, and evaluation of the intervention. Ideally, the results from these evaluations will be used to support the broadening of the scope and scale of interventions in Chicago and elsewhere. Through innovation challenges the Urban Labs research-practitioner partnership has helped design, implement, and evaluate, through randomized controlled trials, a mental health center for released inmates transitioning back into the community, a workforce development program for individuals with long-term bouts of unemployment, and a smart meter technology in households to save energy costs—an example of a place-based initiative that, if effective, requires little effort by the individual households and has the potential to produce household savings and mitigate social environmental costs associated with the greenhouse effects of extra energy use.

One of the more relevant examples to the work we are espousing can be seen in the Urban Labs partnership in New York City with the mayor's office that oversees criminal justice, the police department, and the housing authority to see whether increasing street lighting could impact crime around public housing complexes. In partnership with city agencies, the Urban Labs designed a randomized controlled trial of providing extra street lighting in public housing developments. The trial consisted of randomizing thirty-nine developments to receive roughly ten extra street light towers, while thirty-eight control sites received no additional lighting. Preliminary results suggest that the extra lighting resulted in a 7-percent reduction in crime overall, and a 39-percent reduction in crime that took place outdoors of housing complexes at night. A survey of residents found that respondents appreciated the lighting.[11] New York City installed over three hundred high-powered safety lights at a cost of roughly $80 million as a consequence of what was learned from this experimental evaluation.[12] The results from this study are also now being discussed to support an even larger renovation of street lighting around public housing developments in New York City.

This example from the Urban Labs provides the kind of research-practitioner partnership that could be modeled elsewhere. The project was formed because the Urban Labs had an embedded group of researchers working in the mayor's office. Ideally, grounded partnerships start with embedded researchers in city agencies and established partnerships with local research universities and think tanks. These research-practitioner partnerships could then lead to pilot experiments to figure out what will work in a particular context. Ideally, the results from collaborative efforts will provide convincing evidence with key stakeholders that can sway policy makers to overcome concerns about costs and make place-based changes in cities.

While the models we note here are successful examples of research-practitioner partnerships that have resulted in the design, implementation, and evaluation of policies and programs in urban areas, place-based initiatives represent the minority of these projects. We hope that over time more place-based initiatives will be attempted. Ideally, these designs can also foster a greater interest in field experiments in urban planning. Imagine how much better city neighborhoods could have been if practicing planners in the 1950s had first experimented with the construction of the superblock before deciding that clearing out poor neighborhoods and replacing them with high-rise public housing was preferable to remediation of existing properties. The past doesn't need to be the prologue to the future of place-based design. Urban planners can be the champions of field experiments, as this scientific model can provide even stronger evidence for getting designs implemented and expanded to provide equitable benefits to entire communities.

The health benefits realized in the examples showcased in this book are connected to recent movements in medical treatment, as physicians are increasingly recommending that their patients spend time in nature as part of their recovery—what some have called the "nature cure."[13] Perhaps our desire for green space, connected sidewalks, and social interaction is rooted in our basic DNA, or the hereditary selection of habitat. Pulitzer Prize–winning biologist Edward O. Wilson notes that children from around the world, when shown pictures of various environments, tend to choose ecosystems that have three common factors: a "vantage point looking down," a vista with a view of parkland with grass and scattered trees, and "proximity to a body of water, whether stream, pond, lake, or ocean."[14] These children's choices are rooted in the human ancestral heritage in the savannas of Africa. Is it any wonder that people are then attracted to properties with a view overlooking beaches, lakes, rivers, and parklands? This has been one of the defining problems of mankind and her environment: the conflict between the environmental and economic efficiency of compact, dense urban environments, and the inclination of humans to be healthier and happier in and around natural landscapes.

Our ever-expanding need for better places will only come from one of humankind's most impressive endeavors: the highly structured process of science. Just as our modern, information-driven society has created a population of exacting, discriminating consumers of goods and services, it too can lead to a demand for better places. Once people become more aware of the impact that their surroundings are having on their health, safety, and well-being, they will clamor for more; they will ask for better-designed and more precisely conceived places. The way we change the elements of places should rely on the scientific process to best fulfill the ultimate promise of providing future humankind with healthy places to live.

NOTES

Preface

1. Schneekloth, Lynda H., and Robert G. Shibley, *Placemaking: The art and practice of building communities* (New York: Wiley, 1995); Brown, Lance Jay, David Dixon, and Oliver Gillham, *Urban design for an urban century: Placemaking for people* (Hoboken, NJ: Wiley, 2009); Thomas, Derek, *Placemaking: An urban design methodology* (New York: Routledge, 2016).

2. Corburn, Jason, *Healthy city planning: From neighbourhood to national health equity* (New York: Routledge, 2013).

3. Corburn, Jason, *Toward the healthy city: People, places, and the politics of urban planning* (Cambridge, MA: MIT Press, 2009).

4. Our contention in this book echoes a recent call in the medical journal the *Lancet* that science should be used as a guide to city planning policy and practice for creating healthy and safe cities (see Sallis, James F., Fiona Bull, Ricky Burdett, Lawrence D. Frank, Peter Griffiths, Billie Giles-Corti, and Mark Stevenson, "Use of science to guide city planning policy and practice: How to achieve healthy and sustainable future cities," *Lancet* 388, no. 10062 (2016): 2936–47).

5. Roof, Karen, and Ngozi Oleru, "Public health: Seattle and King County's push for the built environment," *Journal of Environmental Health* 71, no. 1 (2008): 24–27.

Chapter 1. Our Surroundings, Ourselves

1. "Police investigating rape in vacant lot," *Chicago Tribune*, August 16, 1999, http://articles.chicagotribune.com/1999-08-16/news/9908160095_1_raped-vacant-lot-police.

2. Gammon, Crystal, "Pollution, poverty, and people of color: Asthma and the inner city," *Scientific American*, June 20, 2012, http://www.scientificamerican.com/article/pollution-poverty-people-color-asthma-inner-city/.

3. Kleiman, James, "Boy, 17, killed in Wayne car crash," NJ Advanced Media for NJ.com, April 5, 2014, http://www.nj.com/passaic-county/index.ssf/2014/04/teen_killed_in_wayne_car_crash.html.

4. Pacheco, Liz, "Blight's out," *Grid*, January 14, 2013, http://www.gridphilly.com/grid-magazine/2013/1/14/blights-out.html.

5. "Unnatural causes," PBS Special, video, April 10, 2008, http://www.unnaturalcauses.org/assets/uploads/file/UC_Transcript_5.pdf.

6. Schwartz, John, "Young Americans lead trend to less driving," *New York Times*, May 13, 2013, http://www.nytimes.com/2013/05/14/us/report-finds-americans-are-driving-less-led-by-youth.html.

7. DiMassa, Car Mia, and Richard Winston, "L.A.'s business improvement districts help reduce crime, study finds," *Los Angeles Times*, February 20, 2009, http://articles.latimes.com/2009/feb/20/local/me-bids-crime20.html; see Lee, Wonhyung, "Struggles to form business improvement districts (BIDs) in Los Angeles," *Urban Studies* 53, no. 16 (2016): 3423–38.

8. Myers, Sage R., Charles C. Branas, Benjamin C. French, Michael L. Nance, Michael J. Kallan, Douglas J. Wiebe, and Brendan G. Carr, "Safety in numbers: Are major cities the safest places in the United States?" *Annals of Emergency Medicine* 62, no. 4 (2013): 408–18.

9. Furstenberg, Frank F., Thomas D. Cook, Jacquelynne Eccles, Glen H. Elder, Arnold Sameroff, Monika Ardelt, W. Todd Bartko et al., *Managing to make it: Urban families and adolescent success* (Chicago: University of Chicago Press, 1999).

10. This material was adapted from our editorial: Branas, Charles C., and John M. MacDonald, "A simple strategy to transform health, all over the place," *Journal of Public Health Management and Practice: JPHMP* 20, no. 2 (2014): 157–59.

11. Institute of Medicine, *The future of the public's health in the 21st century* (Washington, DC: National Academies Press, 2003).

12. LaPlante, John, and Barbara McCann, "Complete streets: We can get there from here," *ITE Journal* 78, no. 5 (2008): 24-28.

13. Lynott, Jana, Jessica Haase, Kristin Nelson, Amanda Taylor, Hannah Twaddell, Jared Ulmer, Barbara McCann, and Edward R. Stoll, *Planning complete streets for an aging America* (Washington, DC: AARP Public Policy Institute, 2009).

14. Welsh, Wayne N., Robert Stokes, and Jack R. Greene, "A macro-level model of school disorder," *Journal of Research in Crime and Delinquency* 37, no. 3 (2000): 243–83.

15. Lanza, Mike, *Playborhood: Turn your neighborhood into a place for play* (New York: Free Play, 2012).

16. The chlorination of public water in the United States started in the early 1900s in Jersey City as a result of partnership between a physician and an engineer working for a local water company. See McGuire, M., *The chlorine revolution: The history of water disinfection and the fight to save lives* (New York: American Water Works Association, 2013).

17. Branas and MacDonald, "A simple strategy to transform health."

18. Schweig, Sarah, "Healthy communities may make safe communities: Public health approaches to violence prevention," *NIJ Journal* 273 (2014): 52–59.

19. Baker, Susan P, "Childhood injuries: The community approach to prevention," *Journal of Public Health Policy* 2, no. 3 (1981): 235–46.

20. Card, Alan J., "Sustainability of public health programs," *American Journal of Public Health* 102, no. 5 (2012): 776.

21. Frieden, Thomas R., "A framework for public health action: The health impact pyramid," *American Journal of Public Health* 100, no. 4 (2010): 590–95.

22. Thaler, Richard H., and Cass R. Sunstein, *Nudge: Improving decisions about health, wealth, and happiness* (New York: Penguin, 2009).

23. Robertson, Leon S., "Fact and fancy in the formation of public policy," *American Journal of Public Health* 70, no. 6 (1980): 627.

24. "Obesity prevention source: Making healthy choices easy choices," Harvard T. H. Chan School of Public Health, http://www.hsph.harvard.edu/obesity-prevention-source/policy-and-environmental-change/.

25. Baker, Susan P., "Childhood injuries: The community approach to prevention," *Journal of Public Health Policy* 2, no. 3 (1981): 235–46.

26. Anderson, Martin, *The federal bulldozer: A critical analysis of urban renewal, 1949–1962* (Cambridge, MA: MIT Press, 1964).

27. Arnstein, Sherry R., "A ladder of citizen participation," *Journal of the American Institute of Planners* 35, no. 4 (1969): 216–24.

28. For an excellent historical example of Jane Jacobs's battle with Robert Moses's plans for a Lower Manhattan highway, see Paletta, Anthony, "Story of cities #32: Jane Jacobs v. Robert Moses, battle of New York's urban titans," *Guardian,* April 28, 2016, https://www.theguardian.com/cities/2016/apr/28/story-cities-32-new-york-jane-jacobs-robert-moses.

29. Garfield, Leanna, "American highways are so expensive that cities are tearing them down—here's what they're turning into," *Business Insider*, May 6, 2018, http://www.businessinsider.com/highway-closing-city-transformation-2018–5.

30. For an explanation of the Empower Zones initiative during the Clinton Administration, see https://www.hud.gov/program_offices/comm_planning/economicdevelopment/programs/rc/ezcontacts.

31. For an explanation of the Promise Zones initiatives, see https://www.hudexchange.info/programs/promise-zones/promise-zones-overview/.

32. Busso, Matias, Jesse Gregory, and Patrick Kline, "Assessing the incidence and efficiency of a prominent place-based policy," *American Economic Review* 103, no. 2 (2013): 897–947.

33. Glaeser, Edward L., and Joshua D. Gottlieb, "The economics of placemaking policies," working paper no. w14373, National Bureau of Economic Research, 2008.

34. Anderson, *The federal bulldozer*.

35. For an explanation of the Choice Neighborhoods program, see: https://www.hud.gov/cn.

36. See https://www.hud.gov/sites/documents/FY16CN_IMPLEMGRANTPROJ.PDF; https://www.hud.gov/sites/documents/FY16CN_IMPLEMGRANTPROJ.PDF; and https://www.hud.gov/sites/documents/PROJSUMMARIESFY15.PDF.

37. Garvin, Alexander, *The American city: What works, what doesn't* (New York: McGraw-Hill, 2002).

38. Branas, Charles C., Michelle C. Kondo, Sean M. Murphy, Eugenia C. South, Daniel Polsky, and John M. MacDonald, "Urban blight remediation as a cost-beneficial solution to firearm violence," *American Journal of Public Health* 106, no. 12 (2016): 2158–64.

Chapter 2. A New Movement Based on Old Ideas

1. "Better Living Through Chemistry," Wikipedia entry, https://en.wikipedia.org/wiki/Better_Living_Through_Chemistry (last updated December 24, 2017).

2. Frumkin, Howard, Lawrence Frank, and Richard J. Jackson, *Urban sprawl and public health: Designing, planning, and building for healthy communities* (Washington, DC: Island, 2004).

3. Anderson, James M., John M. MacDonald, Ricky Bluthenthal, and J. Scott Ashwood, "Reducing crime by shaping the built environment with zoning: An empirical study of Los Angeles," *University of Pennsylvania Law Review* 161, no. 3 (2013): 699–756.

4. Hirt, Sonia, "The devil is in the definitions: Contrasting American and German approaches to zoning," *Journal of the American Planning Association* 73, no. 4 (2007): 436–50.

5. Fogelson, Robert M., *Downtown: Its rise and fall, 1880–1950.* (New Haven, CT: Yale University Press, 2003).

6. Fogelson, *Downtown.*

7. Yen, Irene H., and S. Leonard Syme, "The social environment and health: A discussion of the epidemiologic literature," *Annual Review of Public Health* 20, no. 1 (1999): 287–308.

8. Juergensmeyer, Julian C., and Thomas E. Roberts, *Land use planning and development regulation law,* 3rd ed., Hornbook Series (Eagan, MN: West Academic, 2013); Frumkin, Frank, and Jackson, *Urban sprawl and public health.*

9. Juergensmeyer and Roberts, *Land use planning and development regulation law.*

10. Glaeser, Edward L., and Bryce A. Ward, "The causes and consequences of land use regulation: Evidence from Greater Boston," *Journal of Urban Economics* 65, no. 3 (2009): 265–78; Glaeser, Edward L., and Joshua D. Gottlieb, "The wealth of cities: Agglomeration economies and spatial equilibrium in the United States," *Journal of Economic Literature* 47, no. 4 (2009): 983–1028.

11. For a discussion of the broader trends in what might be called the urbanization of the suburbs, see Ehrenhalt, Alan, *The great inversion and the future of the American city* (New York: Vintage, 2012).

12. Dunham-Jones, Ellen, and June Williamson, *Retrofitting suburbia: Urban design solutions for redesigning suburbs* (Marblehead, MA: John Wiley & Sons, 2008).

13. Schroeder, Steven A, "We can do better—improving the health of the American people," *New England Journal of Medicine* 357, no. 12 (2007): 1221–28; Corburn, Jason, "Confronting the challenges in reconnecting urban planning and public health," *American Journal of Public Health* 94, no. 4 (2004): 541–46; Constable, George, and Bob Somerville, eds., *A century of innovation: Twenty engineering achievements that transformed our lives* (Washington, DC: Joseph Henry, 2003).

14. Garvin, *The American city.*

15. Calthorpe, Peter, *The next American metropolis: Ecology, community, and the American dream* (New York: Princeton Architectural, 1993).

16. LeGates, Richard T., and Frederic Stout, eds., *The city reader* (New York: Routledge, 2015).

17. Fogelson, Richard, *Planning the capitalist city* (Princeton, NJ: Princeton University Press, 1986); Boyer, M. Christine, *Dreaming the rational city: The myth of American city planning* (Cambridge, MA: MIT Press, 1986).

18. Fishman, Robert, *Urban utopias in the twentieth century: Ebenezer Howard, Frank Lloyd Wright, and Le Corbusier* (Cambridge, MA: MIT Press, 1982).

19. Jacobs, Jane, *The death and life of great American cities* (New York: Random House, 1961), 17.

20. Fishman, *Urban utopias in the twentieth century.*

21. Calthorpe, *The next American metropolis.*

22. Frank, Lawrence D., Martin A. Andresen, and Thomas L. Schmid, "Obesity relationships with community design, physical activity, and time spent in cars," *American Journal of Preventive Medicine* 27, no. 2 (2004): 87–96.

23. Hall, Peter, *Cities of tomorrow*, 3rd ed. (Oxford: Blackwell, 2002).

24. Bors, Philip, Mark Dessauer, Rich Bell, Risa Wilkerson, Joanne Lee, and Sarah L. Strunk, "The Active Living by Design national program: Community initiatives and lessons learned," *American Journal of Preventive Medicine* 37, no. 6 (2009): S313-21.

25. "Planning and Designing the the Physically Active Community," American Planning Association, https://www.planning.org/research/active/.

26. Jeffery, C. Ray, *Crime prevention through environmental design* (Beverly Hills, CA: Sage, 1977), 351.

27. Casteel, Carri, and Corinne Peek-Asa, "Effectiveness of crime prevention through environmental design (CPTED) in reducing robberies," *American Journal of Preventive Medicine* 18, no. 4 (2000): 99–115.

28. Cozens, Paul Michael, Greg Saville, and David Hillier, "Crime prevention through environmental design (CPTED): a review and modern bibliography," *Property Management* 23, no. 5 (2005): 328–56; Carter, Sherry Plaster, Stanley L. Carter, and Andrew L. Dannenberg, "Zoning out crime and improving community health in Sarasota, Florida: Crime prevention through environmental design," *American Journal of Public Health* 93, no. 9 (2003): 1442–45.

29. Crow, Wayman, and James Bull, *Robbery deterrence: An applied behavioral science demonstration—final report* (La Jolla, CA: Western Behavioral Science Institute, 1975).

30. Johnson, Shane D., and Kate J. Bowers, "Permeability and burglary risk: Are cul-de-sacs safer?" *Journal of Quantitative Criminology* 26, no. 1 (2010): 89–111.

31. Rengert, George, "The journey to crime," in *Punishment, places, and perpetrators: Developments in criminology and criminal justice research*, ed. Bruinsma, G., et al., 169–81 (New York: Routledge, 2012).

32. For an excellent explanation of the supply and demand of criminal opportunities and a basic economic model of crime, see Cook, Philip J., "The demand and supply of criminal opportunities," *Crime and Justice: An Annual Review of Research* 7 (1986): 1–28.

33. Taylor, Ralph B., and Adele Harrell, *Physical environment and crime* (Washington, DC: US Department of Justice, Office of Justice Programs, National Institute of Justice, 1996).

34. See, e.g., http://www.cpted.net (International CPTED Association).

35. MacDonald, John, "Community design and crime: The impact of housing and the built environment," *Crime and Justice* 44, no. 1 (2015): 333–83.

36. Cahill, Meagan, Samantha S. Lowry, and P. Mitchell Downey, "Movin' out: Crime and HUD's HOPE VI initiative," Urban Institute, Washington, DC, 2011, http://www.urban.org/research/publication/movin-out-crime-and-huds-hope-vi-initiative.

37. Policy Guides, American Planning Association (APA), https://www.planning.org/policy/guides/.

Chapter 3. Establishing Evidence

1. Morens, David M, "Commentary: Cholera conundrums and proto-epidemiologic puzzles—the confusing epidemic world of John Lea and John Snow," *International Journal of Epidemiology* 42, no. 1 (2013): 43–52.

2. Snow, John, *On the mode of communication of cholera* (London: John Churchill, 1855).

3. "Dr. John Snow named the greatest Doctor," UCLA Department of Epidemiology, Fielding School of Public Health, March 2003, http://www.ph.ucla.edu/epi/snow/snowgreatestdoc .html.

4. Morens, "Commentary."

5. Koch, Tom, "The map as intent: Variations on the theme of John Snow," *Cartographica: The International Journal for Geographic Information and Geovisualization* 39, no. 4 (2004): 1–14.

6. Kukaswadia, Atif, "John Snow: The first epidemiologist," Public Health Perspectives, March 11, 2013, http://blogs.plos.org/publichealth/2013/03/11/john-snow-the-first -epidemiologist/.

7. "Cholera fact sheet," World Health Organization, January 17, 2019,. http://www.who.int /mediacentre/factsheets/fs107/en/.

8. "Removal of the pump handle," UCLA Department of Epidemiology, Fielding School of Public Health, https://www.ph.ucla.edu/epi/snow/removal.html.

9. Dannenberg, Andrew L., Richard J. Jackson, Howard Frumkin, Richard A. Schieber, Michael Pratt, Chris Kochtitzky, and Hugh H. Tilson, "The impact of community design and land-use choices on public health: A scientific research agenda," *American Journal of Public Health* 93, no. 9 (2003): 1500–1508.

10. MillionTreesNYC, New York City Department of Parks and Recreation, https://www .nycgovparks.org/trees/milliontreesnyc.

11. The point about selection undermining statistical models is discussed in detail in lots of research-method texts including Angrist, Joshua D., and Jörn-Steffen Pischke, *Mostly harmless econometrics: An empiricist's companion* (Princeton, NJ: Princeton University Press, 2008).

12. Angrist, Joshua D, "Treatment effect heterogeneity in theory and practice," *Economic Journal* 114, no. 494 (2004): C52–83.

13. Shadish, William R., Thomas D. Cook, and Donald Thomas Campbell, *Experimental and quasi-experimental designs for generalized causal inference* (Boston: Houghton Mifflin, 2002).

14. Deaton, Angus, and Nancy Cartwright, "Understanding and misunderstanding randomized controlled trials," *Social Science & Medicine* 210 (2018): 2–21; Sampson, Robert J., "Gold standard myths: Observations on the experimental turn in quantitative criminology," *Journal of Quantitative Criminology* 26, no. 4 (2010): 489–500.

15. Tabulations made from https://www.ucrdatatool.gov/Search/Crime/Local /RunCrimeJurisbyJurisLarge.cfm.

16. Zimring, Franklin E, *The city that became safe: New York's lessons for urban crime and its control* (Oxford: Oxford University Press, 2011).

17. Shadish, Cook, and Campbell, *Experimental and quasi-experimental designs for generalized causal inference*, 5.

18. US Preventive Services Task Force, http://www.uspreventiveservicestaskforce.org.

19. Shadish, Cook, and Campbell, *Experimental and quasi-experimental designs for generalized causal inference*.

20. See discussion in Shadish, Cook, and Campbell, 6.

21. Rubin, Donald B, "For objective causal inference, design trumps analysis," *Annals of Applied Statistics* 2, no. 3 (2008): 808–40.

22. South, Eugenia C., Michelle C. Kondo, Rose A. Cheney, and Charles C. Branas, "Neighborhood blight, stress, and health: A walking trial of urban greening and ambulatory heart rate," *American Journal of Public Health* 105, no. 5 (2015): 909–13.

23. Moving to Opportunity (MTO) for Fair Housing Demonstration Program, http://www.nber.org/mtopublic/.

24. Ludwig, Jens, Lisa Sanbonmatsu, Lisa Gennetian, Emma Adam, Greg J. Duncan, Lawrence F. Katz, Ronald C. Kessler et al., "Neighborhoods, obesity, and diabetes—a randomized social experiment," *New England Journal of Medicine* 365, no. 16 (2011): 1509–19; Ludwig, Jens, Greg J. Duncan, Lisa A. Gennetian, Lawrence F. Katz, Ronald C. Kessler, Jeffrey R. Kling, and Lisa Sanbonmatsu, "Neighborhood effects on the long-term well-being of low-income adults," *Science* 337, no. 6101 (2012): 1505–10.;

25. Ludwig, Jens, Greg J. Duncan, Lisa A. Gennetian, Lawrence F. Katz, Ronald C. Kessler, Jeffrey R. Kling, and Lisa Sanbonmatsu, "Long-term neighborhood effects on low-income families: Evidence from Moving to Opportunity," *American Economic Review* 103, no. 3 (2013): 226–31.

26. Ludwig et al., "Neighborhoods, obesity, and diabetes."

27. Kessler, Ronald C., Greg J. Duncan, Lisa A. Gennetian, Lawrence F. Katz, Jeffrey R. Kling, Nancy A. Sampson, Lisa Sanbonmatsu, Alan M. Zaslavsky, and Jens Ludwig, "Associations of housing mobility interventions for children in high-poverty neighborhoods with subsequent mental disorders during adolescence," *JAMA* 311, no. 9 (2014): 937–47.

28. Sciandra, Matthew, Lisa Sanbonmatsu, Greg J. Duncan, Lisa A. Gennetian, Lawrence F. Katz, Ronald C. Kessler, Jeffrey R. Kling, and Jens Ludwig, "Long-term effects of the Moving to Opportunity residential mobility experiment on crime and delinquency," *Journal of Experimental Criminology* 9, no. 4 (2013): 451–89.

29. Chetty, Raj, Nathaniel Hendren, and Lawrence F. Katz, "The effects of exposure to better neighborhoods on children: New evidence from the Moving to Opportunity experiment," *American Economic Review* 106, no. 4 (2016): 855–902.

30. Wilkerson, Isabel, *The warmth of other suns: The epic story of America's great migration* (New York: Vintage, 2011); Coates, Ta-Nehisi, "The case for reparations," *Atlantic*, June 2014, https://www.theatlantic.com/magazine/archive/2014/06/the-case-for-reparations/361631/.

31. Sampson, Robert J, "Moving to inequality: Neighborhood effects and experiments meet social structure," *American Journal of Sociology* 114, no. 1 (2008): 189–231.

32. Boruch, Robert F, *Randomized experiments for planning and evaluation: A practical guide*, vol. 44 (Thousand Oaks, CA: Sage, 1997).

33. Manzi, Jim, *Uncontrolled: The surprising payoff of trial-and-error for business, politics, and society* (New York: Basic Books, 2012).

34. Garvin, Eugenia C., Carolyn C. Cannuscio, and Charles C. Branas. "Greening vacant lots to reduce violent crime: A randomised controlled trial," *Injury prevention* 19, no. 3 (2013): 198–203.

35. Jackson, Richard J., Arthur M. Wendel, and Andrew L. Dannenberg, "Healthy places research: Emerging opportunities," in *Making Healthy Places*, ed. Dannenberg, Andrew L., Howard Frumkin, and Richard Jackson, 335–49 (Washington, DC: Island, 2011).

36. Manzi, *Uncontrolled*.

37. Mohler, George O., Martin B. Short, Sean Malinowski, Mark Johnson, George E. Tita, Andrea L. Bertozzi, and P. Jeffrey Brantingham, "Randomized controlled field trials of predictive policing," *Journal of the American Statistical Association* 110, no. 512 (2015): 1399–411.

38. US Code of Federal Regulations, Title 45 Part 46 amended at 70 FR 36328, June 23, 2005.

39. Israel, Barbara A., Amy J. Schulz, Edith A. Parker, and Adam B. Becker, "Review of community-based research: Assessing partnership approaches to improve public health," *Annual Review of Public Health* 19, no. 1 (1998): 173–202.

40. Weiss, Carol H, "Have we learned anything new about the use of evaluation?" *American Journal of Evaluation* 19, no. 1 (1998): 21–33.

41. See the following organizations for examples: http://www.blueprintsprograms.com /criteria; and http://toptierevidence.org/.

42. Braga, Anthony A., Brandon C. Welsh, and Cory Schnell, "Can policing disorder reduce crime? A systematic review and meta-analysis," *Journal of Research in Crime and Delinquency* 52, no. 4 (2015): 567–88.

43. Lehrer, Jonah, "The Truth Wears Off," *New Yorker*, December 5, 2010, http://www .newyorker.com/magazine/2010/12/13/the-truth-wears-off.

44. Ioannidis, John P. A., "Why most published research findings are false," *PLoS Medicine* 2, no. 8 (2005): e124.

45. "Clinical Trials," US National Library of Medicine, https://clinicaltrials.gov.

46. "About us: Our global community," Cochrane, http://www.cochrane.org/about-us /cochrane-groups.

47. http://www.cochrane.org/about-us/cochrane-groups.

48. Bogar, Sandra, and Kirsten M. Beyer, "Green space, violence, and crime: A systematic review," *Trauma, Violence & Abuse* 17, no. 2 (2016): 160–71.

49. Glass, Gene V, "Primary, secondary, and meta-analysis of research," *Educational Researcher* 5, no. 10 (1976): 3–8, 3.

50. Haidich, Anna-Bettina, "Meta-analysis in medical research," *Hippokratia* 14, no. supplement 1 (2010): 29.

51. Berk, Richard A., Alec Campbell, Ruth Klap, and Bruce Western, "The deterrent effect of arrest in incidents of domestic violence: A Bayesian analysis of four field experiments," *American Sociological Review* 57, no. 5 (1992): 698–708.

52. Wilson, James Q., *Thinking about crime* (New York: Vintage, 1983), 47.

53. What Works Clearinghouse (WWC), Institute of Education Sciences, https://ies.ed .gov/ncee/wwc/.

54. Sherman, Lawrence W., Denise C. Gottfredson, Doris L. MacKenzie, John Eck, Peter Reuter, and Shawn D. Bushway, *Preventing crime: What works, what doesn't, what's promising* (Washington, DC: National Institute of Justice, 1998); Burns, Patricia B., Rod J. Rohrich, and Kevin C. Chung, "The levels of evidence and their role in evidence-based medicine," *Plastic and Reconstructive Surgery* 128, no. 1 (2011): 305.

55. What Works Clearinghouse Procedures and Standards Handbook, version 3.0, B.2, Institute of Education Sciences, https://ies.ed.gov/ncee/wwc/Docs/referenceresources/wwc_procedures _v3_0_standards_handbook.pdf.

56. Liberman, A. M., "Advocating evidence-generating policies: A role for the ASC," *Criminologist* 34, no. 1 (2009): 1–3.

57. Gartlehner, Gerald, Richard A. Hansen, Daniel Nissman, Kathleen N. Lohr, and Timothy S. Carey, "Criteria for distinguishing effectiveness from efficacy trials in systematic reviews," *Technical Reviews*, no. 12, introduction (1). Agency for Healthcare Research and Quality, Rockville, Maryland, April 2006, http://www.ncbi.nlm.nih.gov/books/NBK44024/.

Chapter 4. Cities in Ruin

1. See picture images at Merchand Meffre, "The ruins of Detroit: 2010–2015," http://www.marchandmeffre.com/detroit. See also Strangleman, Tim, "'Smokestack nostalgia,' 'ruin porn,' or working-class obituary: The role and meaning of deindustrial representation," *International Labor and Working-Class History* 84 (2013): 23–37; and Millington, Nate, "Post-industrial imaginaries: Nature, representation, and ruin in Detroit, Michigan," *International Journal of Urban and Regional Research* 37, no. 1 (2013): 279–96.

2. Hendrix, Steve, "Life, death, and demolition," *Washington Post*, February 2, 2017, https://www.washingtonpost.com/graphics/local/baltimore-life-death-and-demolition/.

3. Allen, Franklin, James R. Barth, and Glenn Yago, *Fixing the housing market: Financial innovations for the future* (Upper Saddle River, JR: Pearson Prentice Hall, 2012).

4. Fishman, *Urban utopias in the twentieth century*.

5. Sugrue, Thomas J, *The origins of the urban crisis: Race and inequality in postwar Detroit* (Princeton, NJ: Princeton University Press, 2014).

6. Keys, Benjamin J., Tanmoy Mukherjee, Amit Seru, and Vikrant Vig, "Did securitization lead to lax screening? Evidence from subprime loans," *Quarterly Journal of Economics* 125, no. 1 (2010): 307–62.

7. Krieger, James, and Donna L. Higgins, "Housing and health: Time again for public health action," *American Journal of Public Health* 92, no. 5 (2002): 758–68.

8. Corburn, *Healthy city planning*.

9. Brown, Dixon, and Gillham, *Urban design for an urban century*.

10. Jacobs, *The death and life of great American cities*.

11. Biles, Roger, *From tenements to the Taylor homes: In search of an urban housing policy in twentieth-century America* (University Park: Penn State University Press, 2010).

12. Brown, Dixon, and Gillham, *Urban design for an urban century*.

13. Wilson, *Thinking about crime*.

14. Kotlowitz, Alex, *There are no children here: The story of two boys growing up in the other America* (New York: Anchor, 1991).

15. A Chicago Housing Authority public housing project that was built in the 1950s to provide transitional housing for the influx of working poor African Americans from the Southern US states. See also Cohen, Adam, and Elizabeth Taylor, *American pharaoh: Mayor Richard J. Daley—his battle for Chicago and the nation* (New York: Little, Brown, 2001).

16. "Elevators and New York City housing: A dangerous combination?," Orlow Firm, https://orlowlaw.com/elevators-and-new-york-city-housing-a-dangerous-combination/.

17. Kuo, Frances E., William C. Sullivan, Rebekah Levine Coley, and Liesette Brunson, "Fertile ground for community: Inner-city neighborhood common spaces," *American Journal of Community Psychology* 26, no. 6 (1998): 823–51.

18. Newman, Oscar, *Defensible space: Crime prevention through urban design* (New York: Macmillan, 1972).

19. For a critique of the garden city planning model, see Jacobs, *The death and life of great American cities*. Jacobs also argued that the garden city model fostered crime.

20. Newman, *Defensible space: Crime prevention through urban design*, 18.

21. Merry, Sally E., "Defensible space undefended: Social factors in crime control through environmental design," *Urban Affairs Quarterly* 16, no. 4 (1981): 397–422.

22. Schill, Michael H., "Distressed public housing: Where do we go from here?" *University of Chicago Law Review* 60, no. 2 (1993): 497–554.

23. MacDonald, "Community design and crime."

24. Babwin, Don, "Chicago remembers Jane Byrne (1933–2014), city's only female mayor (1979–83)," *Christian Science Monitor*, November 15, 2014.

25. Popkin, Susan J., Diane K. Levy, Laura E. Harris, Jennifer Comey, Mary Cunningham, and Larry Buron, HOPE VI Panel Study, Baseline Report, Urban Institute, Washington, DC, 2002, http://webarchive.urban.org/UploadedPDF/410590_HOPEVI_PanelStudy.pdf.

26. Aliprantis, Dionissi, and Daniel Hartley, "Blowing it up and knocking it down: The local and city-wide effects of demolishing high concentration public housing on crime," *Journal of Urban Economics* 88 (2015): 67–81.

27. Krieger and Higgins, "Housing and health."

28. Details on this study can be found at http://www.nber.org/mtopublic/.

29. The authors refer to this measure as "subject well-being": Ludwig et al., "Long-term neighborhood effects on low-income families."

30. Ludwig et al., "Neighborhoods, obesity, and diabetes."

31. Kessler et al., "Associations of housing mobility interventions for children in high-poverty neighborhoods with subsequent mental disorders during adolescence."

32. Sciandra et al., "Long-term effects of the Moving to Opportunity residential mobility experiment on crime and delinquency."

33. Ludwig et al., "Long-term neighborhood effects on low-income families"; Gennetian, Lisa A., Lisa Sanbonmatsu, Lawrence F. Katz, Jeffrey R. Kling, Matthew Sciandra, Jens Ludwig, Greg J. Duncan, and Ronald C. Kessler, "The long-term effects of Moving to Opportunity on youth outcomes," *Cityscape* (2012): 137–67; Sanbonmatsu et al., "The long-term effects of moving to opportunity on adult health and economic self-sufficiency."

34. Chetty and Katz, "The effects of exposure to better neighborhoods on children."

35. Chetty, Raj, and Nathaniel Hendren, "The impacts of neighborhoods on intergenerational mobility I: Childhood exposure effects," *Quarterly Journal of Economics* 133, no. 3 (2018): 1107–62.

36. Sharkey, Patrick, "The intergenerational transmission of context," *American Journal of Sociology* 113, no. 4 (2008): 931–69; Sharkey, Patrick, *Stuck in place: Urban neighborhoods and the end of progress toward racial equality* (Chicago: University of Chicago Press, 2013).

37. Wilkerson, *The warmth of other suns*.

38. Németh, Jeremy, and Joern Langhorst, "Rethinking urban transformation: Temporary uses for vacant land," *Cities* 40 (2014): 143–50.

39. See Bucchianeri, Grace W., Kevin C. Gillen, and Susan M. Wachter, "Valuing the conversion of urban greenspace," Prudential Financial Inc., University of Pennsylvania, 2012, https://phsonline.org/uploads/resources/Bucchianeri_Gillen_Wachter_Valuing_Conversion_Urban_Greenspace_Fin.al_Draft_KG_changesacceptes.pdf; Branas, Charles C., David Rubin, and

Wensheng Guo, "Vacant properties and violence in neighborhoods," University of Pennsylvania ScholarlyCommons, Cartographic Modeling Papers #5, 2012, https://repository.upenn.edu/cgi/viewcontent.cgi?article=1004&context=cml_papers; Cohen, Deborah, Suzanne Spear, Richard Scribner, Patty Kissinger, Karen Mason, and John Wildgen, "'Broken windows' and the risk of gonorrhea," *American Journal of Public Health* 90, no. 2 (2000): 230; Spelman, William, "Abandoned buildings: Magnets for crime?" *Journal of Criminal Justice* 21, no. 5 (1993): 481–95.

40. Cohen, James R., "Abandoned housing: Exploring lessons from Baltimore," *Housing Policy Debate* 12, no. 3 (2001): 415–48.

41. US Government Accountability Office, "Vacant properties: Growing number increases communities' costs and challenges," Washington, DC, 2011.

42. Phipatanakul, Wanda, "Environmental factors and childhood asthma," *Pediatric Annals* 35, no. 9 (2006): 647–56.

43. "HOPE VI—Public and Indian Housing," HUD.gov, https://www.hud.gov/program_offices/public_indian_housing/programs/ph/hope6.

44. Barnett, Erica C., "Once one of Seattle's highest crime areas, High Point has transformed into a thriving, diverse community," *Seattle Magazine*, September 2017, https://www.seattlemag.com/news-and-features/once-one-seattles-highest-crime-areas-high-point-has-transformed-thriving-diverse.

45. "High Point: Awards," Seattle Housing Authority, https://www.seattlehousing.org/about-us/redevelopment/high-point-redevelopment/high-point-awards.

46. Schwartz, Alex F., *Housing policy in the United States* (New York: Routledge, 2014).

47. Krieger, James W., Tim K. Takaro, Lin Song, and Marcia Weaver, "The Seattle-King County Healthy Homes Project: A randomized, controlled trial of a community health worker intervention to decrease exposure to indoor asthma triggers." *American Journal of Public Health* 95, no. 4 (2005): 652–59.

48. Krieger, James K., Tim K. Takaro, Carol Allen, Lin Song, Marcia Weaver, Sanders Chai, and Phillip Dickey, "The Seattle-King County Healthy Homes Project: Implementation of a comprehensive approach to improving indoor environmental quality for low-income children with asthma," *Environmental Health Perspectives* 110, supplement no. 2 (2002): 311–22.

49. "Seattle's High Point Development Project," US Department of Housing and Urban Development, Office of Policy Development and Research (PDR&R), HUD User, https://www.huduser.gov/portal/casestudies/study_04092012_1.html.

50. "Breathe-Easy Homes," Seattle Housing Authority, https://www.seattlehousing.org/about-us/redevelopment/high-point-redevelopment/breathe-easy-homes.

51. Takaro, Tim K., James Krieger, Lin Song, Denise Sharify, and Nancy Beaudet, "The Breathe-Easy Home: The impact of asthma-friendly home construction on clinical outcomes and trigger exposure," *American Journal of Public Health* 101, no. 1 (2011): 55–62.

52. Breysse, Jill, Sherry Dixon, Joel Gregory, Miriam Philby, David E. Jacobs, and James Krieger, "Effect of weatherization combined with community health worker in-home education on asthma control," *American Journal of Public Health* 104, no. 1 (2014): e57–e64.

53. "Vacant properties: Growing number increases communities' costs and challenges," US Government Accountability Office, Washington, DC, 2011.

54. "Vacant land management in Philadelphia: The costs of the current system and the benefits of reform," Redevelopment Authority of the City of Philadelphia, Philadelphia Association of Community Development Corporations, Econsult Corporation, Penn Institute for Urban Research, May 8, 2010, http://planphilly.com/uploads/media_items/http-planphilly-com-sites-planphilly-com-files-econsult_vacant_land_full_report-pdf.original.pdf.

55. MacDonald, "Community design and crime."

56. "Vacant Property Strategy," Department of Licenses and Inspections, Philadelphia, 2011. http://www.phila.gov/li/aboutus/Pages/VacantPropertyStrategy.aspx.

57. Kondo, Michelle C., Danya Keene, Bernadette C. Hohl, John M. MacDonald, and Charles C. Branas, "A difference-in-differences study of the effects of a new abandoned building remediation strategy on safety," *PloS One* 10, no. 7 (2015): e0129582.

58. See http://www.census.gov/housing/hvs/files/qtr113/q113press.pdf, 4, table 3.

59. Lens, Michael C., "The impact of housing vouchers on crime in US cities and suburbs," *Urban studies* 51, no. 6 (2014): 1274–89; Cubbin, Catherine, Felicia B. LeClere, and Gordon S. Smith, "Socioeconomic status and injury mortality: Individual and neighborhood determinants," *Journal of Epidemiology & Community Health* 54, no. 7 (2000): 517–24.

60. Newman makes similar points in his work in arguing that the design of defensible space is more important for poor residents because they lack the resources to pay for doormen, security guards, childcare, and other services that the middle and upper classes rely on to maintain their safety. See Newman, Oscar, *Creating defensible space* (Washington, DC: US Department of Housing and Urban Development, Office of Policy Development and Research, 1996).

61. Ley, David, *The new middle class and the remaking of the central city* (New York: Oxford University Press, 1996).

62. Hwang, Jackelyn, and Jeffrey Lin, "What have we learned about the causes of recent gentrification?" *Cityscape* 18, no. 3 (2016): 9–26.

63. Martin, Isaac William, and Kevin Beck, "Gentrification, property tax limitation, and displacement," *Urban Affairs Review* 54, no. 1 (2018): 33–73.

64. Zuk, Miriam, Ariel H. Bierbaum, Karen Chapple, Karolina Gorska, and Anastasia Loukaitou-Sideris, "Gentrification, displacement, and the role of public investment," *Journal of Planning Literature* 33, no. 1 (2018): 31–44; Martin and Beck, "Gentrification, property tax limitation, and displacement."

65. Ellen, Ingrid Gould, and Katherine M. O'Regan, "How low-income neighborhoods change: Entry, exit, and enhancement," *Regional Science and Urban Economics* 41, no. 2 (2011): 89–97; McKinnish, Terra, Randall Walsh, and T. Kirk White, "Who gentrifies low-income neighborhoods?" *Journal of Urban Economics* 67, no. 2 (2010): 180–93; Ding, Lei, Jackelyn Hwang, and Eileen Divringi, "Gentrification and residential mobility in Philadelphia," *Regional Science and Urban Economics* 61 (2016): 38–51.

66. Hwang, Jackelyn, and Robert J. Sampson, "Divergent pathways of gentrification: Racial inequality and the social order of renewal in Chicago neighborhoods," *American Sociological Review* 79, no. 4 (2014): 726–51.

67. Sharkey, Patrick, "An alternative approach to addressing selection into and out of social settings: Neighborhood change and African American children's economic outcomes," *Sociological Methods & Research* 41, no. 2 (2012): 251–93.

68. Hwang, Jackelyn, "Pioneers of gentrification: Transformation in global neighborhoods in urban America in the late twentieth century," *Demography* 53, no. 1 (2016): 189–213.

69. Hwang and Lin, "What have we learned about the causes of recent gentrification?"

70. Williams, Timothy, "Cities mobilize to help those threatened by gentrification, *New York Times*, March 3, 2014, https://www.nytimes.com/2014/03/04/us/cities-helping-residents-resist-the-new-gentry.html.

71. Schwartz, Heather L., Liisa Ecola, Kristin J. Leuschner, and Aaron Kofner. "Is inclusionary zoning inclusionary? A guide for practitioners." Technical Report, RAND Corporation, Santa Monica, California, 2012.

72. Dawkins, Casey, Jae Sik Jeon, and Gerrit-Jan Knaap, "Creating and preserving affordable homeownership opportunities: Does inclusionary zoning make sense?" *Journal of Planning Education and Research* 37, no. 4 (2017): 444–46.

73. Freeman, Lance, and Jenny Schuetz, "Producing affordable housing in rising markets: What works?" *Cityscape* 19, no. 1 (2017): 217–36.

74. Wolf-Powers, Laura, "Community benefits agreements and local government: A review of recent evidence," *Journal of the American Planning Association* 76 no. 2 (2010): 141–59.

75. Been, Vicki, "Community benefits: A new local government tool or another variation on the exactions theme," *University of Chicago Law Review* 77 (2010): 5–35.

76. Sharkey, Patrick, *Uneasy peace: The great crime decline, the renewal of city life, and the next war on violence* (New York: W. W. Norton, 2018).

77. Williams, "Cities mobilize to help those threatened by gentrification."

78. Lions, Siobhan, "What 'ruin porn' tells us about ruins—and porn," CNN, November 1, 2017, http://www.cnn.com/2015/10/12/architecture/what-ruin-porn-tells-us-about-ruins-and-porn/.

Chapter 5. The Nature Cure

1. Branas, Charles C., Therese S. Richmond, Dennis P. Culhane, Thomas R. Ten Have, and Douglas J. Wiebe, "Investigating the link between gun possession and gun assault," *American Journal of Public Health* 99, no. 11 (2009): 2034–40.

2. See Sustainable Cities Collective, http://www.sustainablecitiescollective.com/deeproot/1078476/when-parking-meant-space-trees.

3. Block dimensions were determined by the length of surveyor's measuring chains in the late 1800s. These chains were 66 feet in length; thus blocks were laid out through much of the city as 10 chain lengths by 5 chain lengths. See "Street and site plan design standards," City of Chicago, 2007, https://www.chicago.gov/content/dam/city/depts/cdot/StreetandSitePlanDesignStandards407.pdf.

4. The term "emerald necklace" comes from the urban planner Frederick Law Olmstead's design for a ring of park around Boston, now a major attraction for visitors and residents. See Beveridge, Charles E., *Frederick Law Olmsted: Designing the American landscape* (New York: Rizzoli, 2005).

5. See National Climate Assessment US Global Change Research Report, 2014, http://nca2014.globalchange.gov/.

6. Clean Waters Comprehensive Monitoring Plan, Green City, Philadelphia Water Department, 2012.

7. Kondo, Michelle C., Sarah C. Low, Jason Henning, and Charles C. Branas, "The impact of green stormwater infrastructure installation on surrounding health and safety," *American Journal of Public Health* 105, no. 3 (2015): e114–21.

8. Katz, Bruce, and Jennifer Bradley, *The metropolitan revolution: How cities and metros are fixing our broken politics and fragile economy* (Washington, DC: Brookings Institution, 2013).

9. Dilworth, Richardson, Robert Stokes, Rachel Weinberger, and Sabrina Spatari, "The place of planning in sustainability metrics for public works: Lessons from the Philadelphia region," *Public Works Management & Policy* 16, no. 1 (2011): 20–39.

10. Kennedy, Christopher, John Cuddihy, and Joshua Engel-Yan, "The changing metabolism of cities," *Journal of Industrial Ecology* 11, no. 2 (2007): 43–59.

11. Steinhauer, Jennifer, "City says its urban jungle has little room for palms," *New York Times*, November 25, 2006, http://www.nytimes.com/2006/11/26/us/26palm.html?_r=0.

12. Greenworks Progress Report, City of Philadelphia, 2013, https://www.phila.gov/media/20160419140528/2013-greenworks-progress-report.pdf.

13. Crowther, Thomas W., Henry B. Glick, Kristofer R. Covey, Charlie Bettigole, Daniel S. Maynard, Stephen M. Thomas, Jeffrey R. Smith, et al., "Mapping tree density at a global scale," *Nature* 525, no. 7568 (2015): 201.

14. Conniff, Richard, "Trees shed bad rep as accessories to crime," environmentYale, Yale School of Forestry and Environmental Studies, 2012, http://environment.yale.edu/envy/stories/trees-shed-bad-wrap-as-accessories-to-crime.

15. Donovan, Geoffrey H., and Jeffrey P. Prestemon, "The effect of trees on crime in Portland, Oregon," *Environment and Behavior* 44, no. 1 (2012): 3–30.

16. At distances of 50 meters, 100 meters, and 200 meters.

17. Kuo, Frances E., and William C. Sullivan, "Environment and crime in the inner city: Does vegetation reduce crime?" *Environment and Behavior* 33, no. 3 (2001): 343–67.

18. Kuo, Frances E., and William C. Sullivan, "Aggression and violence in the inner city: Effects of environment via mental fatigue," *Environment and Behavior* 33, no. 4 (2001): 543–71.

19. Belluck, Pam, "End of a ghetto: A special report—razing the slums to rescue the residents," *New York Times*, September 6, 1998, http://www.nytimes.com/1998/09/06/us/end-of-a-ghetto-a-special-report-razing-the-slums-to-rescue-the-residents.html?pagewanted=all.

20. Heckert, Megan, and Jeremy Mennis, "The economic impact of greening urban vacant land: A spatial difference-in-differences analysis," *Environment and Planning A* 44, no. 12 (2012): 3010–27.

21. Bonham, J. Blaine Jr, and Patricia L. Smith. "Transformation through greening," in *Growing greener cities: Urban sustainability in the twenty-first century*. ed. E. Birch and S. Wachter, 227–43 (Philadelphia: University of Pennsylvania Press, 2008).

22. Trey Popp, "The park of a thousand pieces," *Pennsylvania Gazette*, July 2011, http://www.upenn.edu/gazette/0711/feature3_1.html.

23. Kondo, Michelle, Bernadette Hohl, SeungHoon Han, and Charles Branas, "Effects of greening and community reuse of vacant lots on crime," *Urban studies* 53, no. 15 (2016): 3279–95; Endo, Arata, "A study on the vacant land management project on Philadelphia, USA," *Journal of Architecture and Planning of Japan* 76 no. 668 (2011): 1875–83.

24. Wachter, Susan, "The determinants of neighborhood transformation in Philadelphia: Identification and analysis—the new Kensington pilot study," Working paper, Wharton School of Business, University of Pennsylvania, 2004.

25. Heckert and Mennis, "The economic impact of greening urban vacant land."

26. Branas, Charles C., Rose A. Cheney, John M. MacDonald, Vicky W. Tam, Tara D. Jackson, and Thomas R. Ten Have, "A difference-in-differences analysis of health, safety, and greening vacant urban space," *American Journal of Epidemiology* 174, no. 11 (2011): 1296–1306.

27. South, Eugenia C., Michelle C. Kondo, Rose A. Cheney, and Charles C. Branas, "Neighborhood blight, stress, and health: A walking trial of urban greening and ambulatory heart rate," *American Journal of Public Health* 105, no. 5 (2015): 909–13.

28. Branas, Charles C., Eugenia South, Michelle C. Kondo, Bernadette C. Hohl, Philippe Bourgois, Douglas J. Wiebe, and John M. MacDonald, "Citywide cluster randomized trial to restore blighted vacant land and its effects on violence, crime, and fear," *Proceedings of the National Academy of Sciences* 115, no. 12 (2018): 2946–51.

29. Moyer, Ruth, John M. MacDonald, Greg Ridgeway, and Charles C. Branas, "Effect of remediating blighted vacant land on shootings: A citywide cluster randomized trial," *American Journal of Public Health* 109, no. 1 (2019): 140–44.

30. Kuo, Frances E., Magdalena Bacaicoa, and William C. Sullivan, "Transforming inner-city landscapes: Trees, sense of safety, and preference," *Environment and Behavior* 30, no. 1 (1998): 28–59.

31. Ulrich, Roger S., "Visual landscapes and psychological well-being," *Landscape Research* 4, no. 1 (1979): 17–23.

32. Moore, Ernest O., "A prison environment's effect on health care service demands," *Journal of Environmental Systems* 11, no. 1 (1981): 17–34.

33. South et al., "Neighborhood blight, stress, and health."

34. South, Eugenia C., Bernadette C. Hohl, Michelle C. Kondo, John M. MacDonald, and Charles C. Branas, "Effect of greening vacant land on mental health of community-dwelling adults: A cluster randomized trial," *JAMA Network Open* 1, no. 3 (2018): e180298.

35. Healthy Trees, Healthy People (HtHt), Portland State University, http://www.treesandhealth.org/.

36. Poland, Therese M., and Deborah G. McCullough, "Emerald ash borer: Invasion of the urban forest and the threat to North America's ash resource," *Journal of Forestry* 104, no. 3 (2006): 118–24.

37. See the Emerald Ash Borer Information Network, http://www.emeraldashborer.info/#sthash.YkLEoegg.dpbs.

38. Donovan, Geoffrey H., David T. Butry, Yvonne L. Michael, Jeffrey P. Prestemon, Andrew M. Liebhold, Demetrios Gatziolis, and Megan Y. Mao, "The relationship between trees and human health: Evidence from the spread of the emerald ash borer," *American Journal of Preventive Medicine* 44, no. 2 (2013): 139–45. For Donovan's own explanation, see "How removing trees can kill you," PBS NewsHour, June 20, 2013, http://www.pbs.org/newshour/rundown/can-lack-of-trees-kill-you-faster/.

39. Kondo, Michelle C., SeungHoon Han, Geoffrey H. Donovan, and John M. MacDonald, "The association between urban trees and crime: Evidence from the spread of the emerald ash borer in Cincinnati," *Landscape and Urban Planning* 157 (2017): 193–99.

40. A video explanation of this study is available at https://www.youtube.com/watch?v=-wHn5QFHpcg.

Chapter 6. Driving Ambivalence

1. Badger, Emily, "The many reasons millenials are shunning cars," *Washington Post*, October 14, 1014, https://www.washingtonpost.com/news/wonk/wp/2014/10/14/the-many-reasons-millennials-are-shunning-cars/

2. Nader, Ralph, *Unsafe at any speed: The designed-in dangers of the American automobile* (New York: Grossman, 1965).

3. Peltzman, Sam, "The effects of automobile safety regulation," *Journal of Political Economy* 83, no. 4 (1975): 677–725.

4. Robertson, Leon S., "Reducing death on the road: The effects of minimum safety standards, publicized crash tests, seat belts, and alcohol," *American Journal of Public Health* 86, no. 1 (1996): 31–34.

5. Cohen, Alma, and Liran Einav, "The effects of mandatory seat belt laws on driving behavior and traffic fatalities," *Review of Economics and Statistics* 85, no. 4 (2003): 828–43.

6. Ewing, Reid, and Eric Dumbaugh, "The built environment and traffic safety: A review of empirical evidence," *Journal of Planning Literature* 23, no. 4 (2009): 347–67.

7. Abrams, Robin Fran, Emil Malizia, Arthur Wendel, James Sallis, Rachel A. Millstein, Jordan A. Carlson, Carolyn Cannuscio et al., *Making healthy places: Designing and building for health, well-being, and sustainability* (Washington, DC: Island, 2012).

8. Frank, Lawrence D., Thomas L. Schmid, James F. Sallis, James Chapman, and Brian E. Saelens, "Linking objectively measured physical activity with objectively measured urban form: Findings from SMARTRAQ," *American Journal of Preventive Medicine* 28, no. 2 (2005): 117–25.

9. Mokdad, Ali H., Earl S. Ford, Barbara A. Bowman, William H. Dietz, Frank Vinicor, Virginia S. Bales, and James S. Marks, "Prevalence of obesity, diabetes, and obesity-related health risk factors, 2001," *JAMA* 289, no. 1 (2003): 76–79; Colditz, Graham, and Claire Y. Wang, "Economic costs of obesity," In *Obesity Epidemiology*, ed. Hu, Frank, 261–74 (New York: Oxford University Press, 2008).

10. Finkelstein, Eric A., Justin G. Trogdon, Joel W. Cohen, and William Dietz, "Annual medical spending attributable to obesity: Payer-and service-specific estimates," *Health Affairs* 28, no. 5 (2009): w822–31.

11. Cawley, John, and Chad Meyerhoefer, "The medical care costs of obesity: An instrumental variables approach," *Journal of Health Economics* 31, no. 1 (2012): 219–30. (The study uses the age of an oldest biological child as a predictor of one's obesity.)

12. Frumkin, Howard, "Urban sprawl and public health," *Public Health Reports*, 117, no. 3 (2002): 201.

13. See Frank, Lawrence D., "Land use and transportation interaction: Implications on public health and quality of life," *Journal of Planning Education and Research* 20, no. 1 (2000): 6–22; Cervero, Robert, and Roger Gorham, "Commuting in transit versus automobile neighborhoods," *Journal of the American Planning Association* 61, no. 2 (1995): 210–25.

14. Jackson, Kenneth T., *Crabgrass frontier: The suburbanization of the United States* (Oxford: Oxford University Press, 1987).

15. Nolan Hicks, Caitlin Nolan, and Barry Paddock, "*Daily News* probe finds mixed results for Bill deBlasio's vision zero plan," *New York Daily News*, May 26, 2015.

16. Furness, Zack, *One less car: Bicycling and the politics of automobility*, vol. 29 (Philadelphia: Temple University Press, 2010).

17. Giles-Corti, Billie, and Robert J. Donovan, "Relative influences of individual, social environmental, and physical environmental correlates of walking," *American Journal of Public Health* 93, no. 9 (2003): 1583–89; Gauvin, Lise, Lucie Richard, Cora Lynn Craig, Michaël Spivock, Mylène Riva, Mathieu Forster, Sophie Laforest, et al., "From walkability to active living potential: An 'ecometric' validation study," *American Journal of Preventive Medicine* 28, no. 2 (2005): 126–33; Hoehner, Christine M., Laura K. Brennan Ramirez, Michael B. Elliott, Susan L. Handy, and Ross C. Brownson, "Perceived and objective environmental measures and physical activity among urban adults," *American Journal of Preventive Medicine* 28, no. 2 (2005): 105–16; Frank, Lawrence D., James F. Sallis, Terry L. Conway, James E. Chapman, Brian E. Saelens, and William Bachman, "Many pathways from land use to health: Associations between neighborhood walkability and active transportation, body mass index, and air quality," *Journal of the American Planning Association* 72, no. 1 (2006): 75–87.

18. Committee on Physical Activity, Health, Transportation, and Land Use, "Does the built environment influence physical activity? Examining the evidence," Transportation Research Board Special Report 282, Institute of Medicine of the National Academies, Washington, DC, 2005, http://onlinepubs.trb.org/onlinepubs/sr/sr282.pdf.

19. Haskell, William L., I-Min Lee, Russell R. Pate, Kenneth E. Powell, Steven N. Blair, Barry A. Franklin, Caroline A. Macera, Gregory W. Heath, Paul D. Thompson, and Adrian Bauman, "Physical activity and public health: Updated recommendation for adults from the American College of Sports Medicine and the American Heart Association," *Circulation* 116, no. 9 (2007): 1081.

20. Siegel, Paul Z., Robert M. Brackbill, and Gregory W. Heath, "The epidemiology of walking for exercise: Implications for promoting activity among sedentary groups," *American Journal of Public Health* 85, no. 5 (1995): 706–10; Bauman, Adrian E., James F. Sallis, David A. Dzewaltowski, and Neville Owen, "Toward a better understanding of the influences on physical activity: The role of determinants, correlates, causal variables, mediators, moderators, and confounders," *American Journal of Preventive Medicine* 23, no. 2 (2002): 5–14; Frank, Lawrence D., "Economic determinants of urban form: Resulting trade-offs between active and sedentary forms of travel," *American Journal of Preventive Medicine* 27, no. 3 (2004): 146–53.

21. Levine, Jonathan, and Lawrence D. Frank, "Transportation and land-use preferences and residents' neighborhood choices: The sufficiency of compact development in the Atlanta region," *Transportation* 34, no. 2 (2007): 255–74.

22. Tudor-Locke, Catrine, and David R. Bassett, "How many steps/day are enough?" *Sports Medicine* 34, no. 1 (2004): 1–8; Besser, Lilah M., and Andrew L. Dannenberg, "Walking to public transit: Steps to help meet physical activity recommendations," *American Journal of Preventive Medicine* 29, no. 4 (2005): 273–80; Wener, Richard E., and Gary W. Evans, "A morning stroll: Levels of physical activity in car and mass transit commuting," *Environment and Behavior* 39, no. 1 (2007): 62–74.

23. Brown, B. B., and C. M. Werner, "Before and after a new light rail stop: Resident attitudes, travel behavior, and obesity," *Journal of the American Planning Association* 75, no. 1 (2008): 5–12.

24. Saelens, Brian E., Anne Vernez Moudon, Bumjoon Kang, Philip M. Hurvitz, and Chuan Zhou, "Relation between higher physical activity and public transit use," *American Journal of Public Health* 104, no. 5 (2014): 854–59.

25. See "Light Rail Transit: Myths and Realities," Federal Reserve Bank of St. Louis, 2003-4, https://www.stlouisfed.org/publications/bridges/winter-20032004/lightrail-transit-myths-and-realities.

26. Stokes, Robert J., John MacDonald, and Greg Ridgeway, "Estimating the effects of light rail transit on health care costs," *Health & Place* 14, no. 1 (2008): 45–58.

27. Frazier, Eric, "Dirt moving for light rail to UNCC—raising high hopes for development," *Charlotte Observer*, August 30, 2014, http://www.charlotteobserver.com/news/business/biz-columns-blogs/article9159005.html

28. Stokes, Robert J., John MacDonald, and Greg Ridgeway, "Estimating the effects of light rail transit on health care costs."

29. See Wikipedia's entry for the Charlotte Area Transit System, http://en.wikipedia.org/wiki/Lynx_Rapid_Transit_Services (last updated April 17, 2019).

30. MacDonald, John M., Robert J. Stokes, Deborah A. Cohen, Aaron Kofner, and Greg K. Ridgeway, "The effect of light rail transit on body mass index and physical activity," *American Journal of Preventive Medicine* 39, no. 2 (2010): 105–12.

31. Given that housing prices didn't jump appreciably until after the light rail opened suggests that the anticipation of a future rail line didn't likely affect those living in the area in the pre–opening period. See Billings, Stephen B., "Estimating the value of a new transit option," *Regional Science and Urban Economics* 41, no. 6 (2011): 525–36.

32. The study used propensity score weighting to assure that the groups were statistically comparable on a number of variables.

33. Boarnet, Marlon G., "Metropolitan Los Angeles and transportation planning: Back to the future," in *Planning Los Angeles*, ed. Sloane, David (Chicago: American Planning Association, 2012).

34. Metro Interactive Estimated Ridership Stats, http://isotp.metro.net/MetroRidership/Index.aspx.

35. LA County Metropolitan Transportation Authority FY 2002 On-Board Bus Survey Regional Weekday Travel Patterns Report, Vol. 1, Rea & Parker Research, San Diego, California, May 2003, http://media.metro.net/projects_studies/research/images/reports/mta_bus_regional_weekday_travel_patterns.pdf.

36. Spears, Steven, Douglas Houston, and Marlon G. Boarnet, "Illuminating the unseen in transit use: A framework for examining the effect of attitudes and perceptions on travel behavior," *Transportation Research Part A: Policy and Practice* 58 (2013): 40–53.

37. Ridgeway, Greg, and John M. MacDonald, "Effect of rail transit on crime: A study of Los Angeles from 1988 to 2014," *Journal of Quantitative Criminology* 33, no. 2 (2017): 277–91.

38. Boarnet, Marlon G., Xize Wang, and Douglas Houston, "Can new light rail reduce personal vehicle carbon emissions? A before-after, experimental-control evaluation in Los Angeles," *Journal of Regional Science* 57, no. 3 (2017): 523–39.

39. Spears, Steven, Marlon G. Boarnet, and Douglas Houston, "Driving reduction after the introduction of light rail transit: Evidence from an experimental-control group evaluation of the Los Angeles Expo Line," *Urban Studies* 54, no. 12 (2017): 2780–99.

40. Hong, Andy, Marlon G. Boarnet, and Douglas Houston, "New light rail transit and active travel: A longitudinal study," *Transportation Research Part A: Policy and Practice* 92 (2016): 131–44.

41. Morabia, Alfredo, Franklin E. Mirer, Tashia M. Amstislavski, Holger M. Eisl, Jordan Werbe-Fuentes, John Gorczynski, Chris Goranson, Mary S. Wolff, and Steven B. Markowitz, "Potential health impact of switching from car to public transportation when commuting to work," *American Journal of Public Health* 100, no. 12 (2010): 2388–91.

42. The American Time Use Survey shows Americans work 4.41 days a week (http://www .bls.gov/tus/). If one multiples 4.41 by 52 weeks by 124 calories the total number of calories burned over a year is equivalent to 24,436 calories.

43. Johnson and Bowers, "Permeability and burglary risk."

44. Murphy, Dean E., "Barricades, police visits give hope to crime-plagued neighborhood," *Los Angeles Times*, June 22, 1991, http://articles.latimes.com/1991-06-22/local/me-825_1 _south-central-community.

45. Murphy, "Barricades, police visits give hope to crime-plagued neighborhood."

46. Map of Reporting District 1345, *Los Angeles Times*, http://maps.latimes.com/lapd /reporting-district/1345/. The specific roadways are Hooper and Central Avenue.

47. Lasley, James R., "Using traffic barriers to design out crime," report to the National Institute of Justice, California State University, Fullerton, 1996, 15.

48. In the aftermath of the 1992 Los Angeles Riots the barriers were in a state of "disrepair," and most were removed by 1995.

49. Lasley, James R., "Using traffic barriers to design out crime," report to the National Institute of Justice, California State University, Fullerton, 1996, table 2; Lasley, James R. " 'Designing out' gang homicides and street assaults," National Institute of Justice Research in Brief, 1998.

50. Lasley, James R., "Using traffic barriers to design out crime," 21.

51. American Public Transportation Association: 2013 Public Transportation Fact Book, Washington, DC, October, 2013. See also the American Public Transportation Association Quarterly Ridership Report: http://www.apta.com/resources/statistics/Pages /ridershipreport.aspx.

52. Ewing, Reid, and Robert Cervero, "Travel and the built environment: A meta-analysis," *Journal of the American Planning Association* 76, no. 3 (2010): 265–94.

Chapter 7. Good Clean Fun

1. Florida, Richard, *The rise of the creative class and how it's transforming work, leisure, community and everyday life* (New York: Basic Books, 2002).

2. Stokes, Robert, "The challenges of using BIDs in lower-income areas: The case of Germantown, Philadelphia," *Drexel Law Review* 3 (2010): 325-337.

3. Twinam, Tate, "Danger zone: Land use and the geography of neighborhood crime," *Journal of Urban Economics* 100 (2017): 104–19.; Chang, Tom Y., and Mireille Jacobson, "Going to pot? The impact of dispensary closures on crime," *Journal of Urban Economics* 100 (2017): 120–36.

4. Stokes, Robert J., "Business improvement districts and inner-city revitalization: The case of Philadelphia's Frankford special services district," *International Journal of Public Administration* 29, nos. 1–3 (2006): 173–86.

5. Thorsby, Devon, "How commercial real estate is changing residential housing," *US News and World Report*, May 19, 2016, http://realestate.usnews.com/real-estate/articles/how-commercial-real-estate-is-changing-residential-housing/.

6. Hoyt, Lorlene, "Collecting private funds for safer public spaces: An empirical examination of the business improvement district concept," *Environment and Planning B: Planning and Design* 31, no. 3 (2004): 367–80; Brooks, Leah, "Volunteering to be taxed: Business improvement districts and the extra-governmental provision of public safety," *Journal of Public Economics* 92, nos. 1–2 (2008): 388–406; Ellen, Ingrid Gould, Amy Ellen Schwartz, Ioan Voicu, Leah Brooks, and Lorlene Hoyt, "The impact of business improvement districts on property values: Evidence from New York City [with comments]," *Brookings-Wharton Papers on Urban Affairs* (2007): 1–39.

7. Mitchell, Jerry, "Business improvement districts and the 'new' revitalization of downtown," *Economic Development Quarterly* 15, no. 2 (2001): 115–23; Houston, Lawrence O., Jr., "What do BIDs do? What can BIDs do?" Inspired Leaders Shaping Cities, 2017, https://www.ida-downtown.org/eweb/DynamicPage.aspx?webcode=houstounBIDs.

8. "Business improvement districts," LA City Clerk, https://clerk.lacity.org/business-improvement-districts; http://clerk.lacity.org/stellent/groups/departments/@clerk_bid_contributor/documents/contributor_web_content/lacityp_027503.pdf.

9. For details on BIDs in Los Angeles see MacDonald, John, Ricky N. Bluthenthal, Daniela Golinelli, Aaron Kofner, Robert J. Stokes, and Leo Beletsky, *Neighborhood effects on crime and youth violence: The role of business improvement districts in Los Angeles* (Santa Monica, CA: Rand, 2009).

10. Los Angeles Citywide Business Improvement District Program FAQ, https://clerk.lacity.org/sites/g/files/wph606/f/lacityp_025636.pdf.

11. For a full discussion of the history of the Figuero BID, see Holter, Daryl, "BIDS: A quiet revolution in urban management," working paper, UCLA School of Public Affairs, 2002, http://escholarship.org/uc/item/7bg1w1ph.

12. Los Angeles Citywide Business Improvement District Program FAQ, https://clerk.lacity.org/sites/g/files/wph606/f/lacityp_025636.pdf.

13. Figueroa Corridor Business Improvement District Newsletter, spring 2014, http://media.wix.com/ugd/07e1b9_f4d11f9da4264a01b2deb61c9c1a5189.pdf.

14. See Figueroa Corridor website for details: https://www.figueroacorridor.org/what.

15. *Hollywood Entertainment BID Newsletter* 17, no. 2 (Summer 2014): 7. http://onlyinhollywood.org/hollywood-bid/newsletter/.

16. Hollywood Property Alliance 2013 Annual Report, http://onlyinhollywood.org/wp-content/uploads/2014/03/jointannualdocsm.pdf.

17. For a description of Clean Street, see http://www.cleanstreet.com/.

18. See quote at https://historiccore.bid/about-the-bid/.

19. AlliedUniversal Security Systems, http://www.universalpro.com/UPS_index.html.

20. This is the case for private spaces where victims can sue place managers for negligence if they are injured or victimized in controlled areas. As BID security are often private contractors patrolling public spaces, the legal issues related to civil liability standards regarding safety get blurred.

21. MacDonald, John, Daniela Golinelli, Robert J. Stokes, and Ricky Bluthenthal, "The effect of business improvement districts on the incidence of violent crimes," *Injury Prevention* 16, no. 5 (2010): 327–32.

22. Cook, Philip J., and John MacDonald, "Public safety through private action: An economic assessment of BIDS," *Economic journal* 121, no. 552 (2011): 445–62.

23. Unfortunately, police data were not collected as part of this study to capture public intoxication offenses. It is unclear how reliable reports for public intoxication would be relative to a measure of arrests. BIDs could cause an increase in public intoxication arrests even if overall public intoxication started to decline.

24. Han, Sehee, Göktuğ Morçöl, Don Hummer, and Steven A. Peterson, "The effects of business improvement districts in reducing nuisance crimes: Evidence from Philadelphia," *Journal of Urban Affairs* 39, no. 5 (2017): 658–74.

25. Ellen et al., "The impact of business improvement districts on property values."

26. A preliminary analysis of crime reductions in New York City in the 1990s finds that police precincts in which BIDs were formed that spend a considerable share of their budgets on private security had larger reductions in crime than other parts of the city. Meltzer, Rachel, et al., "Private investment in the public's interest? The case of business improvement districts and crime in New York City," May 8, 2017, https://www.rachelmeltzer.com/uploads/1/4/5/3/14532900/appendix_20_nyc_bids_crime_nta_submission_5-8-17.pdf.

27. See discussion in Cohen et al., "Parks and physical activity."

28. For an overview of the history of park and playground planning in the United States, see Garvin, *The American city.*

29. Foglesong, *Planning the capitalist city.*

30. Garvin, *The American city.*

31. Rogers, Cleveland, "Robert Moses: An *Atlantic* portrait," *Atlantic*, February 1939, http://www.theatlantic.com/magazine/archive/1939/02/robert-moses/306543/.

32. For the impressive financial resources of Central Park, see http://www.centralparknyc.org/assets/pdfs/990-forms/990-Public-Inspection.pdf.

33. Godbey, Geoffrey, Alan R. Graefe, and Stephen W. James, *The benefits of local recreation and park services: A nationwide study of the perceptions of the American public* (Arlington, VA: National Recreation and Park Association, 1992).

34. ParkScore, Detroit, The Trust for Public Land, 2018, http://parkscore.tpl.org/city.php?city=Detroit.

35. ParkScore, Los Angeles, The Trust for Public Land, 2018, http://parkscore.tpl.org/city.php?city=Los%20Angeles.

36. Scott, David, and Wayne Munson, "Perceived constraints to park usage among individuals with low incomes," *Journal of Park and Recreation Administration* 12, no. 4 (1994): 79–96.

37. Cohen et al., "Parks and physical activity."

38. Bedimo-Rung, Ariane L., Andrew J. Mowen, and Deborah A. Cohen, "The significance of parks to physical activity and public health: A conceptual model," *American Journal of Preventive Medicine* 28, no. 2 (2005): 159–68.

39. Cohen, Deborah A., Thomas L. McKenzie, Amber Sehgal, Stephanie Williamson, Daniela Golinelli, and Nicole Lurie, "Contribution of public parks to physical activity," *American Journal of Public Health* 97, no. 3 (2007): 509–14.

40. Cohen, Deborah A., J. Scott Ashwood, Molly M. Scott, Adrian Overton, Kelly R. Evenson, Lisa K. Staten, Dwayne Porter, Thomas L. McKenzie, and Diane Catellier, "Public parks and physical activity among adolescent girls," *Pediatrics* 118, no. 5 (2006): e1381–89.

41. Cohen, Deborah A., Daniela Golinelli, Stephanie Williamson, Amber Sehgal, Terry Marsh, and Thomas L. McKenzie, "Effects of park improvements on park use and physical activity: Policy and programming implications," *American Journal of Preventive Medicine* 37, no. 6 (2009): 475–80.

42. Cohen, Deborah A., Amber Sehgal, Stephanie Williamson, Terry Marsh, Daniela Golinelli, and Thomas L. McKenzie, "New recreational facilities for the young and the old in Los Angeles: Policy and programming implications," *Journal of Public Health Policy* 30, no. 1 (2009): S248–63.

43. Cohen, Deborah A., Bing Han, Kathryn Pitkin Derose, Stephanie Williamson, Terry Marsh, Jodi Rudick, and Thomas L. McKenzie, "Neighborhood poverty, park use, and park-based physical activity in a Southern California city," *Social Science & Medicine* 75, no. 12 (2012): 2317–25.

44. Han, Bing, Deborah A. Cohen, Kathryn Pitkin Derose, Terry Marsh, Stephanie Williamson, and Laura Raaen, "How much neighborhood parks contribute to local residents' physical activity in the City of Los Angeles: A meta-analysis," *Preventive Medicine* 69 (2014): S106–10.

45. Andersen, Ross E., Shawn C. Franckowiak, Julia Snyder, Susan J. Bartlett, and Kevin R. Fontaine, "Can inexpensive signs encourage the use of stairs? Results from a community intervention," *Annals of Internal Medicine* 129, no. 5 (1998): 363–69.

46. Soler, Robin E., Kimberly D. Leeks, Leigh Ramsey Buchanan, Ross C. Brownson, Gregory W. Heath, David H. Hopkins, and Task Force on Community Preventive Services, "Point-of-decision prompts to increase stair use: A systematic review update," *American Journal of Preventive Medicine* 38, no. 2 (2010): S292–300.

47. Blamey, Avril, Nanette Mutrie, and Aitchison Tom, "Health promotion by encouraged use of stairs," *Bmj* 311, no. 7000 (1995): 289–90.

48. Brownell, Kelly D., Albert J. Stunkard, and Janet M. Albaum, "Evaluation and modification of exercise patterns in the natural environment," *American Journal of Psychiatry* 137, no. 12 (1980): 1540-45; Coleman, Karen J., and Eugenia C. Gonzalez, "Promoting stair use in a US–Mexico border community," *American Journal of Public Health* 91, no. 12 (2001): 2007–9.

49. Sallis, James F, Adrian Bauman, and Michael Pratt, "Environmental and policy interventions to promote physical activity," *American Journal of Preventive Medicine* 15, no. 4 (1998): 379–97.

50. Cohen, Deborah A., Bing Han, Kathryn Pitkin Derose, Stephanie Williamson, Terry Marsh, and Thomas L. McKenzie. "Physical activity in parks: A randomized controlled trial using community engagement." *American Journal of Preventive Medicine* 45, no. 5 (2013): 590–97.

51. This study estimated energy expenditure using the metabolic equivalent of a task (MET). This is a simple way to translate how much energy is expended with common tasks (see http://en.wikipedia.org/wiki/Metabolic_equivalent). The study used 1.5 METS for observed sitting, 3 for observed walking or moderate activity, and 6 for vigorous activity like running or playing sports.

52. MacVean, Mary, "Better park signs can spur more people to exercise, study says," *Los Angeles Times,* October 17, 2013, http://articles.latimes.com/2013/oct/17/news/la-sn-parks-usage-20131017.

53. See http://www.thehighline.org/visit.

54. Stokes, Robert. "The challenges of using BIDs in lower-income areas: The case of Germantown, Philadelphia," *Drexel Law Review* 3, no. 1 (2010): 325–37.

Chapter 8. Embracing Change

1. Merton, Robert K., "The unanticipated consequences of purposive social action," *American Sociological Review* 1, no. 6 (1936): 894–904.

2. Anderson, Elijah, "The cosmopolitan canopy," *Annals of the American Academy of Political and Social Science* 595, no. 1 (2004): 14–31.

3. Oldenburg, Robert, *The great good place: Café, coffee shops, community centers, beauty parlors, general stores, bars, hangouts, and how they get you through the day* (St. Paul, MN: Paragon House, 1989).

4. Rodin, Judith, "The 21st-century urban university: New roles for practice and research," *Journal of the American Planning Association* 71, no. 3 (2005): 237–49.

5. Ehlenz, Meagan M. "Neighborhood revitalization and the anchor institution: Assessing the impact of the University of Pennsylvania's West Philadelphia initiatives on University City," *Urban Affairs Review* 52, no. 5 (2016): 714–50.

6. Kromer, John, and Lucy Kerman, "West Philadelphia initiatives: A case study in urban revitalization," Working paper, Fels Institute of Government, University of Pennsylvania, 2005.

7. See "Living in Philadelphia," Penn Off-Campus Services, University of Pennsylvania, http://www.business-services.upenn.edu/offcampusservices/cms/wp-content/uploads/grad -housing-guide-draft-2012.pdf.

8. MacDonald, John M., Jonathan Klick, and Ben Grunwald, "The effect of private police on crime: Evidence from a geographic regression discontinuity design," *Journal of the Royal Statistical Society: Series A (Statistics in Society)* 179, no. 3 (2016): 831–46.

9. Steif, Kenneth, "Toward school improvement districts: Evaluating the costs and benefits of a university-funded public school intervention," working paper, University of Pennsylvania, 2012.

10. "Let the Penn Alexander kindergarten registration madness begin," West Philly Local, January 18, 2013, http://www.westphillylocal.com/2013/01/18/let-the-penn-alexander -kindergarten-registration-madness-begin/.

11. See data available at the Philadelphia School District web profile: https://webapps.philasd .org/school_profile/view/1280.

12. Levy, Diane K., Jennifer Comey, and Sandra Padilla, "In the face of gentrification: Case studies of local efforts to mitigate displacement," *Journal of Affordable Housing and Community Development Law.* 16 no. 3 (2006): 238–315.

13. See discussion in Levy, "In the face of gentrification."

14. Bar, François, and John Seely Brown, "Is downtown LA's Figueroa Corridor the next Silicon Valley?" *Los Angeles Times,* March 18, 2014, http://articles.latimes.com/2014/mar/18/news /la-ol-downtown-figueroa-corridor-innovation-silicon-valley-20140318.

15. Pool, Bob, "Catapulted to new heights," *Los Angeles Times,* July 13, 2017, http://articles .latimes.com/2007/jul/13/local/me-felix13.

16. Cavanaugh, Kerry, "Build my Figueroa, and let LA's cyclists, and walkers, flourish," *Los Angeles Times,* February 26, 2014, http://www.latimes.com/opinion/opinion-la/la-ol-my -figueroa-debate-walkers-20140225-story.html.

17. "LA's plan to make Figueroa a 'complete street' makes sense," *Los Angeles Times* (editorial), February 26, 2014, http://www.latimes.com/opinion/editorials/la-ed-my-figueroa-bike-lanes-complete-street-20140226-story.html.

18. Bar and Brown, "Is downtown LA's Figueroa Corridor the next Silicon Valley?"

19. Levy, "In the face of gentrification."

20. Cowman, Amy, "Light rail development brings boom to quiet neighborhoods," Delaware Online, February 3, 2015, https://www.delawareonline.com/story/news/local/2015/02/03/light-rail-development-brings-boom-to-quiet-neighborhoods/22816411/.

21. Billings, Stephen B, "Estimating the value of a new transit option," *Regional Science and Urban Economics* 41, no. 6 (2011): 525–36.

22. Cowman, Amy, "Light rail development brings boom to quiet neighborhoods."

23. Stokes, Robert J., John MacDonald, and Greg Ridgeway, "Estimating the effects of light rail transit on health care costs," *Health & Place* 14, no. 1 (2008): 45–58.

24. Weber, Rachel, "Equity and entrepreneurialism: The impact of tax increment financing on school finance," *Urban Affairs Review* 38, no. 5 (2003): 619–44.

25. Gillen, Kevin, "Fiscal analysis of Philadelphia's ten-year property tax abatement: Updated statistics on the size and distribution of tax-abated properties in Philadelphia," working paper, Fels Institute of Government, University of Pennsylvania, 2104.

26. Econsult Corporation, "Building Industry Association: Philadelphia tax abatement analysis," consulting report, Philadelphia, Pennsylvania, 2006.

27. Blanchard, Olivier Jean, "Crowding out," in *The New Palgrave Dictionary of Economics*, 2nd ed., ed. Durlauf, Steven, and Lawrence E. Blume (Palgrave Macmillan, 2008).

28. Vigdor, Jacob L., Douglas S. Massey, and Alice M. Rivlin, "Does gentrification harm the poor? [with comments]," *Brookings-Wharton Papers on Urban Affairs* (2002): 133–82.

29. Hwang and Lin, "What have we learned about the causes of recent gentrification?"

30. Glaeser, Edward, and Jacob Vigdor, *The end of the segregated century: Racial separation in America's neighborhoods, 1890–2010* (New York: Manhattan Institute for Policy Research, 2012).

31. Sharkey, Patrick. *Stuck in place: Urban neighborhoods and the end of progress toward racial equality* (Chicago: University of Chicago Press, 2013).

Epilogue

1. Kaiser, Edward J., David R. Godschalk, and F. Stuart Chapin, *Urban land use planning*, vol. 4. (Urbana: University of Illinois Press, 1995).

2. Kochtitzky, Chris S., H. Frumkin, R. Rodriguez, A. L. Dannenberg, J. Rayman, K. Rose, R. Gillig, and T. Kanter, "Urban planning and public health at CDC," *MMWR Supplements* 55, no. 2 (2006): 34–38.

3. See Robert Wood Johnson's Active Living by Design: http://activelivingbydesign.org/project/robert-wood-johnson-foundation-active-living-by-design/

4. See "Healthy communities," Robert Wood Johnson Foundation, http://www.rwjf.org/en/our-focus-areas/focus-areas/healthy-communities.html.

5. See the CDC Healthy Community Design Initiative: https://www.cdc.gov/healthyplaces/default.htm.

6. National Research Council, *Improving health in the United States: The role of health impact assessment* (Washington, DC: National Academies Press, 2011).

7. Arnold Ventures, http://www.arnoldfoundation.org/initiatives/.

8. Barragan, Blanca, "Watts is working on a huge, neighborhood-wide makeover," Curbed (Los Angeles), May 22, 2015, http://la.curbed.com/archives/2015/05/watts_is_working_on _a_huge_neighborhoodwide_makeover.php.

9. "Jordan Downs," Curbed (Los Angeles), http://la.curbed.com/places/jordan-downs.

10. USC Prince Center for Social Innovation, University of Southern California, https:// socialinnovation.usc.edu/.

11. "The impact of street lighting on crime in New York City housing," University of Chicago Crime Lab New York, October 2017, https://urbanlabs.uchicago.edu/attachments/ef4ec9dc a5bb0cd02019a0299f6fabf081ee548c/store/50eab357f0ee925539c8e72d1f0d6380d7ac0670bec3 1b63473c1dd7c5e2/Lights+report_10.20.17.pdf.

12. NYC Housing Authority press release, August 4, 2015, https://www1.nyc.gov/site/nycha /about/press/pr-2015/NYCHA-announces-80mil-for-public-safety-lighting-20150804.page.

13. Hamblin, James, "The nature cure," *Atlantic*, October 2015, http://www.theatlantic.com /magazine/archive/2015/10/the-nature-cure/403210/.

14. Wilson, Edward O., *The meaning of human existence* (New York: W. W. Norton, 2014).

INDEX

Active Design, 17; healthy places and, 22–24
"Active Living by Design," 22, 149
active-living design programs, 23–24, 11; transportation-oriented, 140
aggregation fallacy, 50–51
air pollution, from fossil fuel emissions, 82
Angrist, Josh, 33
ash trees, loss of, 42
asthma, 1; housing design and, 75; incidence of, 65–66; study of housing effects on, 67–70

balance: definition of, 32; of experimental and control groups, 38–39
Berk, Richard, 50–51
"Better Living Through Chemistry" movement, 29–31
Beyer, Kirsten, 49
biases, in place-based programs, 47–48; in RCTs, 34–35. *See also* selection bias
BIDs. *See* business improvement districts (BIDs)
bike lanes, 103; replacing car lanes in Figueroa BID, 143–44
biking: in crime reduction, 113–14; urban design encouraging, 103–4
block dimensions, determination of, 169n3
body mass index (BMI), in transit users, 107–9
Bogar, Sandra, 49
Boston, MA: Charlesbank Gymnasium in, 128; ring of parks around, 169n4

Breathe-Easy Homes (BEHs), 65–70; childhood asthma and, 67–70; compared to clinical intervention, 69
broken windows theory, 70–74
Brownsville housing project, 60–61
Bryant Park, 137
building codes, early 20th-century creation of, 13
built environment: crime and safety effects of, 70–74; health impact of, x, 58–70; reducing access to, 25; rehabilitation opportunities for, 55–56. *See also* cities; housing
Built Green 3-star standard, 66
business districts. *See* commercial districts
business improvement districts (BIDs), 120–21; in crime reduction, 121–26; park management and design in, 126, 127–36; private security in, 176n20; public intoxication arrests in, 177n23
business location decisions, 118

Calthorpe, Peter, 18
Camden, NJ, vacant-lot greening in, 93
Campbell Collaboration, 49
car-dependent culture, xii, 4, 102–3; crime and, 113–14; health impact of, 3, 15–16; light rail transit reducing, 112–13. *See also* cars
carbon footprints, reducing, 82
Carlin, George, 79
cars: design and safety standards for, 101–2; designing out to reduce crime, 113–14; reducing reliance on, 4, 102–3